Realist Thought from Weber to Kissinger

REALIST
THOUGHT
from
WEBER
to
KISSINGER

Michael Joseph Smith

Louisiana State University Press
Baton Rouge and London

Designer: Albert Crochet
Typeface: ITC Sabon
Typesetter: Donnelley Rocappi Inc.
Printer: Thomson-Shore, Inc.
Binder: John H. Dekker & Sons

Publication of this book has been
assisted by a grant from
the Andrew W. Mellon Foundation.

LIBRARY OF CONGRESS CATALOGING IN PUBLICATION DATA

Smith, Michael Joseph, 1951–
  Realist thought from Weber to Kissinger.

  (Political traditions in foreign policy series)
  Bibliography: p.
  Includes index.
  1. International relations—Research.   2. Realism.
I. Title.   II. Series.
JX1291.S46   1986   327'.072   86-15180
ISBN 0-8071-1321-2

For Stanley Hoffmann,
Teacher, example, friend

Contents

Acknowledgments

Several people have helped me throughout the process of producing this book with their gifts of love, friendship, and knowledge, and thanking them in print is a pleasure I have been anticipating for rather too long.

My parents, Harold and Evelyn, first taught me to cherish and respect learning and have encouraged me in all I have tried to do, teaching me all the while the meaning of unselfish love.

Unless one is a poet (and sometimes even then), words of gratitude to one's spouse inevitably sound sentimental or contrived; suffice it therefore to say that without Deborah I cannot imagine how this book could have been completed.

While working on this project, I was fortunate enough to be associated with the Social Studies program at Harvard University, first as a graduate student teaching fellow and then as a faculty member sharing an appointment with the Government Department. Before their departure, Michael Walzer and Robert Amdur established an atmosphere of rigorous interdisciplinary inquiry (leavened by humor and devoted attention to box scores) from which I learned enormously. Certainly the experience of teaching Social Studies 10 deepened my understanding of the importance of social theory. Two friends who remain in the program, Michael Donnelly and Cheryl Welch, have helped perhaps more than they know, and I thank them warmly.

Finally, I bow in the direction of my teachers. At Oxford, Professor Alastair Buchan first kindled my interest in the American realists and, before his untimely death, supervised an M.Phil. thesis on a similar subject. During my time at Oxford, I had the privilege to study political theory with Zbigniew Pelczynski, whose lively imagination on all political questions continues to inspire. Hedley Bull also helped by providing a set of remarkably incisive criticisms and by being extraordinarily generous with his time during a sabbatical leave. His recent death has deprived us all of a uniquely civilized mind.

Although I have never formally studied with him, Kenneth W. Thompson has, through his own books, taught every student of realism. As editor of the Political Traditions in Foreign Policy Series, he read my manuscript with great care and broad-mindedness and offered a host of probing questions and criticisms. If I am occasionally overly hard on the realists it is because I was too stubborn to take many of his well-founded criticisms.

I have dedicated this volume to my teacher and colleague Stanley Hoffmann in the hope that it is worthy of him. The late Jacob Talmon once said that there are two ways to teach: like a haberdasher who supplies a ready-made suit straight off the peg, or like a gardener who plants a seed and anxiously waits for it to grow in its own time at its own pace. Since I first took "War" in my sophomore year at Harvard, Stanley Hoffmann has carefully tended this particular seedling. His generosity and friendship are invaluable, and my gratitude to him runs deeper than I can say.

Realist Thought from Weber to Kissinger

1

Modern Realism
in Context

As an approach to the theory and practice of international relations, realism has had enormous influence and remains important today. The roots of the idea can be traced as far back as Thucydides or Saint Augustine, and modern partisans of realism have not hesitated to claim this venerable historical pedigree. As opposed to utopians, idealists, optimists, and reformers of every stripe, realists say they accept and understand the world as it is; this understanding provides the foundation for all their ideas.

In its most basic outline, the realist picture of the world begins with a pessimistic view of human nature. Evil is inevitably a part of all of us which no social arrangement can eradicate: men and women are not perfectible. The struggle for power—which defines politics—is a permanent feature of social life and is especially prominent in the relations between states. In the realm of international politics, states are the only major actors, and no structure of power or authority stands above them to mediate their conflicts; nor would they peacefully consent to the creation of such a structure, even if it could be shown to be workable. States act according to their power interests, and these interests are bound at times to conflict violently. Therefore, even if progress toward community and justice is possible *within* states, the relations *between* them are doomed to a permanent competition that often leads to war. However deplorable, this permanent competition remains an unavoidable reality that no amount of moral exhortation or utopian scheming can undo. Only by appreciating its source and its permanence can interstate conflict be moderated.

As a body of thought about international relations, realism contains three main aspects, which various theorists emphasize differently. First, and most broadly, realism purports to be a general theory explaining the essence of international politics. Second, some writers draw on the precepts of realism—without necessarily regarding it as a general theory—to advocate, criticize, or justify specific policies for a given state. Finally, the notion of realism is often advanced as a particular solution to the vexed problem of the place of moral considerations in foreign policy. These three aspects obviously need not conflict, and some authors, most notably Hans Morgenthau, have tried ambitiously to combine all three. But other writers have concentrated on one or another of these aspects, and their different emphases—together with their varying initial assumptions—have resulted in distinct varieties of realism.

My goal in this book is to analyze the ideas of several key modern exponents of realism, beginning with Max Weber and ending with Henry Kissinger. I shall examine the assumptions, explore the implications, and consider the internal coherence of each author's version of realism with the object of assessing the ultimate value and significance of the overall approach. Realists have argued that their ideas demonstrate consistency, prudence, and—as the term "realism" suggests—accuracy in far greater measure than other explanations of international politics; my goal is to scrutinize that claim by tracing the modern development of the concept.

The figures I have chosen to treat in depth—Weber, E. H. Carr, Reinhold Niebuhr, Hans Morgenthau, George Kennan, and Kissinger—obviously do not exhaust the list of contemporary realists; at the risk of sacrificing depth for breadth, one could add Georg Schwarzenberger, Martin Wight, Arnold Wolfers, John Herz, or Raymond Aron, to name but a few prominent writers of roughly the same generation. But the six central figures to be considered here do fairly represent the range and depth of modern realist thought. Moreover, their preeminence in the field—their seminal importance and influence on others—is without question. Certainly American realism in its original form has been virtually identified with Niebuhr, Morgenthau, and Kennan. Indeed, rather to the chagrin of behaviorally oriented scholars—for whom realism amounts to *ex cathedra* pronouncement instead of "scientific" theory—Morgenthau's great *Politics Among Nations* continues to be cited as the field's "most influential textbook" and Morgenthau himself as the scholar who has contributed most to the field.[1]

Though they clearly share the same general approach, these writers sometimes prove to be inconsistent both internally and taken together. Realists reach surprisingly dissimilar conclusions on a wide range of issues more frequently than one would assume if one were to take at face value

1. John A. Vasquez, *The Power of Power Politics: A Critique* (New Brunswick, N.J., 1983), 17, 26.

their general statements about the governing propositions of world politics; at the same time the similarities in approach are noticeable enough to justify considering them as a coherent school. Part of the task of the chapters that follow will be to explain these similarities and differences among the realists: are they simply the product of idiosyncratic concerns or do they suggest difficulties with the notion of realism? One of the themes to emerge from this study of realism concerns the elusiveness of the concept. It is easy enough to present a common set of assumptions about the inescapability of evil and the ubiquity of power, assumptions that lead to similar conclusions about prudent calculations of interest and the pitfalls of moralism. Realists all agree with Pascal that "he who plays the angel ends up the beast."

But closer examination of individual writers reveals a wide range of fundamental postulates claimed to support these assumptions. Realism can appear as theological dogma, applied social theory, diplomatic pragmatism, political science, or philosophy of history. As a result, it can be unclear whether one is dealing with a theory, a doctrine, or merely an approach to difficult international problems. Indeed, recently there have even been attempts to distinguish "structural realism" from "classical realism," or "practical realism" from "technical realism."[2] No such attempt at typology or classification will be offered here; in my view these dichotomies are rarely helpful and inevitably sacrifice the nuances at the heart of realist thought. It is far better, I think, to acknowledge that each thinker has a different version and justification of realism and that these differences are ill served by schemes of classification, which can be Procrustean.

Nevertheless, the variety of guises in which realism appears has dictated my approach in the book. I shall present each author, at least initially, in his own terms; to understand the reasons for disagreements among the realists it is necessary first to grasp their individual starting points and their choice of discourse. Thus part of each chapter will be exegetic so that each author can emerge in his own light before he is criticized and compared with others. As the study progresses, the comparisons will multiply and the criticisms will develop until the final chapter, when I shall characterize the essence and limitations of the approach and briefly suggest some alternatives to its more problematic formulations.

2. Robert O. Keohane, "Theory of World Politics: Structural Realism and Beyond," in Ada W. Finifter (ed.), *Political Science: The State of the Discipline* (Washington, 1984); Richard K. Ashley, "Political Realism and Human Interests," *International Studies Quarterly*, XXV (June, 1981), 204–36.

Antecedents in Classical Political Thought:
Thucydides, Machiavelli, and Hobbes

Before plunging into the argument on modern realism, it is worth pausing briefly to consider realism in its classical guise. Modern realists draw consciously from classical theorists, in particular from Thucydides, Machiavelli, and Hobbes—thinkers who obviously differ in many important ways but who share a characteristic approach to international relations.

Perhaps the most quoted sentence from *The Peloponnesian War* concerns power: "What made war inevitable was the growth of Athenian power and the fear which this caused in Sparta."[3] Thus Thucydides, like all realists who followed him, emphasized the primary and inescapable importance of power. But this is only the most obvious way that Thucydides can be considered the first realist. In his conception of international order, his notion of state honor and interest, and his view of the radically circumscribed place of morality in foreign policy, he effectively defined a paradigm of realist thought. And underlying all this is a dark vision of human nature which lends a tragic consistency to his account.

Order in the Greek city-state system described by Thucydides depended upon a hierarchy of power. Two rival alliance systems coexisted as long as both perceived a rough equilibrium of power. The democratic power, Athens, proved decidedly undemocratic in its treatment of its diverse allies, whereas oligarchic Sparta treated its alliance of similar oligarchies as an association of rough equals. In the one case, hierarchy was enforced—Athens exacted high tribute from its allies—whereas in the other it was built in by the character of the regimes; in both alliances hierarchy was the governing principle of order. In modern jargon, the system was bipolar with one bloc of homogeneous regimes led by a conservative land power and the other bloc led by a restless, innovative sea power. A clash between them seemed inevitable.

All this is familiar: indeed a recent work analyzing the character of crises has criticized Thucydides for being too deterministic.[4] But even if he regards the underlying cause to be "the growth of Athenian power and the fear which this caused in Sparta" Thucydides hardly neglects the immediate events precipitating the conflict. And it is striking that those events all

3. Thucydides, *History of the Peloponnesian War*, trans. Rex Warner, ed. M. I. Finley (Harmondsworth, 1972), I, §24, p. 49.
4. Richard N. Lebow, *Between Peace and War: The Nature of International Crisis* (Baltimore, 1981).

involved attempts by smaller powers to subvert the hierarchy, to manipulate the competing alliances to their own benefit. Without rehearsing the complex sequence of events that led to war, the immediate trouble began when Corcyra, a small neutral state, got into a dispute with Corinth—its "mother country" and an important Spartan ally—after a revolt in another colony, Epidamnus. The Corinthians resented the independence displayed by the Corcyreans; their resentment turned to a bitter desire for vengeance after the Corcyreans defeated them in a naval battle. They turned to Sparta for help, and the worried Corcyreans went to Athens to seek the protection of the Athenian alliance.

The fascinating speeches of the importuning smaller powers reveal the essence of Thucydides' portrait of state behavior. The Corcyreans make a frank appeal to the Athenians: "By giving us this help you will be acting in your own interests." Almost in passing, they attempt to allay any lingering Athenian notions of justice by portraying themselves as "victims of aggression," but the heart of their argument lies in their appeal to Athenian power interests. They even present a kind of domino theory, evoking a logic of inevitable escalation: "Sparta is frightened of you and wants war . . . Corinth is your enemy and is also influential at Sparta. Corinth has attacked us first in order to attack you afterwards." Against arguments that accepting Corcyra's offer of alliance would breach the treaty governing relations between Athens and Sparta, the Corcyreans repeat their appeal to power: "Whether you feel apprehensive [about the treaty] or not you will certainly have become stronger . . . this fact will make your enemies think twice before attacking you." Thus the Corcyreans both play on Athenian fears for their security and dangle before them an opportunity to strengthen themselves in a war with Sparta that they present as inevitable.[5]

In contrast to this appeal to "interest defined in terms of power" (as Hans Morgenthau would later put it) the Corinthians in their speech to Athens invoke legality and a basic notion of fairness in dealing with other states. They tell the Athenians not to subvert the hierarchical order that has maintained the status quo between the alliances: "What you ought not to do is to establish a precedent by which a power may receive into its alliance the revolted subjects of another power." They argue that accepting Corcyra would violate the spirit of the treaty, and they warn that "though Corcyra is trying to frighten you into doing wrong by this idea of

5. Thucydides, *History*, I, §§32, 33, 36, pp. 54, 55, 57.

a coming war, there is no certainty that a war will come." In essence the Corinthians present an alternative view of security, a view based on stable hierarchy, fairness, and adherence to existing norms and treaties. They urge Athens not to "aid and abet" Corcyrean crimes. "The power that deals fairly with its equals," they assert, "finds a truer security than the one which is hurried into snatching some apparent but dangerous advantage."[6]

The Athenian decision to "snatch" the Corcyrean advantage tells us much about Thucydides' realism: faced with a choice between a concrete gain in power or fidelity to interstate agreements, states inevitably choose power. The logic of fear and escalation always pushes out the logic of moderation and peaceful diplomacy. Even the inherently cautious Spartans, whose allies must goad them into action, were eventually provoked into responding to the Athenian challenge. Thus differences in domestic regime or national character may be interesting, but the nature of the international system overwhelmingly dictates foreign policy. Modern realists share this fundamental assertion of the priority of the international system; but Thucydides does not stop here. He goes on to explain the *result* of war—as opposed to its *outbreak*—largely by pointing to the crucial domestic differences between Athens and Sparta. After the death of Pericles, Athenian waywardness and democratic factionalism led to the disastrous Sicilian Expedition and ultimately to defeat at the hands of the stolid, but steady and methodical, Spartans.

Another major aspect of Thucydides' contribution to realist thought is his consistent assertion of the radically limited role morality plays in the deliberations of states. Nowhere has this idea been presented more baldly than in the Melian dialogue. The Athenians (in a way quite uncharacteristic for modern states) do not even trouble to frame hypocritical justifications for their harsh demands on Melos. "We on our side will use no fine phrases," they tell the Melians, "since you know as well as we do that, when these matters are discussed by practical people, the standard of justice depends on the equality of power to compel and that in fact the strong do what they have the power to do and the weak accept what they have to accept."[7] Justice and honor are irrelevant in the face of power, and the Athenians sweep away the Melian arguments framed in those terms. It is as if the Athenian generals did not dare to engage in common moral discourse; as Michael Walzer has written, "moral talk is coercive; one thing

6. *Ibid.*, I, §§41–43, pp. 60–61.
7. *Ibid.*, V, §89, pp. 401–402.

leads to another."[8] But whether they wanted to avoid having to give reasons for their demands or simply felt themselves too powerful to have to bother, their message is clear: in international politics only the weak resort to moral argument. The strong rely on their power; as Joseph Stalin once reportedly responded to criticism from the Vatican, "How many divisions has the Pope?"

Indeed, throughout Thucydides' account, when one encounters overtly moral language, either the weak employ it in (usually vain) appeals to the strong, or leaders use it for suspect purposes of arousal or ideological justification. Thus in his Funeral Oration, Pericles celebrates Athenian honor and virtue. He calls Athens "an education to Greece" and praises the men who have "nobly fought and nobly died" on behalf of "our constitution and the way of life which has made us great." In this speech Pericles claims that "we make friends by doing good to others, not by receiving good from them." He speaks in high moral terms to bolster morale at a difficult time; one can almost sense him calculating the uplifting effect of his words.[9] But when he discusses actual policy, when persuasion really counts, Pericles prefers the cool language of interest. Consider this later speech after the plague in Athens: "Do not imagine that what we are fighting for is simply the question of freedom or slavery: there is also involved the loss of our empire and the dangers arising from the hatred which we have incurred in administering it. . . . Your empire is now like a tyranny: it may have been wrong to take it; it is certainly dangerous to let it go."[10] Gone is the notion that Athens made friends by doing good; instead he appeals to the hard facts of fear and interest. Thucydides makes it clear that he prefers Pericles in this mode. In the passage following the speech, he writes that "in what was nominally a democracy, power was really in the hands of the first citizen"; as long as it stayed there Athens was well-governed and the war well-fought. Pericles was a great statesman who understood how to marshal power on behalf of the interests of the state.

Thucydides demonstrates his attitude to overt moralizing even more vividly in his account of the Mytilenian Debate. After an unsuccessful revolt in Mytilene, the Athenians ordered the execution of all males in the city and the enslavement of the women and children—the fate later to be

---

8. Michael Walzer, *Just and Unjust Wars: A Moral Argument with Historical Illustrations* (New York, 1977), 12.

9. Thucydides, *History*, II, §§41, 36, pp. 147, 145.

10. *Ibid.*, II, §65, p. 163.

dealt to the Melians. But on this occasion, the people of Athens had second thoughts: they "began to think how cruel and unprecedented such a decision was—to destroy not only the guilty but the entire population of a state." They decided on a new debate of the order. The speech by Cleon in favor of the punishment which Thucydides chooses to report (or reconstruct) is a tour de force of brutality cloaked in righteous indignation. After telling the assembly that "you are simply victims of your own pleasure in listening and are more like an audience sitting at the feet of a professional lecturer than a parliament discussing matters of state," Cleon argues that "no single city has ever done you the harm that Mytilene has done. . . . They made up their minds to put might first and right second, choosing the moment when they thought they would win, and then making their unprovoked attack upon us." They deserve their punishment; in any case, "it is a general rule of human nature that the people despise those who treat them well and look up to those who make no concessions." Cleon offers a quasi-moral argument on behalf of the punishment: "If they were right in revolting, you must be wrong in holding power." He concludes by urging the Athenians "not to be traitors to your own selves" and to uphold their interest in power as well as their honor as the leader of an alliance: "Make an example of them to your other allies [by] plainly showing that revolt will be punished by death."[11]

Cleon's speech conceals an argument for unyielding exercise of power in the language of morality—evidence enough of Thucydides' mistrust of "morality." More striking is the tone taken by the moderate in the debate. Almost incredibly, Diodotus never refers to the very reason the debate was called—the widespread feeling that the punishment was unwarranted and cruel, that it amounted to state-sponsored murder. Rather, like Pericles in his last speech, he uses the cool language of self-interest, the rational discourse of cost-benefit analysis: "If we are sensible people, we shall see that the question is not so much whether they are guilty as whether we are making the right decision for ourselves. I might prove that they are the most guilty people in the world, but it does not follow that I shall propose the death penalty, unless that is in your interests; I might argue that they deserve to be forgiven, but should not recommend forgiveness unless that seemed to me the best thing for the state."[12] It seems clear from this debate

11. *Ibid.*, III, §§36, 38–41, pp. 212–16.
12. *Ibid.*, III, §44, p. 219.

that Thucydides believes that "good" or moderate policy follows from the prudent consideration of interest, not from the direct application of morality or idealism. Diodotus "wins" the debate not because he has a better moral case but because he is able to convince the assembly that his policy represents a more prudent calculation of Athenian interests. Thucydides seems convinced that such prudent calculation is the best hope for moderation given the facts of international competition and human nature.

On the question of human nature, Thucydides establishes a tone that other realists follow. He doubts that people can restrain their desire for power without external restrictions; nor has he any great faith in democracy, as the passage on the leadership of Pericles demonstrates. His most explicit treatment of human nature *per se* comes in the midst of his chilling account of the civil war in Corcyra:

> With the ordinary conventions of civilized life thrown into confusion, human nature, always ready to offend even where laws exist, showed itself proudly in its true colors, as something incapable of controlling passion, insubordinate to the idea of justice, the enemy to anything superior to itself; for, if it had not been for the pernicious power of envy, men would not so have exalted vengeance above innocence and profit above justice. Indeed, it is true that in these acts of revenge on others men take it upon themselves to begin the process of repealing those general laws of humanity which are there to give a hope of salvation to all who are in distress, instead of leaving those laws in existence, remembering that there may come a time when they, too, will be in danger and will need their protection.[13]

This passage is telling not only for its unflattering portrayal of human nature ("always ready to offend") but also for its prudential justification of what Thucydides calls the "general laws of humanity." We should obey those laws because it serves our interest to do so: someday we may need their protection. Thucydides here anticipates the Hobbesian conception of natural law as dictates of prudence.

Thus in three important ways Thucydides laid the foundation for modern realism. First, his account of the outbreak of war emphasizes the key importance of the structure of the international system and argues that almost regardless of their internal character, states define their interests in terms of power and fear for their security. Second, throughout his history he betrays a profound suspicion of overt moralizing and an implicit normative preference for moderation based upon unsentimental calculations

13. *Ibid.,* III, §84, p. 245.

of interest. The distinction between Athenian behavior toward Mytilene and Melos was a prudent calculation of interest in the first case; in the Melian dialogue the Athenian generals burke this calculation, content to exercise their superior power almost unthinkingly. The lesson of both cases is that straightforward appeals to morality either fail completely or, as in Cleon's speech, incite to immoderation and brutality. Finally, Thucydides rejects in advance idealistic notions about the benign and perfectible character of human nature. We are unable ourselves to control our passions; at best, laws backed by power will tame our "insubordination to the idea of justice."

Underlying Thucydides' history is a sense of brooding tragedy, a profound regret that this is the way of the world. No such tragic sense pervades the work of Machiavelli. Instead, Machiavelli presents a political science of the differences between state morality and the morality of ordinary men and women. Apart from his unquestioned faith in, and ardent desire for, a strong, well-ordered state, Machiavelli offers no universal standard of judgment. What follows is a frankly dual standard of morality. States in their interest may do things that no moral individual would. Harsh actions may be necessary: as Hegel put it in a comment on Machiavelli, "gangrenous limbs cannot be cured by lavender water."[14] To be sure, the appearance of virtue can be useful to a leader, and *The Prince* includes several examples of how to seem virtuous. Nor need a leader do evil gratuitously; but a "prince cannot observe all things which are considered good in men, being often obliged, in order to maintain the state, to act against faith, against charity, against humanity, and against religion."[15]

Thus morality in Machiavelli's usage is entirely instrumental: it is part of a prince's arsenal, to be used to greater or lesser effect. In no sense does it restrain state behavior—nor should one expect it to do so because the state in Machiavelli's treatment is beyond such restraint. As Carl Friedrich has written, "The state is for Machiavelli the supreme and all-inclusive good and therefore no genuine good can be found outside the state. As a result, Machiavelli sees no need for 'justifying' the means which are required for building and maintaining a state." From this perspective, any action that can be regarded as important for the survival of the state carries with it a built-in justification—although it is important to emphasize that

14. Z. A. Pelczynski (ed.), *Hegel's Political Writings* (Oxford, 1964), 220–21.
15. Niccolò Machiavelli, *The Prince and the Discourses*, ed. Max Lerner (New York, 1950), chap. 18, p. 65.

Machiavelli offers no argument on behalf of his high valuation of the state. This treatment of the state as a supreme work of art seems to preclude any attempt either in *The Prince* or *The Discourses* to explain why the well-ordered state is so self-evidently to be sought and maintained; as J. P. Plamenatz puts it, "Machiavelli took it for granted that strong government is desirable," simply assuming "that nearly everyone wants to belong to a powerful and respected political community."[16]

As with Thucydides, the key to understanding state behavior is the calculation of power, interest, and consequences. Machiavelli regards this as a simple fact, observable to all but the most blinkered moralist. But unlike Thucydides, Machiavelli does not appear to be troubled by this state of affairs: he is far more interested in advising a would-be prince to transform the sorry condition of the Italy of his day into a strong state worthy of the name. He moves rather easily from describing the necessary dual standard of morality to constructing a "how to" for princes—thus the cynical advice for which *The Prince* is so infamous. In this sense Machiavelli can be considered not only the first political scientist but the first "policy scientist," eager to urge particular policies on those in power.

Some interpreters, most notably Friedrich Meinecke, have found in Machiavelli's notion of *virtù* the kernel of an argument about inescapable *raison d'état*. Meinecke opens his learned treatise on the concept with a chapter on Machiavelli which seeks to establish that although Machiavelli himself never used the term, he nevertheless was the first major thinker to deal with the ideas fundamental to it. Late in the book he cites a chapter of the *Discourses* to illustrate the statesman's basic dilemma in acting for the state: "Where the very safety of the country depends on the resolution to be taken, no considerations of justice or injustice, humanity or cruelty, nor of glory or of shame, should be allowed to prevail. But putting all other considerations aside, the only question should be, What course will save the life and liberty of the country?"[17]

Meinecke treats the passage as a gloss on the personal sacrifices of value a true leader must make; he had in mind Theobald von Bethmann-Hollweg's decision to launch unconditional submarine warfare during World War I. But surely this interpretation reads too much back into Machiavelli,

16. Carl J. Friedrich, *Constitutional Reason of State: The Survival of the Constitutional Order* (Providence, R.I., 1957), 23; J. P. Plamenatz, *Man and Society* (2 vols.; London, 1963), I, 15, 19.
17. Machiavelli, *Discourses*, Book III, chap. 41, p. 528.

who nowhere describes a painful conflict of values. He simply asserts that the state must take precedence. To be sure, the language is apparently normative ("the only question *should* be"), but there is no sense of any consistent external standard of morality that would justify placing the state's interest above one's personal values. For Machiavelli, politics and morality operate in quite different spheres, and those interested in the latter should stay out of the former. On this point, Friedrich's conclusion seems to me more persuasive: "For Machiavelli . . . the problem of reason of state does not exist in its more pointed and typical form, because the necessity of acting in accordance with the state's requirements needs no justification."[18]

Whether or not Machiavelli can be considered the progenitor of more advanced notions of *raison d'état*, it is clear that he regarded the successful pursuit of foreign policy as inconsistent with ordinary conceptions of morality. In this important sense the "Machiavellian problem" of statecraft remains with us to the present day, and as we shall see, each of the modern realists attempts to deal with it in his own way. One point deserves emphasis here: nothing in Machiavelli suggests that prudence and a Thucydidean reluctance to moralize when defining policy together lead to moderation in the relations among states. On the contrary, Machiavelli seems to regard interstate conflict as inevitably intense, even agonistic. The wise prince will always be prepared for war and for the seizure of momentary advantage: "Let no state believe that it can always follow a safe policy, rather let it think that all are doubtful. This is found in the nature of things, that one never tries to avoid one difficulty without running into another, but prudence consists in being able to know the nature of the difficulties and taking the least harmful as good."[19] Machiavelli offers little respite from conflict; but unlike Thucydides, Hobbes, or the modern realists, this prospect seems not to bother him—there is glory to be had for the wise, *virtù*-bearing prince on whom fortune smiles.

In the very different world of Thomas Hobbes, glory is "exultation of mind" and is part of the larger system of "Appetites, and Aversions, Hopes and Feares" which defines human nature. Few thinkers are as systematic as Hobbes in the construction of their arguments, and like many of the realists who followed him, he begins with human nature. His account of men

18. Friedrich Meinecke, *Machiavellism*, trans. Douglas Scott (New Haven, 1952), 356; Friedrich, *Constitutional Reason*, 23.

19. Machiavelli, *The Prince*, chap. 21, p. 85.

and women as the sum of passions, and of human reason as a calculating machine driven by the alternate pursuit and avoidance of appetites and aversions, stands in the foreground of his conception of politics, society, and the state. Hobbes is less concerned with states *per se* than with individuals, for whom life in the state of nature is, in his unforgettable phrase, "solitary, poor, nasty, brutish, and short."[20]

Few contemporary realists would share Hobbes's picture of human nature, but his analysis of the state of nature remains the defining feature of realist thought. His notion of the international state of nature as a state of war is shared by virtually everyone calling himself a realist.[21] Hobbes's analysis involves making an analogy from the situation for individuals living in the state of nature to states—which "because of their Independency, are in continuall jealousies, and in the state and posture of Gladiators; having their weapons pointing, and their eyes fixed on one another; that is their Forts, Garrisons and Guns upon the Frontiers of their Kingdomes; and continuall Spyes upon their neighbours; which is a posture of War." In fact, Hobbes uses international relations to buttress his account of the individual state of nature: to those who doubt that so horrible a condition ever prevailed he points to the existing structure of international politics. States have always faced one another without a power or authority above them to hold their ambitions in check; it is worth remembering that Hobbes produced a remarkably vivid translation of *The Peloponnesian War.* Such a state of nature amounts to a constant state of war and hence lies beyond notions of right and wrong and justice and injustice for "where there is no common Power, there is no Law: where no Law, no Injustice."[22]

Nevertheless it is clear that for Hobbes, if not necessarily for later realists, the horrors of the state of nature for individuals—the conditions that prevail, say, in a civil war—far exceed those of the state of nature for nations. Why should this be so? First, individuals in a state of nature have no protection whatsoever: even the strongest man has to sleep. Without "a common Power to keep them all in awe" men and women can never be assured of their own security. Natural law amounts merely to reason-

20. Thomas Hobbes, *Leviathan,* ed. C. B. Macpherson (Harmondsworth, 1968), chaps. 6, 13, pp. 125, 127, 186.
21. See Hedley Bull, *The Anarchical Society: A Study of Order in World Politics* (New York, 1977), chap. 2, for a discussion of three traditions of political thought on international relations, of which the Hobbesian or realist tradition is the first.
22. Hobbes, *Leviathan,* chap. 13, pp. 187–88.

able—but unenforceable—dictates of prudence. Individuals go naked in a brutal world of power; that is why they are willing to alienate all their rights, save self-preservation, to a sovereign who will at least protect them from themselves.

Despite the international state of nature, citizens of constituted states are not so exposed. Hobbes rather cryptically says that because states "uphold the industry of their subjects, there does not follow from the [international state of nature] that misery which accompanies the Liberty of particular men."[23] In short, states insulate individuals from the rigors of international competition; for Hobbes the dangers of domestic anarchy pressed more urgently than those of interstate conflict. Had he lived on the Continent during the Thirty Years' War, his ideas might have been different.[24] But from the viewpoint of a timid man horrified by the excesses of the English Civil War, the international state of nature was manageable and could be lived with in a way impossible for individuals lacking any government. States at least provide domestic order, and individual sovereigns have an interest in protecting the realm of their sovereignty; it is even possible to treat Hobbes as providing a rationale for balance-of-power diplomacy.[25]

Modern realists adopt in one form or another two key Hobbesian ideas—his description of the international state of nature as a state of war and his radical skepticism about the possibility of moral behavior in such a milieu. For individual writers, the state of war is more or less intense, but the structural predisposition toward war—the autonomy of units and the absence of a common power or set of norms above them—remains a constant. On the moral question, modern realists are not so united. Hans Morgenthau, for example, shares Hobbes's skepticism about law without power and his insistence upon a single code of morality that can or cannot be applied. In contrast, E. H. Carr seems more in tune with Machiavelli's notion of a dual morality for states and individuals. But there is no question that the ideas of Hobbes, like those of Thucydides and Machiavelli before him, helped to constitute a rich mine of political thought which all modern realists draw from. How did they do so? How have modern realists managed to define what Robert O. Keohane has called "the principal

23. *Ibid.*
24. For an analysis along these lines see Arnold Wolfers, *Discord and Collaboration* (Baltimore, 1962), 233–52.
25. Stanley Hoffmann, *The State of War: Essays on the Theory and Practice of International Politics* (New York, 1965), chap. 3; Bull, *Anarchical Society,* chap. 2.

tradition for the analysis of international relations in Europe and its off-shoots in the New World"?[26]

From Weber to Kissinger

To understand the characteristic approach of contemporary realists the best place to begin is with Max Weber. Although he is surprisingly neglected among scholars of international relations, of all the authors to be considered here Weber has obviously had the greatest influence on all the social sciences. In an essay concerned only with realism in international affairs, it is impossible to treat him with anything approaching full justice or even "in his own terms"—these terms are simply too broad and complex. Rather, I shall present Weber as the modern figure who first set out the defining ideas of realism in a careful and systematic way. Even if others, particularly Reinhold Niebuhr and George Kennan, reached their own versions of realism in a way that owed little to Weber directly, the fact remains that Weber's delineation of the issues established the terms of realist discourse that endure to the present day. Equally, one need not argue that the elements of Weber's approach are wholly original with him; it is enough to say that the ensemble of his ideas on the subject was important and influential.

Five themes of Weber's political writings combine to form his contribution to realism: (1) his definitions of the state and politics, (2) his view of international politics as an unending struggle between nations, (3) his deep commitment to the advance of German culture and nationality, that is, his nationalism, (4) his concern for leadership in all its aspects, a concern with several sources and consequences, and (5) his formulation of the moral problem in statecraft as a conflict between an ethic of conviction and an ethic of responsibility.

Weber's definitions of the state as "the human community that (successfully) claims the monopoly of the legitimate use of physical force" and of politics as "striving to share power or striving to influence the distribution of power either among states or among groups in a state" have both proven influential on later realists.[27] Taken together they have focused attention on the state as a unitary actor in international relations (leading

26. Keohane, "Theory of World Politics," in Finifter (ed.), *Political Science*, 503.
27. Max Weber, "Politics as a Vocation," in H. H. Gerth and C. Wright Mills (eds.), *From Max Weber: Essays in Sociology* (London, 1948), 78.

to the so-called billiard-ball model) and at the same time on the universal aspect of struggle in all politics—domestic and international. There is a tension between these views, which affects nearly all the realists. The first definition points to the differences between states—their varying skills and capacities to compete—and suggests an important distinction between domestic and international politics; the latter inclusive definition of politics seems to eradicate this distinction. I shall probe this ambiguity in Weber and in all the realists who follow.

The next two of these themes—international relations as unending struggle and nationalism—are hardly original to Weber, but they inform his theoretical concerns so pervasively that it would be impossible to understand his political sociology in general, and the other three themes in particular, without appreciating their character and consequences. Their effect is especially evident in Weber's concern for leadership. To be sure, that concern, as we shall see in Chapter 2, runs through his political sociology; his conception of legitimacy and his dread of bureaucratization both suggest a crucial role for leadership. But his oft-expressed worries that Germany's leaders were inadequate to the task of promoting German interests and that Germany's political institutions disadvantaged her in the international competition are at least as important in animating his treatment of the problem of leadership. Weber argued for democratic parliamentary reform on the grounds that reform would produce more competent and responsible leaders, who, he hoped, would then do a better job at guiding Germany's foreign policy.

The final way in which Weber set the agenda for modern realism results from his sharp distinction between an ethic of conviction or ultimate ends and the ethic of responsibility. The distinction has been immensely influential and is a veritable leitmotif of realism. Nearly all realists begin by criticizing misguided moralism or liberal illusions of perfectionism. Yet the actual content of the ethics of responsibility is unclear in Weber; whether other realists are more successful in providing this content will be a major concern throughout the book.

After the development of Weber's ideas in Chapter 2, the next chapter will consider briefly a group of interwar writers usually called "idealists." In particular, I shall examine the writings of Sir Alfred Zimmern, the young Arnold Toynbee, David Davies, and such advocates of Wilsonianism and the League of Nations as James T. Shotwell and Nicholas Murray Butler. However brief, this consideration is necessary to establish the context in which later realists, including E. H. Carr, Niebuhr, and Morgenthau, were writing. As Raymond Aron has pointed out, a characteristic of all the realists is their tendency to "think against."[28] Each of them was concerned to puncture idealistic illusions—whether they be about the effects of "world opinion," about peace through law, or about unending progress through the Social Gospel. I shall characterize these "illusions" in Chapter 3 so as better to understand the specifically negative inspiration of later writers.

The first of these men to be considered, in Chapter 4, is the English historian E. H. Carr. Carr worked for the British Foreign Office between 1916 and 1936, when he resigned to take up the Woodrow Wilson Chair of International Politics at University College of Wales in Aberystwyth. Carr's *Twenty Years' Crisis* was an early milestone in realist thought. The book was important for several reasons. Published on the eve of World War II, it provided a theoretical foundation for the foreign policy of British rulers in the late 1930s; indeed, in its first edition there are several approving references (later excised) to Neville Chamberlain's attempt at appeasement. More generally, the book stands as a lucid and elegant statement of flexible realism, which perhaps more than later realist works is sensitive to the importance of economics in the interstate competition. As a former diplomat, Carr had little taste for dogmatic policies based on unbending moral principle; like Weber he advocated an ethic of responsibility. In a sense, Carr translated the thumping cadences of German *Realpolitik* into the measured phrases of English pragmatism: he made the frequently amoral character of international affairs seem at the same time inevitable and yet subject to reason. Carr wrote several other books on international relations *per se* (for example, *Conditions of Peace, Nationalism and After*) before 1951, when he turned his scholarly attention to his monumental history of the Soviet Union. Carr is an important bridge between Weber and German *Machtpolitik* on one side and American realism on the other.

Probably the most important figure in American realism was the theologian Reinhold Niebuhr. In contrast to the cool skepticism of Carr, Niebuhr built his position on theology and on what he called "the rock bottom problem of human nature"; his realism has the cast of prophecy. Born in 1892, Niebuhr received his Bachelor of Divinity and M.A. degrees

28. Raymond Aron, *Peace and War: A Theory of International Relations*, trans. R. and A. B. Fox (Garden City, N.Y., 1966), 596.

from Yale University in 1914. A year later, he went to Detroit, where he was the pastor of a small church with an active congregation. As Niebuhr describes it, World War I and the harsh social realities of Detroit "undermined my youthful optimism" and demonstrated "the irrelevance of the mild moralistic idealism, which I had identified with the Christian faith, to the power realities of our modern technical society."[29] In 1928, Niebuhr joined the faculty of Union Theological Seminary, where he remained until his retirement.

Niebuhr was a prolific writer, with sixteen books and more than fifteen hundred essays and articles to his credit. In 1939 Edinburgh University invited him to give the prestigious Gifford Lectures in Theology; the two volumes of *Nature and Destiny of Man*, representing the summa of Niebuhr's *oeuvre*, were the result. Over the course of his career Niebuhr moved from a mild commitment to Marxism in the 1930s to become a staunch advocate of the American achievement of "relative social justice." Niebuhr based his realism on an Augustinian view of human nature and sin as well as a prophetic hope for salvation in humility. He never identified himself with the entire program of American realism, yet as George Kennan has put it, "he is the father of us all": his effect on other writers was enormous. Because much of Niebuhr's realism crystallized through his participation in the debate about American policy immediately after World War II, I shall pay particular attention to his work up to 1952, when he reached a watershed with the publication of *The Irony of American History*. Together with George Kennan and Hans Morgenthau, Niebuhr tried to provide American foreign policy with a moral basis that accurately reflected the realities of power in a divided world.

The treatment of Niebuhr will be followed by chapters on Hans Morgenthau and George Kennan. Of all the realists, Morgenthau was the most ambitious intellectually: he tried avowedly to combine all three aspects of realism. First, he offered a general theory of international relations: *Politics Among Nations* was, and in a new edition edited by his friend and former student Kenneth W. Thompson remains, the standard textbook in the field. Second, he claimed to have a solution for the moral problem in international relations with his idea of the "moral dignity of the national interest." This idea deserves particular scrutiny. Finally, and arguably most interestingly, Morgenthau was active throughout his career in debates

29. Reinhold Niebuhr, "An Intellectual Autobiography," in Charles W. Kegley and Robert W. Bretall, *Reinhold Niebuhr: His Religious, Social and Political Thought* (New York, 1956), 4–5.

about current American foreign policy. He always argued that his specific recommendations for policy grew out of the superiority of his theoretical approach, in particular his conception of "interest defined in terms of power"; but his disagreements with other realists suggest it was less a master key to wisdom than a personal one. All these issues will be canvassed in Chapter 6.

Unlike Morgenthau, the former diplomat George Kennan made no claim to comprehensive theory; more than anything else his realism was a reaction to what he regarded as naive and moralistic American diplomacy. His concern was to debunk this moralism and to make room for a traditional diplomacy, whose function was to mute conflict and enshrine moderation. Throughout his career Kennan has tried to influence policy on issues he regarded as vital—indeed, now in his eighties, he is still trying. Ironically, he provided the code word "containment" for the diplomatic inflexibility of the Cold War and an oversimplified picture of the Soviet Union. A point of this chapter will be to account for this irony by illuminating Kennan's own idiosyncratically moral view of the world and by contrasting this view with that of his contemporaries Niebuhr and Morgenthau.

The subject of Chapter 8 will be the ideas and statecraft of Henry Kissinger. Just as many scholars were trying to move beyond the realist tradition, and just as the founding fathers themselves were having profound doubts about an application of realism that led to protracted and divisive war in Vietnam, he came into power with Richard Nixon in 1969. Kissinger was determined to apply the precepts of realism (or what he called geopolitics), and he believed that he had the skill and support to do so with subtlety and consistency. His ideas on power, prestige, and the importance of the great powers all belong, I shall argue, in the realist tradition, even if Kissinger himself prefers the term "geopolitics." In addition, his romantic notions about the importance and possibilities of leadership echo Weber's trust in the responsible and charismatic leader. The main goal of the chapter, therefore, will be to demonstrate the continuing survival and relevance of realist ideas as developed by Kissinger. As its second purpose, the chapter will consider not only how far Kissinger's policies reflected his ideas but also how far the difficulties inherent in the ideas resulted in fundamental problems of policy. Kissinger's problems with detente, his inability to build a sound domestic base for his policies, and his unusually personal approach to the ethical dilemmas of statecraft can all be traced to his own cast of realist ideas.

Moreover, the attitude of the original American realists to Kissinger's leadership recalls Weber's profound ambivalence about the legacy of Otto von Bismarck. In theory, Bismarck embodied Weber's criteria for responsible, charismatic leadership. For as long as he was in power, Bismarck dominated the German political system, presiding over its unification and determining its character. His foreign policy was masterful and always reflected a careful weighing of consequences—seemingly the essence of Weber's ethic of responsibility. Yet, as we shall see, Weber judged Bismarck harshly, blaming him for imperial Germany's attenuated institutions and its overall political immaturity.

Similarly, Kennan and especially Morgenthau criticized Kissinger for his basic conceptual mistakes, his overreliance on military means, and his pursuit of "an unviable conception of stability." Despite the assurance of its assumptions and recommendations, realism would seem very difficult to practice properly. Realists have always had a hard time reconciling the exigencies of domestic politics with their austere vision of the requirements of success in international relations. This difficulty goes back at least as far as Weber's Freiburg Inaugural in 1895, when he (unsuccessfully) urged Prussian Junkers to forego cheap Polish labor for the sake of Germany's national interest. Kissinger is the latest, though certainly not the last, figure to face the problem of trying to balance "realistic" foreign policy with the demands of his domestic polity.

Having traced the evolution of realist ideas from Weber to Kissinger, the book will conclude with a general assessment of the approach in each of the aspects I have identified. Rather than preview the argument here, perhaps a word or two explaining my larger purpose may be in order. Above all, I wish to examine and reconstruct as fairly, carefully, and critically as possible the central corpus of realist thought as a prerequisite for assessing its overall contribution. Too often, in my view, realist ideas are presented crudely or reduced to a least common denominator, which is then denounced for its oversimplifications. To be sure, there are many valid criticisms of realism, and I shall be adding some of my own. But as Keohane—himself a critic of the realist approach in his early work—has recently written, "Periodic attacks on Realism have taken place; yet the very focus of these critiques seems only to reconfirm the centrality of Realist thinking in the international political thought of the West."[30]

---

30. Keohane, "Theory of World Politics," in Finifter (ed.), *Political Science*, 503; for his earlier critique see Joseph S. Nye and Robert O. Keohane, *Power and Interdependence: World Politics in Transition* (Boston, 1977).

Thus the first justification of a study of this kind is that realism still has much to teach. Despite its shortcomings, realism has asked some very important questions, identified some crucial and lasting problems, and presented a vision of international relations that remains vitally relevant—even if it is not complete. No fair-minded person can fail to admire the historical breadth and sheer culture of George Kennan, the profound faith of Reinhold Niebuhr, or the erudition and forceful advocacy of Hans Morgenthau. Second, the realists have had enormous influence on the theory and teaching of international relations, and judging by the continuing debates in scholarly journals, they remain important today. As Stanley Hoffmann put it half-flippantly in 1977, it is as if "scholars were competing for a prize to the best discourse . . . about 'Persistence or Demise of the Realist Paradigm.'" The contest has gone on, and even intensified; but let us hope that Hoffmann is not borne out in his suspicion that the verdict will be spoken "in incomprehensible gibberish."[31] Realism continues to spark research and controversy. Its "doctrines," Hedley Bull has written, "profoundly affected a whole generation of students"; moreover, "the lessons of the realists have to be learnt afresh by every new generation."[32] It is therefore important to understand these lessons in all their complexity to determine if and how we are to move beyond them in an illuminating way.

Thus it is important to study the realists because their ideas persist. One need only glance at a newspaper to recognize that some form of realism still retains a hold on the popular and journalistic discourse on the subject, indeed that many contemporary statesmen avowedly share its vision. Commentators of every stripe continue to cite the central figures of modern realism in support of their views.[33] Given this persistence, careful scrutiny of the premises, development, lessons, and inconsistencies of realist thought is unquestionably worthwhile and even necessary. The arguments developed by the realists have gone in many different directions, and despite their apparent claim that the overt pursuit of morality should have no

31. Stanley Hoffmann, "An American Social Science: International Relations," *Daedalus*, CVI (Summer, 1977), 53; for evidence of the recent debate see Richard K. Ashley, "The Poverty of Neo-Realism," and the series of replies in *International Organization*, XXXVIII (Spring, 1984).

32. Hedley Bull, "The Theory of International Politics, 1919–1969," in Brian Porter (ed.), *The Aberystwyth Papers: International Politics, 1919–1969* (London, 1972), 38–39.

33. Irving Kristol, for example, invoked what he called Reinhold Niebuhr's "moral realism" in support of his approval of the 1983 American invasion of Grenada ("Toward a Moral Foreign Policy," *Wall Street Journal*, November 15, 1983, p. 8); also see Charles Krauthammer's polemic, "The Poverty of Realism," *New Republic*, February 17, 1986, pp. 14–22.

place in foreign policy, a moral vision informs the entire realist approach. What is this vision, and where does it lead? Ought we to share it? Together with those already defined, these questions and issues will engage the chapters ahead.

2

Max Weber and the Modern Discourse of Realism

"Nobody was more realistic than Max Weber," Karl Jaspers has written, but Weber "distinguished between a reality that is inescapable and a reality that is an expression of ideas, opinions, and wills which it is possible to influence and transform."[1] Jaspers points out that Weber was concerned with both realities: as a scholar he sought to identify the boundaries of inescapability, and as a political man—a polemicist with deep convictions about Germany's fate in the modern world—he marshaled his formidable powers of persuasion in an attempt to affect the second reality. This double concern imparts a sense of commitment and urgency to Weber's political writings that, for the most part, is missing from his more explicitly theoretical work. Weber's realism resonates with integrity and engagement.

My goal in this chapter is to present the outlines of Weber's realism as a way to highlight the concerns of later realists. I shall begin by considering Weber's definition of politics and the state to introduce his view of international relations. The depth and complexity of Weber's values will perhaps become most apparent in the discussion of his nationalism that follows. Weber was no ordinary chauvinist, yet it remains possible to argue that the interest of the German state was his ultimate value. His worries about Germany lent his general preoccupation with leadership—the next section of the chapter—immediacy and relevance: throughout World War I and after, Weber's essays and lectures on the subject of leadership were explicit attempts to shape Germany's postwar institutions. Following this discussion of Weber's view of the necessity of genuine leadership, I shall examine his treatment of its character. Weber contrasts the true politician with a vocation who lives *for* politics with the bureaucratic manager

1. Karl Jaspers, "Max Weber as Politician, Scientist, Philosopher" in *Three Essays: Leonardo, Descartes, Weber*, trans. Ralph Manheim (New York, 1964), 224.

who lives *off* politics. In addition, he formulates the moral problem in statecraft as a dichotomy between an ethic of conviction and an ethic of responsibility—a formulation that has dominated subsequent realists' treatment of the issue. After setting out these issues, the chapter will conclude with some preliminary critical remarks.

Politics, the State, and the International Struggle

Weber's view of the character of the international milieu follows from his definitions of politics and of the state. As set out in "Politics as Vocation," both definitions emphasize the struggle for power. Weber begins by noting that only a definition according to means makes sense: "Sociologically, the state cannot be defined in terms of what it does. There is scarcely any task that some political association has not taken in hand, and there is no task that one could say has always been exclusive and peculiar to those institutions which are designated as political. . . . Ultimately one can give a sociological definition of the modern state only in terms of the specific *means* peculiar to it, as to every political association: namely, the use of physical force."[2]

Weber goes on to note that if "the only social institutions which existed did not know the use of violence, the concept of the state would be eliminated, and a condition would emerge that could be designated 'anarchy' in the specific sense of the word." Thus the use of violence is "intimately related" to the state, and thus Weber's well-known definition:

> A state is a human territory which successfully claims the monopoly of the legitimate use of physical force within a given territory. . . . The state is considered the sole source of the "right" to use force. Hence "politics" for us means striving to share power or striving to influence the distribution of power either among states or among groups within a state. . . . When a question is said to be a "political" question . . . what is always meant is that interests in the distribution, maintenance, or transfer of power are decisive for answering the questions and determining the decisions.[3]

2. Weber, "Politics as a Vocation," in Gerth and Mills (eds.), *From Max Weber*, 77–78; translation slightly adapted: *cf.* Max Weber, *Gesammelte Politische Schriften*, ed. Johannes Winckelmann (2d ed., Tübingen, 1958), 494.
3. *Ibid.* Weber's wording here follows that in the subsequently published *Economy and Society*, ed. Guenther Roth and Claus Wittich (2 vols.; Berkeley and Los Angeles, 1978), 54–56.

In a passage from *Economy and Society* justifying his definition, Weber writes that "this usage thus seeks to bring out the common features of domination, the way it is exercised by the state, irrespective of the ends involved. Hence it is legitimate to claim that the definition put forward here is only a more precise formulation of what is meant in everyday usage in that it gives sharp emphasis to what is most characteristic of this means [of domination]: the actual or threatened use of force."[4] Weber therefore deliberately chose to underline the importance of force and the struggle for power in his definitions. Moreover, his account of the emergence of the modern state concentrates on the methods used by leaders to monopolize the legitimate use of force within a given territory: "To this end the state has combined the material means of organization in the hands of its leaders, and it has expropriated all autonomous functionaries of estates who formerly controlled these means in their own right. The state has taken their positions and now stands in the top place."[5]

As these definitions suggest, Weber regarded the power aspect of all politics to be inescapable. As he wrote to Robert Michels in 1908, "All ideas aimed at abolishing the dominance of men over men are 'Utopian.'"[6] On this important issue, Weber stands as a vintage realist: power is the essence of his view of politics. Of course, that power may be exercised only indirectly—"force is not the normal or only means of the state" but "a means specific to the state."[7] Most states, by virtue of their successful claim to legitimacy, can rely on the habitual obedience of their citizens by establishing legal codes in which the threat of physical coercion is only implicit. But however structured or mitigated, competition for power pervades all political life.

Nowhere is this pervasiveness more apparent than in international politics. Weber's position here is straightforward: states are locked in a struggle for survival. As he put it in the Freiburg Inaugural (1895), "For those who dream of peace and happiness, there stands written over the door of the unknown future of human history: 'abandon hope all ye that enter

---

4. *Economy and Society*, 55.
5. "Politics as a Vocation," in Gerth and Mills (eds.), *From Max Weber*, 83.
6. Quoted by Wolfgang J. Mommsen, *Max Weber und die Deutsche Politik, 1890–1920* (Tübingen, 1959), 392.
7. "Politics as a Vocation," in Gerth and Mills (eds.), *From Max Weber*, 78.

here.'"[8] Nor does this position simply represent an overexuberant, youthful call to arms, for in 1919 he wrote that "peace is nothing more than a
change in the character of conflict."[9]

Weber's analysis of the international competition is usually embedded
in his treatment of the problems facing Germany, but on occasion he
presents some general ideas. These ideas usually combine a conventional
balance-of-power view with a characteristic emphasis on the importance
of national honor or prestige. Consider, for example, the following passage from *Economy and Society*:

> Every political structure naturally prefers to have weak rather than strong
> neighbors. Furthermore, as every big political community is a potential aspirant
> to prestige, it is also a potential threat to all its neighbors; hence the big political
> community, simply because it is big and strong, is latently and constantly en-
> dangered. Finally, by virtue of an unavoidable "dynamic of power," wherever
> claims to prestige flare up—and this normally results from an acute political
> danger to peace—they challenge and call forth the competition of all other
> possible bearers of prestige. The history of the last decade [1900–1910], espe-
> cially the relations between Germany and France, shows the prominent effect
> of this irrational element in all political foreign relations.[10]

This passage illustrates Weber's appreciation of so-called systemic factors ("an unavoidable dynamic of power") as well as his emphasis on prestige. In addition, his curious assertion that big powers are "latently and
constantly endangered"—one would have thought that the small and
weak neighbors had more to worry about—recalls Bismarck's famous
"nightmare of coalitions." Weber casts even his general formulations in a
distinctly German mold.

Another aspect of the international struggle for Weber is economic
competition. The Kantian and liberal notion of peace through commerce
gets short shrift: "Even under the guise of 'peace' the economic struggle of
nationalities makes its way. . . . There is no *peace* in the economic *struggle*
for existence; only those who take the appearance of peace for the truth
can believe that the future will bring peace and the enjoyment of life for
our descendants." Weber insists that economic policy is "the servant of

8. Weber, "*Der Nationalstaat und die Volkswirtschaftpolitik,*" in *Politische Schriften,*
12.
9. Quoted in David Beetham, *Max Weber and the Theory of Modern Politics* (London,
1974), 41.
10. *Economy and Society,* 911.

politics—not the everyday politics of temporary power-brokers and classes—but of the continuing power-political interests of the nation."[11]

In holding such austere views, Weber was very much a German of his time; but unlike many of his contemporaries, his view of the international struggle did not rest on racial or Social Darwinist grounds.[12] Weber rejected the notion that history selected superior civilizations for survival; indeed, he feared that higher cultures might prove ill-adapted to modern circumstances. This fear helps to explain the militant tone of the Inaugural Lecture; Weber was concerned that Germany was sinking into "a feeble eudaemonism" that would hinder its progress in the world.[13] Thus a formidable sense of political duty—and, as we shall see shortly, of Germany's particular duty—lay behind Weber's stern admonitions, which in turn reflect his notion of politics as unending struggle.

It is important to emphasize that this notion of the international struggle for power led Weber to evaluate domestic political arrangements and economic policy on the basis of their effect on the power-political interests of the nation. For Weber, as for later realists, domestic politics act as enabling (or constraining) factors in the unending competition among different states. Weber's admiration of British political institutions, for example, stemmed at least partly from his assessment of their efficacy in promoting Britain's power in the world.[14] And his harsh judgment of Bismarck's legacy, and even more of Kaiser Wilhelm II's activities, reflected his conviction that both undermined Germany's prestige and position in the world.[15] Let us now consider Weber's view of what that position should be.

The Character of Weber's Nationalism

What form of nationalism did Weber espouse? The question has aroused considerable scholarly debate. Students and younger colleagues of Weber, many of whom remained close to his widow, Marianne, after his death in

11. *Politische Schriften*, 12, 14.
12. Beetham, *Weber and Modern Politics*, 43; cf. *Politische Schriften*, 9.
13. *Politische Schriften*, 24.
14. Cf. "Politics as a Vocation," in Gerth and Mills (eds.), *From Max Weber*, 104–106, and *Economy and Society*, 912.
15. Weber, "Parliament and Government in a Reconstructed Germany," reprinted as an appendix to *Economy and Society*, 1385–93, 1435–37.

1920, regard Weber to have been the quintessential "good German." Several, notably Karl Jaspers, have argued that Weber's sudden death robbed the Weimar Republic of a potentially great leader. These scholars stress Weber's liberal values, his commitment to parliamentary democracy, and his unquestioned intellectual integrity; for them, Weber represented the best in German culture.[16]

With the publication of *Max Weber und die Deutsche Politik* in 1959, Wolfgang J. Mommsen fundamentally challenged this view. Mommsen focused on the nationalist element in Weber's thought, asserting that a "national power state" (*nationaler Machtstaat*) was Weber's political ideal and the driving force behind his political writings and activities.[17] Predictably, a lively controversy followed. As Raymond Aron put it, "This reinterpretation of Weberian politics caused an outrage because it robbed the new German democracy of a 'founding father,' a glorious ancestor, a spokesman of genius." Aron entered the fracas with a paper, "Max Weber and Power Politics," at a 1964 conference in Heidelberg commemorating Weber's centenary. Aron largely took Mommsen's view, arguing that "Weber had chosen the power of the national state as the ultimate value, and this choice was free and arbitrary."[18]

Recent scholarship has entered what one might call a postrevisionist phase. Mommsen himself has written that his book was influenced by British and American efforts at "democratic re-education" and by a desire to purge Germany of all traces, however ancestral, of National Socialism; the 1959 book was written "from a somewhat more dogmatic point of view than I would entertain nowadays."[19] It is now possible to present a balanced view of Weber's nationalism which recognizes its importance in his thought without magnifying it to proto-Nazi proportions. All responsible scholars agree that Weber would have abhorred Hitler and everything he stood for.

16. Jaspers, *Three Essays*; Karl Loewenstein, *Max Weber's Political Ideas in the Perspective of Our Time*, trans. R. and C. Winsten (Boston, 1966). See also Reinhard Bendix, *Max Weber: An Intellectual Portrait* (Garden City, N.Y., 1959), and Beetham, *Weber and Modern Politics*, chap. 5.

17. Mommsen, *Weber und die Deutsche Politik*, esp. chaps. 3 and 10. An early and unreliable treatment of similar issues can be found in J. P. Mayer, *Max Weber and German Politics: A Study in Political Sociology* (2d ed.; London, 1946).

18. Raymond Aron, *Main Currents in Sociological Thought* (2 vols.; Harmondsworth, 1967), II, 253. Aron, "Max Weber and Power Politics," in Otto Stammer (ed.), *Max Weber and Sociology Today* (New York, 1971), 93.

19. Wolfgang Mommsen, *The Age of Bureaucracy: Perspectives on the Political Sociology of Max Weber* (New York, 1974), 24, 114n.

Weber's view of the nation combines elements of sociological analysis with personal values, and it grows out of the view of politics and the international struggle sketched above. Sociologically Weber identifies three main conditions for nationhood: (1) a common factor (frequently, but not always, language) between people which allows them to distinguish themselves from outsiders, (2) a shared recognition that the common factor acts as a source of value and solidarity (Mommsen characterizes this notion simply as "common cultural heritage"), and (3) a political organization with sufficient power to defend its common culture against outsiders.[20] Weber does not develop these ideas contained in two short (one was unfinished) sections of *Economy and Society*, but he does make some interesting suggestions, particularly with respect to the third condition. Weber seems to posit a notion of "cultural mission": "The idea of the nation for its advocates stands in very intimate relation to its 'prestige' interests. The earliest and most energetic manifestations of the idea . . . have contained the legend of a providential 'mission.' . . . The significance of the 'nation' is usually anchored in the superiority, or at least the irreplaceability, of the culture values that are to be preserved and developed only through the cultivation of the peculiarity of the group."[21]

Weber states the importance of this notion of mission—and of the power required to pursue it—as a matter of empirical observation of the phenomenon of nationhood. As he writes in an earlier chapter, "Time and again we find that the concept 'nation' directs us to political power. Hence the concept seems to refer—if it refers at all to a uniform phenomenon—to a specific kind of pathos which is linked to the idea of a powerful political community of people who share a common language, or religion or common customs, or political memories; such a state may exist or it may be desired."[22] Thus the pursuit of power is closely tied to the very idea of nationhood, once again demonstrating the ubiquity of Weber's view of politics as struggle.

As interesting as these empirical-sociological conditions for nationhood are, they miss the essence of Weber's idea of nation. "The concept," he writes forthrightly, "belongs in the sphere of values." Sociologically one could "analyze all the individual kinds of sentiments of group mem-

---

20. *Economy and Society*, chap. 9, esp. 921–26; and chap. 5, esp. 385–98; Mommsen, *Age of Bureaucracy*, 38.
21. *Economy and Society*, 925.
22. *Ibid.*, 397–98.

bership and solidarity in their generic conditions and in their consequences for the social action of the participants," but this was not Weber's project.[23] To his credit, he carefully separated his analysis from his personal values. Unlike many of his German contemporaries (Heinrich von Treitschke, for example) Weber did not try to dress his nationalism in the garments of a pseudo-science: as he wrote in a well-known passage of "Science as Vocation," "I do not know how one might wish to decide 'scientifically' the value of French and German culture; for here, too, different gods struggle with one another, now and for all times to come."[24]

This last quotation points up the characteristic form of Weber's nationalism. On one hand, Weber eschewed any claim about the superiority of any culture on the basis of "science"—a point rightly made by his defenders.[25] Yet on the other hand, his insistence—on apparently empirical grounds—that the struggle between cultures is unending and agonistic led him to urge that Germany pursue its "cultural mission" with bellicose vigor and, if necessary, force. Weber was deeply committed to German culture and to the advance of the power-political interests of its bearer in a hostile world, the German state.

To develop in all its implications the nature of Weber's commitment would require a multiplication of the many quotations already presented—in the compass of the present study an impossible (and probably undesirable) task. Instead, it seems sensible simply to emphasize its main characteristics. First, Weber's attachment to Germany's national ideals was lifelong; although the tone of the Freiburg address may be extreme, Weber held the sentiments behind it throughout his life. On December 26, 1918, in the midst of Spartacist activities, Weber wrote to a friend that "I believe in the indestructibility of this Germany, and never before have I regarded my being a German as such a gift from heaven as I do in these darkest days of Germany's disgrace."[26]

Substantively, Weber's lifelong commitment rested on his firm belief in the worthiness of German culture and the German national mission. In this regard, Weber was a classic nationalist. He believed that as possessors of a noble culture, Germans had a positive duty to ensure its survival:

23. *Ibid.*, 922, 925.
24. "Science as a Vocation," in Gerth and Mills (eds.), *From Max Weber*, 148.
25. See Beetham, *Weber and Modern Politics*, chap. 5.
26. Quoted in Marianne Weber, *Max Weber: A Biography*, trans. Harry Zohn (New York, 1975; original German ed., 1926), 638.

Future generations, and above all our descendants, will not hold the Danes, the Swiss, the Dutch, and the Norwegians responsible if the mastery of the world—and in the last resort this means the disposal over the civilization of the future—is divided up between the regulations of Russian officials and the conventions of Anglo-Saxon society, with perhaps a dash of Latin *raison*. They will hold *us* responsible, and rightly so: for we are a great power [*Machtstaat*], and unlike the smaller nations we are able to cast our weight in the scale.[27]

Note that Germany's responsibility derives not only from the importance of preserving its culture "in the civilization of the future" but also from its position as a large state, a great power. Great powers have greater responsibilities than lesser powers; and for Weber Germany's responsibilities were greatest.

Like many other Germans of his generation, Weber regarded a world political role for Germany as a matter of entitlement. The strength of German culture, in his view, earned for Germany a prominent place in the world; and a vital way to establish this place was through imperial expansion. As David Beetham points out, Weber's imperialism had two main elements, both of which were evident in his speeches to the Protestant Social Movement in the late 1890s. The first was a straightforward economic argument: "We need more room externally, we need an extension of economic opportunities through the expansion of our markets abroad and that is nowadays in the long run absolutely dependent upon the expansion of our political power abroad." Germany had a late start in the race for colonies, and her geography disadvantaged her, but Weber thought that these disadvantages should provide Germany with greater challenges; they intensified the crucial tasks that lay ahead.[28]

The second element of Weber's imperialism connects directly to his sense of national duty. A strong and expanding economy was a *sine qua non* for a great power of world rank. I have already noted Weber's conviction that economic competition is only an aspect of the struggle for survival; therefore, if Germany were to succeed as a great power, it would need to struggle for new markets and accept the risks attached to developing an export economy: "It is not a policy of comfort and ease that we are after, but one of national greatness, and as a result this is the risk we must take, if we want to pursue a form of national life which is different say,

27. *Politische Schriften*, 140.
28. Beetham, *Weber and Modern Politics*, 134–38; quotation from Weber's 1896 speech to the Protestant Congress, 134.

from the Swiss."[29] This 1897 speech echoes Weber's strictures against "feeble eudaemonism" and his stern reminders that the purpose of German policy was not to "promote well-being" but to "develop the characteristics which make for nobility and human greatness."[30] In this sense, Weber regarded imperialism as a national obligation.

Perhaps the most striking feature of Weber's nationalism is that it was a matter of faith for him. The power interests of the German state, as Aron and Mommsen argue, constituted Weber's "supreme value," a value Weber held throughout his life. But for all its importance, Weber seems to have regarded it as a given: his commitment to the nation is curiously unexamined. To be sure, he recognized its consequences, and indeed enshrined this recognition in the ethic of responsibility; but the value itself Weber accepted without question. It is tempting to say that Weber found meaning in his own life through his devotion to the nation: among the warring gods of values Weber chose the god of nation almost as a matter of personal religion. As he wrote to F. D. Crusius in November, 1918,

> Like Eulenspiegel on the uphill road, I am an *absolute* optimist (but only at long range) as far as our own nation is concerned. We have now seen all its weaknesses, but if one wishes one can also see its fabulous efficiency, simplicity, objectivity, its *capacity*—not the attainment!—for the "beauty of everyday life," in contrast to the intoxication or the playacting of the others.... History, which has already given us—*only* us—a second youth, will give us a third. I have no doubt of it and neither have you—*quand même*.[31]

But if Weber's commitment to the German nation was deep, it was not uncritical. He was not a crude seeker of power for its own sake; in "Politics as Vocation" he writes that "there is no more harmful distortion of political power than ... worship of power *per se*."[32] Foreign policy must be carefully calculated and the responsibility for its consequences fully accepted. Weber mercilessly criticized Kaiser Wilhelm II for his inept interventions and his "hysterical vanity," and throughout World War I he warned against the politics of "national vanity" and the "politics of hate."[33] For Weber, the responsibility of power demanded a brutal hon-

29. 1897 speech quoted in *ibid.*, 136.
30. *Politische Schriften*, 14.
31. Quoted in Marianne Weber, *Weber*, 636.
32. "Politics as a Vocation," in Gerth and Mills (eds.), *From Max Weber*, 116; *Politische Schriften*, 535.
33. Weber, "Germany Among the European Powers" in *Politische Schriften*, 154; *Economy and Society*, 1431–38.

esty—especially from leaders—about Germany's objective situation. The 1918 letter to Crusius quoted above, for example, states that "the self-discipline of truthfulness bids us say that Germany's role in world politics is over."[34] In Weber's view, precisely the absence of such responsibility and truthfulness among Germany's leaders after Bismarck contributed to its eclipse. His concern about leadership followed directly from his assessment of the dangers facing Germany as it sought to realize its national mission in a hostile world. In his treatment of leadership, as in all other aspects of domestic politics and economic policy, Weber employed as his ultimate criterion the German national interest.

The Importance of Leadership

A concern for the character and quality of leadership runs through all of Weber's work; his notion of leadership can be seen as a bridge between his theoretical enterprise and his practical political concerns. Thus from a theoretical point of view, an emphasis on leadership is built into Weber's basic definitions.

Weber distinguished his three pure types of legitimate domination, for example, according to the category of claim made by leaders. To form "a sufficiently reliable basis for a given domination," its rulers attempt "to establish and cultivate the belief in its legitimacy." Weber classifies "the types of domination" according to the kind of claim to legitimacy typically made by each. In other words, he bases his typology on the characteristically different ways leaders attempt to foster a belief in the validity of their rule. Weber concedes that people may submit to rule for many reasons ranging from genuine belief to "weakness and helplessness." "But," he goes on, "these considerations are not decisive for the classification of types of domination." What matters is the category of claim the "persons claiming authority" make; Weber identifies three pure types: traditional, rational-legal, and charismatic. My point is neither to criticize this typology nor to pursue the implications of its criterion for classification but to stress that Weber's very definition of the ideal types of authority led him to concentrate on leadership.[35]

Another important reason for this concentration relates to the entire direction of his sociological analysis. Weber regarded the advance of bu-

34. Marianne Weber, *Weber*, 636.
35. *Economy and Society*, 213–14.

reaucracy in the modern world to be irresistible, and there can be no doubt—as any reader of the closing passages of *The Protestant Ethic and the Spirit of Capitalism* will recall—that he viewed the prospect of its triumph with horror. Indeed, Weber's strongest indictment of socialism was that it would speed the process of bureaucratic rationalization: "If private capitalism were abolished, the state bureaucracy would rule alone."[36] The force most capable of interrupting this inexorable advance, in Weber's view, was genuinely charismatic leadership. As the antithesis of bureaucratic domination, charisma acts as a revolutionary force; in its "purely empirical and value-free sense charisma is indeed the specifically creative revolutionary force of history."[37] Because he dreaded the effects of bureaucratization, Weber sought in his political writings to encourage the emergence of genuinely charismatic leaders. His conception of plebiscitary leadership democracy should be understood in this light.

In addition to these "scientific" grounds for a preoccupation with leadership, Weber's concern was immediate and practical: he was worried about Germany's drift into leaderlessness at a time when the most skillful guidance was essential. The general reasons for this concern, as we have seen, stem from Weber's conception of politics and the international struggle. But how did Germany's domestic structure intensify its difficulties? Why was Germany bereft of real leadership? Weber's answers to these questions are crucial for an understanding of his view of leadership.

The diagnosis of Germany's problems which Weber offered in his political writings had two aspects: the class structure of imperial Germany and its political system. In considering each aspect, Weber's primary concern was the prospect of producing able, responsible, and, if possible, charismatic leaders. When Weber surveyed Germany's three major classes in his Inaugural, he found little reason for optimism. The class that had supplied most of Germany's leadership through the 1890s was the Prussian landed aristocracy, the Junkers. "For a quarter of a century, the highest office in Germany was in the hands of the last and greatest of the Junkers," Bismarck. Weber recognized that this class lay "in its economic death agony, from which no state economic policy can restore it to its former place in society."[38] At the same time, he knew that this class still dominated Germany's leadership and that its home state, Prussia, dominated the country's political system and bureaucracy.

36. *Politische Schriften*, 320.
37. *Economy and Society*, 1117.
38. *Politische Schriften*, 19.

Weber deplored this Prussian and Junker control because "it is danger-ous and, in the long run, contrary to the national interest for an economi-cally declining class to retain political dominance."[39] Why was such control dangerous—especially given the "incomparable grandeur" of Bis-marck's tenure? Weber's answer was straightforwardly Marxian: he thought that the class—particularly a class in the midst of irreversible economic decline—would rule in its own interest. And in fact, Weber believed that the Junkers were placing their class interest above the Ger-man national interest. This conclusion grew out of one of Weber's earliest works—the work that earned him the chair in economic history at Frei-burg—a study of Polish migrant agricultural labor on East Prussian estates. In the study, Weber noted that Junkers were employing cheap Polish labor at the cost of displacing local German workers and wrecking the stability of agrarian life. Even as he quixotically urged the Junkers to halt this damaging process for the sake of the larger interests of Germany, he real-ized that the demise of the estates was inevitable: Junker rule had merely prolonged their existence, first by establishing favorable tariffs, and second by allowing them to rely on the Polish migrant workers. Thus the Junkers had played their historical part, and the time had come for them to pass on the political leadership of Germany to its succeeding economic class, the bourgeoisie.

In a well-known passage of the Inaugural Lecture, Weber identified himself "as a member of the bourgeois class: I feel myself to be such and have been brought up on its opinions and ideals." Nevertheless, Weber was scathing in his discussion of the bourgeoisie as a source for leadership. Bismarck had unified the Reich without them, and therefore the class lacked experience in the rigors of power politics: its members were timid and "politically immature": "Part of the *haute bourgeoisie* longs only too obviously for the appearance of a new Caesar to protect it: to protect it from below, against the rising political masses, and from above, against the social and political assaults which they suspect the German dynasties of making against them. Another part has long been submerged into that political philistinism from which the broad mass of the *petit bourgeoisie* has never stirred."[40]

Weber maintained this harsh judgment of his own class throughout his political writings. He laid part of the blame for the political immaturity of the bourgeoisie at the door of Bismarck: the political system he created

39. *Ibid.*
40. *Ibid.*, 20, 23.

excluded them from meaningful political participation. But even after Bismarck fell in 1890, the middle class acquiesced to the continuation of a system in which "the great capitalist powers stand to a man on the side of a bureaucratic, authoritarian state [*Obrigkeitstaat*] and against parliamentary government." Weber regarded the "cowardice of the bourgeoisie" as an important reason for the "continuation of bureaucratic rule" in Germany.[41] Their fears of the working class, their hankering after aristocratic titles and accoutrements, and their complete lack of effective political instincts all locked the bourgeoisie into impotence. Weber's tone of contempt toward his own class is unmistakable; for leadership he looked elsewhere.

Unfortunately, the rising proletariat was equally unlikely to provide the responsible, charismatic leadership that Germany needed. The false god of socialism held most of the working class in its thrall. Weber's objections to socialism were both substantive and organizational. Substantively, he dismissed the "lofty hopes" for the transformation of capitalist society—either by revolution or evolution—to a free community of producers as illusions of the worst kind. Socialism, he believed, would merely speed the universal bureaucratization of modern society: "It is the dictatorship of the official, not that of the worker, which, for the present at any rate, is on the advance." By abolishing private entrepreneurs, socialism would aid that advance. The position of the worker would remain unchanged or even worsen: "The lot of a miner is not affected in the slightest by whether the pit is privately or state owned . . . under this kind of state socialism, the dependence of the worker is quite substantially increased." Thus as a doctrine socialism, according to Weber, was both wrongheaded and pernicious in its consequences.[42]

The organizational aspects of socialism also worked against the emergence of the kind of leader Weber wished to see at the head of Germany. The Social Democratic party (SPD) in Germany, large and bureaucratically organized, shared what Weber in "Politics as a Vocation" calls a "very petty bourgeois hostility of all parties to leaders." Especially after the death of August Bebel (who "was still a leader . . . however modest his intellect") "the instincts of officialdom dominated the party." The trade unions, as well, produced only organization men, cautious and plodding.

41. *Politische Schriften*, 337, 233.
42. Weber, "Socialism," in J. E. T. Eldridge (ed.), *Max Weber: The Interpretation of Social Reality* (New York, 1972), 208, 209, 203.

Men who lived *off*—rather than *for*—politics controlled both party and unions; their leaders were skillful bureaucrats, not brilliant improvisers capable of inspiring a mass following. Moreover, the *Weltanschauung* of the socialist organization committed it to permanent opposition within a bourgeois political order. The SPD "did not wish to stain itself" by governing in imperial Germany; therefore even if it possessed genuine leaders, the party would have barred them from lending their talents to the German nation.[43]

Having surveyed Germany's classes in vain for real leaders, Weber confirmed his diagnosis of leaderlessness with a pessimistic analysis of the nation's political system. Weber published this analysis in its most systematic form as a series of articles in the *Frankfurter Zeitung* in the summer of 1917, but the substance of his views had not changed for the previous twenty years. What lent the *Frankfurter* articles (published as *Parlament und Regierung im Neugeordneten Deutschland* [Parliament and Government in a Reconstructed Germany] in 1918) their tone of earnest persuasion was Weber's desire to learn from the flaws of the imperial system and to create a new system that would encourage leadership.

The imperial system, of course, did precisely the opposite. Rather than countering the sheeplike tendencies that, as we have seen, for different reasons characterized Germany's classes, the imperial political order enhanced them. The result was rule by bureaucrats. Weber would probably have agreed with Marx's description of imperial Germany in a letter to Engels as "a military despotism bedecked with parliamentary trimmings with an admixture of feudalism influenced by the bourgeoisie, bureaucratically constructed and protected by the police."[44] How did Germany end up with such a system?

Weber blamed Bismarck. Despite his undoubted achievements as the charismatic figure who dominated Germany for twenty-five years, Bismarck created "a nation without any political sophistication."[45] To ensure his personal control, Bismarck surrounded himself with "Conservative lackeys," squashed independent opposition, and emasculated the Reichs-

43. "Politics as a Vocation," in Gerth and Mills (eds.), *From Max Weber*, 114, 112. See A. J. P. Taylor's tart verdict on the SPD leadership in early Weimar: "The Social Democrats were republican, but they lacked all sense of authority: trade union officials, they awaited a boss with whom they could resume bargaining over wage rates" (*The Course of German History* [London, 1946], 185).
44. Quoted by Golo Mann, *A History of Germany Since 1789* (London, 1967), 208.
45. Weber, "Parliament and Government," in *Economy and Society*, 1392.

tag. In the end, he "tragically reaped his own harvest; for he had wanted—and deliberately accomplished—the political impotence of parliament and of the party leaders." Weber excoriated Bismarck for ruling the Catholic Center party after destroying the National Liberals and after the futile *Kulturkampf*; the Center party, according to Weber, was interested only in patronage and provided no real leaders. Bismarck's attempt to eliminate socialism by banning the SPD "drove the working class into the most extreme radicalism of pure party politics" and merely accelerated the growth of the party. Weber describes his social legislation as "very bad demagoguery" and a "grave political error." Bismarck, in short, arrested the political development of Germany and prevented the emergence of genuine leaders. His legacy was "a nation *without any political will* of its own, accustomed to the idea that the great statesmen at the helm would make the necessary political decisions."[46]

After Bismarck was removed in 1890 the true character of his system became painfully clear. Weber regarded the monarchy as a cruel joke, criticizing the "hysterical vanity" of the kaiser and abominating his clumsy forays into foreign policy. Parliament never emerged from its Bismarck-induced impotence and failed to serve as the place to recruit and test new leaders. "Our so-called monarchic government amounts to nothing but a process of *negative selection* which diverts all major talents to the service of capitalist interests. For only in the realm of private capitalism is there today anything approaching a selection of men with leadership talents." This "negative selection" led to unchecked bureaucratic rule in Germany precisely at a time when real political leadership was necessary. Germany's political parties could not counter this rule by bureaucracy, first because it was too deeply entrenched: "Wherever the modern specialized official comes to predominate, his power proves practically indestructible, since the whole organization of even the most elementary want-satisfaction has been tailored to his mode of operation." Second, the parties were characterized by bureaucratic organization—a result of "the rationalization of campaign techniques during the last decades." Thus an impotent parliament, irresponsible and bureaucratized parties, and an overbearing state bureaucracy combined to leave Germany without effective leaders.[47]

46. *Ibid.*, 1386, 1391–92.
47. *Ibid.*, 1413, 1401, 1398.

Weber's Solution: Plebiscitary
Leadership Democracy

To solve Germany's chronic leaderlessness, Weber proposed in his 1917 articles constitutional revisions that would bring about a system he called plebiscitary leadership democracy. The problem went beyond institutional tinkering; as he wrote in the preface to the book form of the *Frankfurter* pieces, "the arguments presented here cannot influence those for whom the historical tasks of the German nation do not rank above all issues of constitutional form."[48] In any case, "forms of constitution," he wrote to a friend in 1917, "are for me technical questions like any other machinery. I'd be just as happy to take the side of the monarch against Parliament, if only he were a politician or showed signs of becoming one."[49] As always, Weber's concern was to enhance Germany's ability to fulfill its "historic tasks" in the face of the acute dangers that threatened his nation throughout the war and after. Plebiscitary leadership democracy seemed to him the best method toward this end.

That Weber's commitment to democracy was at best instrumental bears emphasis. He had no patience with believers in popular sovereignty or the "will of the people." In 1908, he told Robert Michels that "such expressions were fictitious" and that if Michels cherished such illusions, he "still had great disillusion to suffer."[50] Weber proposed democracy because he thought a responsible parliamentary system would produce and train new leaders. Moreover, his view of democracy was conservative, a "doctor's mandate" democracy such as was advanced by British Conservatives or writers like Joseph Schumpeter. A dramatic exchange Weber had with General Erich Ludendorff in 1918 vividly illustrates this view:

Weber: In a democracy the people choose a leader whom they trust. Then the chosen man says, "Now shut your mouths and obey me." The people and the parties are no longer free to interfere in the leader's business.

Ludendorff: I could like such a "democracy"!

Weber: Later the people can sit in judgment. If the leader has made mistakes—to the gallows with him![51]

48. *Ibid.*, 1381.
49. Quoted in Beetham, *Weber and Modern Politics*, 102.
50. Quoted in Mommsen, *Weber und die Deutsche Politik*, 392.
51. Quoted in Marianne Weber, *Weber*, 654.

Obviously this colloquy oversimplifies Weber's view. He did recognize other important independent functions for parliament—in particular overseeing the bureaucracy and safeguarding civil liberties. But it does express the essence of his conception: the primary justification for parliament and democracy was his belief that real leaders would emerge from this system and that Germany's position in the world would therefore be strengthened.

How would the system work? What did Weber mean by "plebiscitary leadership democracy"? First, as in the typology of legitimacy, leaders take the initiative: "It is not the politically passive 'mass' that produces the leader from its midst, but the political leader recruits his following and wins the mass through 'demagogy.'"[52] "Demagogy" in Weber's usage applies to all political systems and suggests that by leadership he meant the capacity to sway the masses and win a following. Thus equipped, the leader could dominate the machinery of government. Plebiscitary democracy as Weber conceived it based its claim to legitimacy not on rational-legal grounds but on the strength of the leader's charisma: it is "a variant of charismatic authority which hides behind a legitimacy that is formally derived from the will of the governed. The leader (demagogue) rules by virtue of the devotion and trust which his political followers have in him personally."[53] The charismatic leader validates his authority by submitting to occasional plebiscites. By demonstrating his independent base, the leader is then better able to lead parliament and dominate the bureaucracy.

The role of parliament is primarily to provide a suitable proving ground for would-be leaders and, moreover, to ensure "the peaceful elimination of the Caesarist dictator once he has lost the trust of the masses." Weber's model here was the English Parliament, which he admired as a source of effective leadership. The British, according to Weber, recognized that "great political decisions . . . are unavoidably made by a few great men" and therefore made the necessary "major concessions to the Caesarist principle of selecting leaders." Weber hoped that an effective parliament would guarantee an orderly succession of charismatic leaders and that the revolutionary aspects of charisma could perhaps be smoothed out, as he thought they were in Britain. But his main concern for Germany was the

52. "Parliament and Government" in *Economy and Society*, 1457.
53. *Economy and Society*, 268.

recruitment of charismatic leaders to the political system, and his ideas for reform reflected this concern.[54]

In the aftermath of the 1918 November Revolution in Germany, Weber's general proposals took concrete form as a result of his participation in the working group that produced the Weimar Constitution. In particular, Weber worked hard to add a popularly elected president to Hugo Preuss's more traditional parliamentary scheme. Weber wanted to graft charisma onto the Weimar system, whose claim to legitimacy would be prosaically rational-legal. The president would be independent of parliament, with power to dissolve it and to choose the leaders of coalitions. Moreover, under Article 48 of the Constitution, the president would have emergency powers to legislate without parliament in times of crisis. Weber hoped that the Weimar presidency would provide a structure for charismatic leadership, which, by virtue of the leader's link to the masses, could tame the bureaucracy and spur self-interested and parochial political parties to consider the broader national interest.

In its basic outline, Weber's notion of plebiscitary leadership democracy attempted to combine charismatic leadership with some democratic safeguards. Mommsen has pointed to the similarities of Weber's idea to the constitution of Charles De Gaulle's Fifth Republic as a way to understand what Weber had in mind.[55] A strong, charismatic leader—who, by definition, possesses a large, devoted following—uses his mass base to set the broad policy for the nation, which indicates its approval in occasional plebiscites. The president stands above the day-to-day details of government and concentrates on matters of greater moment. Of course, the Fifth Republic was designed for De Gaulle. Weber's problem was more difficult: his system needed to produce leaders like De Gaulle to face the task of rebuilding a defeated Germany while preserving its national culture and honor. Such leaders are rare at any time and in any system; Weber hoped that under plebiscitary democracy they could, as it were, be made to order.

The Character of Leadership and the Ethics of Statecraft

We have seen thus far that Weber's preoccupation with leadership had several sources. His definition of politics and the state, his view of the

54. "Parliament and Government," in *Economy and Society*, 1452.
55. Mommsen, *Weber und die Deutsche Politik*, 411.

international struggle for power, and his commitment to the national ideals of the German state all led him to stress the vital importance of leadership for success in the modern world. His analysis in *Parlament und Regierung im Neugeordneten Deutschland* outlined the reasons for Germany's deficiency in leaders and proposed some basic constitutional revisions to attract potential leaders to the political system and to enable them to shape Germany's destiny without obstruction from bureaucrats or petty-minded party politicians. The extent of Weber's reliance on leadership, as well as the reasons behind it, should therefore be clear. But what of the actual character of the leadership? What would real leaders be like and what would they do once in power?

Weber's most sustained and systematic answer to these questions came in his lecture "Politics as a Vocation," given in Munich on January 28, 1919, and published after substantial revision in October of the same year.[56] The context of the lecture is important; Weber spoke to an audience of students polarized by their attitude to Kurt Eisner's revolutionary socialist Bavarian republic. He attempted in the address to persuade the students to place the current issues dividing them into historical perspective and to look beyond their millennial hopes and confront the consequences of their beliefs. The lecture was at once an effort at sociological analysis and political persuasion, and some of Weber's ambivalences are reflected in its structure. It therefore deserves close attention.

In the published version, Weber begins by setting out the definitions of politics and the state discussed above. He then turns to a historical analysis of the development of a separate political class—essential before politics could become a real vocation. Characteristically, Weber treats this development as an outgrowth of the attempt by rising leaders to extend and maintain their domination. Such a leader assembles a staff "personally dependent upon him" and moves to gain a monopoly on the "means of administration, warfare, and financial organization, as well as politically usable goods of all sorts." The process continues until "in the end, the modern state controls the total means of political organization, which actually come together under a single head."[57]

56. For a discussion of the problem of fixing the date of this lecture see Wolfgang Schluchter, "Value Neutrality and the Ethic of Responsibility," in Guenther Roth and Wolfgang Schluchter, *Max Weber's Vision of History: Ethics and Methods* (Berkeley and Los Angeles, 1979), 113–16.
57. "Politics as a Vocation," in Gerth and Mills (eds.), *From Max Weber*, 81–82.

Built into this historical sketch is Weber's contrast between two sorts of politician. The prince who gathers a staff lives *for* politics: "Either he enjoys the naked possession of the power he exerts, or he nourishes his inner balance and self-esteem by the consciousness that his life has *meaning* in the service of a cause." The man who lives for politics under normal circumstances must be wealthy; although he may obviously derive financial gain from his participation in politics, his livelihood does not depend on that participation. Those people recruited by the prince, those who "enter the *service* of political lords," are "professional politicians" of a different kind: they live *off* politics. These people rely on politics to make a living; they are officials theoretically at the disposal of the leader.[58] After making this basic distinction, Weber goes on to trace the importance of controlling patronage as a factor in the political evolution of different states. In Germany, for example, a highly developed officialdom cooperated with the aristocracy to stymie the claims of parliament, whereas in England a powerful Parliament preceded the establishment of a professional bureaucracy. The consequences for parliamentary democracy were momentous, for Weber assumes that a struggle between an "expert officialdom" and the "political leader" is constant.

This struggle results from contrasting conceptions of vocation. The genuine official administers his office *sine ira et studio*—without scorn or bias. "The honor of the civil servant is vested in his ability to execute conscientiously the order of the superior authorities, exactly as if the order agreed with his own conviction." The essence of the true political leader, by contrast, is "to make a stand, to be passionate—*ira et studium*. . . . The honor of the political leader, of the leading statesman, lies precisely in an exclusive *personal* responsibility for what he does, a responsibility he cannot and must not reject or transfer."[59] Weber here describes ideal types as a way implicitly to criticize both the politicians and the bureaucrats of imperial Germany. Bureaucrats tried to be politicians and failed because of their technical approach and unwillingness to accept responsibilities, and politicians behaved too much like timid bureaucrats, acting on narrow grounds with no overall vision of policy.

But having made this neat contrast, Weber then returns to sociological analysis to consider the characteristic sources of modern political leader-

58. *Ibid.*, 84, 83.
59. *Ibid.*, 95.

ship. In the middle third of the lecture Weber surveys journalism, political parties, and parliament as paths to leadership; his approach is comparative and historical and ends with a summary sketch of Germany's difficulties. Compared to his position in the 1917 *Frankfurter Zeitung* articles, Weber in this sketch is pessimistic about the prospects of parliament producing leaders. Proportional representation combined with the usual party-political "horse-trading" would create, in his view, "an unpolitical Parliament in which genuine leadership finds no place. Only the President of the Reich could become the safety-valve of the demand for leadership if he were elected in a plebiscitarian way and not by Parliament."[60]

At this point, having expressed once again his hopes for the Weimar presidency, Weber abruptly shifts from sociological analysis to political persuasion. After his historical outline of the sources of leadership, a discussion of its likely contemporary sources would have followed logically. Weber might have surveyed the current scene in Germany to assess the possibilities for leadership, to consider where the necessary leaders might come from—especially since he continued to deny that they would emerge from the mass of the people. But Weber never supplies an account of the ultimate sources of leadership as much as an institutional analysis of what inhibits or encourages its emergence. Just as he assumes politics is perennial struggle, he assumes there will always be aspiring leaders. In any case, instead of pursuing his analysis Weber mounts the political pulpit.

His subject is the essence of the true politician with a vocation and the proper ethics of statecraft. He identifies three qualities as "decisive for the politician: passion, a feeling of responsibility and a sense of proportion." The passion Weber has in mind is "matter-of-fact" and consists of an "inner devotion to a 'cause,' to the god or demon who is its overlord." The true politician must be able to distance himself from his cause and from his fellow men so he can understand and accept responsibility for his actions; he must be able "to let realities work upon him with inner concentration and calmness." Weber insists that a "passionate devotion" to a cause is essential to the true politician. The exact cause Weber regards "as a matter of faith"; but "some kind of faith must always exist. Otherwise, he will in fact—it is absolutely certain—labor under the curse of creaturely futility present even in his apparently greatest political successes."[61]

60. *Ibid.*, 114.
61. *Ibid.*, 115, 117; translation adapted: *cf. Politische Schriften*, 537.

Weber's politician must therefore possess more than a simple lust for power. As he puts it in *Parliament and Government*, "the struggle for personal power, and the resulting personal responsibility, is the lifeblood of a politician," but that struggle must never "become purely personal self-intoxication." Weber regards a "quite vulgar vanity" as "the deadly enemy of a realistic devotion to a cause." Precisely because power is the motor of all politics as well as its inescapable means, "there is no more harmful distortion of political force than the parvenu-like braggart with power, and the vain self-reflection in the feeling of power, and in general every worship of power *per se*." In these passages Weber distinguishes his view from that of the simple *Machtpolitikers*, for whom power was an end in itself; mere power politicians hide their "inner weakness and impotence . . . behind boastful and entirely empty gesture."[62]

Thus even before he introduces his dichotomy between the ethic of conviction and the ethic of responsibility, Weber foreshadows it in his picture of the ideal politician with a vocation. The extent to which his positive and negative portrayals rest on a contrast between "inner qualities" should be emphasized. The true politician is characterized by his "inner devotion," the "firm taming of his soul," a "personal knowledge of the tragedy with which all action, but especially political action is truly interwoven." The "mere power politician," by contrast, betrays vanity, a "personal need to occupy the limelight . . . inner weakness and impotence."[63] Weber distinguishes the true from the false politician on psychological grounds, on the basis of "inner strength" versus "inner weakness." Although it sounds straightforward enough, the criterion cannot easily be applied; as we shall see, Weber himself occasionally had some difficulty.

After describing the ideal politician in this way, Weber elaborates with a discussion of the relation between politics and ethics culminating in his familiar distinction between absolute and responsible ethics. The absolute ethic of conviction, as Weber defines it, is an ethic of intention. "The absolute ethic simply does not *ask* about consequences. *That* is the decisive point." Those who act on the basis of an ethic of ultimate ends question only the purity of their intentions; consistency is crucial. As Weber says, "this ethic is no joking matter": it is the ethic of the Sermon on the

---

62. *Ibid.*, 116.
63. *Ibid.*, 116–17; translation adapted: *cf. Politische Schriften*, 535–36.

Mount.[64] Only the *intentions* of the leaders of the workers' and soldiers' councils, Weber argues, distinguish their rule from that of the leaders of the old regime. Once again Weber concentrates on the psychology of the leaders to construct his argument, for surely the *process* by which the leaders of the old regime ruled differed sharply from the method of ruling in workers' and soldiers' councils. But what counts for Weber is the attitude of the leader toward politics; the revolutionary leaders, he asserts, convinced of their noble intentions and of the truth of their faith, ignore the consequences of their actions.

As Weber defines it, the ethic of ultimate ends does not attempt to *justify* the use of evil means by the good of the ultimate end. Logically the adherent of the ethic of conviction must "repudiate every action which involved morally dangerous means." To be consistent "one must be saintly in *everything*, at least in intention: one must live like Jesus, or the Apostles or St. Francis and their like, and *then* this ethic has meaning and dignity."[65] In reality, however, few statesmen behave with this consistency. Instead they urge one "last act of violence"; they behave like "millenarian prophets" who promise fulfillment after one last evil. Weber argues forcefully that the slightest concession to the idea that the end justifies the means marks the undoing of the absolute ethic of conviction as a credible ethical standard because it is "impossible to decree ethically which end should justify which means." This conclusion follows from Weber's own conviction that we live in an "ethically irrational" world—an irrationality that "the proponent of the ethics of conviction cannot accept"—and that one's ultimate values, in the end, result from an arbitrary choice among warring gods.[66] Thus followers of an ethic of conviction either betray inconsistency if they advocate evil means or, if they are consistent, they act as saints, not politicians.

But sainthood cannot serve as a political ethic because "the decisive means for politics is violence." The saint must forswear violence; the politician cannot: "The early Christians knew full well that the world is ruled by demons and that he who lets himself in for politics—in other words for power and force as means—concludes a pact with diabolical powers. They

64. *Ibid.*, 120; translation adapted: *cf. Politische Schriften*, 538.
65. *Ibid.*, 122, 119; translation adapted: *cf. Politische Schriften*, 540, 538.
66. *Ibid.*, 123; translation adapted: *cf. Politische Schriften*, 541. On this point see also "Science as a Vocation" in Gerth and Mills (eds.), *From Max Weber*, 129–59, and "Objectivity in Social Science and Social Policy," in *The Methodology of the Social Sciences*, trans. and ed. Edward A. Shils and Henry A. Finch (New York, 1949).

knew as well that for such a man it is *not* true that only good can follow good and only evil from evil—but rather the contrary often holds true. Anyone who cannot see this is indeed a political infant."[67] A political ethic has no choice but to confront the reality that "good" ends often require evil, or at least morally questionable, means.

Weber argues that only an ethic of responsibility confronts this reality squarely. The responsible statesman calculates and accepts the consequences of his policies; he realizes that he must "give an account of the foreseeable results of one's action." Such a leader is willing to risk his personal salvation as a result of his political actions. Again personal qualities are crucial: "What is decisive is the disciplined relentlessness in viewing the realities, and the ability to endure them and to measure up to them inwardly." Weber finds this relentlessness and responsibility absent among the "politicians of intention." He questions their "inner strength" because they pass off responsibility; he characterizes them as "windbags who do not fully realize what they take upon themselves, but who instead intoxicate themselves with romantic sensations." By contrast, the responsible leader is in full command. He realizes he has contracted with diabolical forces and accepts the "inner" burden for the sake of his calling. Indeed, the responsible leader, as we have seen, is devoted to a cause, and this devotion allows him to draw a line, to proclaim, "Here I stand, I can do no other." To the extent that this devotion strengthens the leader and enables him to confront his responsibilities, "the ethic of conviction and the ethic of responsibility are not diametrically opposed, but complementary: together they make a genuine man, a man *capable* of the calling for politics."[68]

In sum, then, the ethic of responsibility is a quintessentially political ethic, because it is an ethic of doing evil when circumstances require it, and evil is an inescapable component of political action. What distinguishes the responsible from the merely well-intentioned statesman is the former's ability to foresee as far as possible the consequences of his actions and his willingness to accept personal responsibility for those consequences— even for those he did not expect. Weber's condemnation of the German leaders who ordered unrestricted submarine warfare follows precisely this formulation: they refused to confront the likely consequences of their

67. "Politics as a Vocation," in Gerth and Mills (eds.), *From Max Weber*, 121, 123; translation adapted: *cf. Politische Schriften*, 542.
68. *Ibid.*, 120, 127; translation adapted: *cf. Politische Schriften*, 546–47.

action—American entry into the war—and they denied responsibility for these consequences once they occurred. And as usual, personal qualities were decisive. Alfred von Tirpitz was fundamentally "irresponsible," and Bethmann-Hollweg "lacks will-power," was "incapable of making decisions," and "simply is not a statesman."[69] Thus the ethic of responsibility ends as a standard of personal fitness for leadership, an ethic of making difficult decisions and later standing by them.

Weber's Responsible Realism: Some Critical Remarks

Weber's approach is open to a number of different criticisms, beginning with his definition of politics and the state and his conception of the international struggle. For example, by treating all politics as struggle one is blinded to distinctions in the levels of force employed and to the varying circumstances that define different kinds of struggle. The notion of politics as struggle is central to later realists, especially Carr and Morgenthau. Since they try to elaborate and improve on Weber's view—not, after all, original to him—it seems wise to defer a fuller discussion of this issue until later. For now, it should simply be noted as a problematic foundation for many of the realists' later ideas. It can certainly be said even at this point that to treat all politics as inexpiable struggle is to propound a self-fulfilling prophecy. The ethical pessimism of the realists results from their stark view of politics in general and international politics in particular.

Of more immediate concern here is Weber's treatment of leadership and his definition of the ethical problem in statecraft. We have seen that Weber's concern for leadership rests on both theoretical and political grounds. Theoretically, Weber saw leadership as the effective force most able to arrest the inexorable triumph of bureaucracy in the modern world. Politically, he regarded leadership as essential for the survival and promulgation of Germany's national ideals. The premises of this approach to leadership can, of course, be challenged. A contemporary critic of Weber, for example, charged that his fear of bureaucratization was vastly overdrawn and was the product of his treating the uniquely arrogant Prussian bureaucracy as a universal phenomenon.[70] A gentler view of international

69. For a discussion of this matter see Marianne Weber, *Weber*, 559–70; remarks about Tirpitz and Bethmann-Hollweg, 574, 577. Also *cf.* "Der Verscharfte U-Bootkrieg," in *Politische Schriften*, 142–57.
70. Beetham, *Weber and Modern Politics*, 85.

politics and a less assertive nationalism would have led to a considerably more serene reading of the chances for the survival of German culture. But let us, for the sake of argument, accept Weber's premises about the importance of leadership.

In this case the crucial issue becomes how to produce, and more important, how to recognize genuine leaders. As we have seen, Weber distinguished the bureaucrat from the charismatic leader and proposed political arrangements to facilitate the emergence and domination of the latter over the former. But the problem of how to recognize the genuine leader with a calling remains. How can we tell the difference between the truly charismatic leader and a plausible phony, between the windbag and the eloquent statesman? Weber can offer no guidance at all on theoretical grounds precisely because legitimacy is defined as a successful claim to authority and because, as a matter of definition, the charisma of the "berserk" or the "shaman" cannot be distinguished from that of the "genuine" hero or prophet: "What is alone important is how the individual is actually regarded by those subject to charismatic authority. . . . Value free sociological analysis will treat all these ["shaman" types or "sophisticated swindlers"] on the same level as it does the charisma of men who are the 'greatest' heroes, prophets, and saviours according to conventional judgments."[71] Thus from a sociological point of view one cannot distinguish Myneer Pieperkorn from Goethe, or Moses from Elmer Gantry—all that matters sociologically is the extent and devotion of the putative leader's following.

Yet Weber did distinguish between leaders: *he* could tell the difference between the "parvenu-like braggart" and the profound leader. Explicitly he offered two related criteria—the "inner qualities" of the leader and the political ethic he espoused. The criterion of personal qualities amounts to no more than a purely subjective judgment about whether a given leader possesses "inner strength" or "inner weakness." Weber never hesitated to make such judgments—more often detecting weakness than strength—but he failed to divulge or defend the specific grounds on which he formed them. And he could make mistakes.

In an incident that reveals much about Weber's political values and his curiously anachronistic sense of national honor and chivalry, in 1919 he went to visit General Ludendorff; part of their exchange was quoted above. Weber's purpose in going was to urge Ludendorff to "offer his

71. *Economy and Society*, 242.

head" to the allies. Obviously believing that Ludendorff possessed the requisite "inner strength," Weber told him that "the honor of the nation can be saved only if you give yourself up." After Ludendorff retorted that "the nation can go jump in the lake," Weber changed his mind about Ludendorff's inner qualities and concluded that he would not be suitable: "If he should again meddle with politics, he must be fought remorselessly."[72] Clearly, recognizing real leaders on the basis of their inwardly "disciplined relentlessness" is a tricky business; people are often not what they seem.

Weber's apparently more straightforward standard for recognizing genuine leaders is their adherence to the ethic of responsibility. Of course, to the extent that one identifies that adherence by the same qualities of inner strength, this standard suffers all the difficulties attached to judging intentions—something Weber rightly regards as impossible or fruitless because nearly everyone professes good intentions. But Weber does not admit that judging inner qualities involves the same problems. These qualities manifest themselves in outward political action, and one is far more likely to extend one's assessment of that action on external grounds to a judgment about inner qualities than vice versa. It is unlikely that Weber would have repeated his mistake about Ludendorff on a figure like Kurt Eisner: his disapproval of Eisner stemmed from his political values, not his judgment of Eisner's inner bearing.

Yet, explicitly, Weber denies that one can judge a figure's acceptance of the ethic of responsibility by the cause he espouses. The leader's cause is "a matter of faith" and "some kind of faith must always exist."[73] Weber cannot judge on the basis of this faith without himself embracing the ethic of conviction—a course he wants to avoid. What matters for the ethic of responsibility is the willingness to calculate and confront the consequences of one's actions. The genuine leader accepts personal responsibility for his policy—even at the cost of his own salvation. This sense of responsibility for consequences marks the difference between the real leader and the well-intentioned statesman-*manqué*. But what defines the sense of responsibility? According to which criteria does the leader weigh the consequences of his actions?

Weber's ethic of responsibility runs aground on precisely these questions, for according to his own definition he is unable to answer them. One

---

72. Marianne Weber, *Weber*, 653–54.
73. "Politics as a Vocation," in Gerth and Mills (eds.), *From Max Weber*, 117; *Politische Schriften*, 535.

can imagine a statesman of great inner strength—a Rosa Luxemburg or a Wilhelm Liebknecht, both of whose genuineness Weber acknowledged—pursuing a policy of socialist revolution with full awareness and acceptance of the consequences of that policy. There is little doubt that Weber would have rejected such a policy. But as long as the leader calculated, and accepted personal responsibility for, the consequences of his policy, he would have fulfilled the ethic of responsibility. Equally, one can imagine a contemporary leader who felt it necessary for reasons of state to launch a nuclear attack; let us further imagine that leader to be a religious man who worried that his action would endanger his personal salvation but who nevertheless ordered the attack. He weighed the consequences and accepted responsibility for them. This leader, too, would have fulfilled the ethic of responsibility. We may nonetheless wish to condemn his action not only on moral but on prudential grounds. It all depends on our criteria for judging consequences. The point is that the ethic of responsibility defines no such criteria. It speaks only to the leader's ability and willingness to *face* consequences; it says nothing about how he *weighs* them. The standards for calculating costs reflect the leader's choice of cause—for Weber a matter of faith. But Weber implicitly identified his own faith—the national ideas of the German state—with the ethic of responsibility. The standard he used to separate the windbag from the heroic leader was his reading of Germany's national interests. As a committed German, Weber judged leaders on the basis of his assessment of their policies for Germany.

Yet Weber nowhere defended his values and refused even to admit that the ethic of responsibility, in the end, expressed his convictions about Germany's national destiny. To have done so would have been to deny his value-free definitions of legitimacy and charisma. He would have been forced to acknowledge that he too followed something of an ethic of conviction and that the real distinction between the leaders he liked and those he abominated reflected more than their ability to face consequences: his distinction was based on the values they pursued. Because Weber chose not to express and justify his own values, and because of his inordinate hopes for charismatic leadership, ultimately he was left in the difficult position of *hoping* that a responsible, charismatic leader would arise and serve Germany's interests. But overtly he is unable to distinguish such a leader from a convincing phony who lacks depth. For as he defines it, the ethic of responsibility speaks only to a leader's ability and willingness to face consequences.

Weber's assessment of Bismarck is instructive in this context. As has been shown, Weber judged Bismarck's legacy to Germany harshly, blaming him for Germany's political immaturity and attenuated institutions. Yet in almost every respect, Bismarck embodied the ethic of responsibility. Throughout his career he was the calculator of consequences *par excellence*; few statesmen in history match his capacity to judge the effects of his policy. Nor did he shirk the responsibility for his policies while he was in office: indeed, the very actions whose long-term consequences Weber deplored represented Bismarck's efforts to concentrate responsibility for policy on himself. Clearly Bismarck was a charismatic figure whose "inner strength" could not be questioned. What Weber did question was Bismarck's overall effect on Germany, which he probably rightly regarded as deleterious. But the point is that Weber's assessment of Bismarck was based on values that go beyond the ethic of responsibility. Weber wanted strong institutions that could produce independent leaders; he wanted responsible political parties, a flexible bureaucracy, and a loyal opposition. All these desiderata are compatible with an ethic of responsibility—provided that one defines his conception of responsibility. And this Weber refused to do: his view of responsible statecraft can be reconstructed only through his disparate political writings. The ethic of responsibility itself offers no guidance.

Two implications follow from Weber's position, the first specific to him and the second in his bequest to later realists. Weber's attempt to enshrine charisma in the Weimar Constitution by adding a plebiscitary presidency and his reliance on charismatic leadership to stem the tide of bureaucracy both found ironic fulfillment in subsequent German history. The two men who occupied the Weimar presidency, Friedrich Ebert and the aged General Paul von Hindenburg, were both in their very different ways the very antithesis of charismatic leadership. In their tenure in office they neither promoted parliamentary responsibility nor effectively countered the bureaucracy; Hindenburg actually helped to doom the republic. And of course the next charismatic leader to come on the scene in Germany was Adolf Hitler—a tragic demonstration of the force of charisma and the consequences of unprincipled *Realpolitik*. Weber obviously would have hated the Nazis and had nothing to do with the failure of Weimar; but it is fair to say that he did not fully appreciate the "demonic" possibilities inherent in his own ideas.

The second implication concerns Weber's legacy to the later realists.

More than any other modern figure Weber established the discourse of the realist approach to international relations. His view of politics as struggle, his definition of the state, and his austere vision of the international competition for survival—a vision that led him to subsume domestic politics and economics into this international struggle—all were adopted more or less intact by later realists. But by far the most influential of Weber's formulations was his rigid division of political ethics into the ethic of conviction and the ethic of responsibility. Virtually to a man, later writers accepted this dichotomy primarily because they saw themselves as arguing against a view that good intentions solved everything. As a result they urged instead an ethic of prudence, of weighing consequences, of accepting the evil inherent in all politics in order to limit it. Unfortunately, as we shall see, these later writers failed to recognize the extent to which Weber's particular values—his unquestioned acceptance of the primacy of the nation-state, his commitment to Germany—informed his very definition of the problem. As Weber used it, the distinction between responsibility and ultimate ends as competing ethics boiled down to a division between competing values: it was less a matter of whether the statesman weighed the consequences than what those consequences would be.

More than anything else, the ethic of responsibility reflected Weber's specific concerns about Germany. He identified responsible statecraft with the pursuit of national ideals—an arguable, but not a self-evident, proposition. By accepting Weber's definition of the ethical problem in statecraft, later realists doomed themselves to repeating his mistake. For, as will become clear, they too espouse values which they build into their approach; they too fail to discuss their values openly or to attempt to defend them against other claims. They present the problem simply as a confrontation between prudence and misguided Messianism. Weber's dichotomy of realism and responsibility versus idealism and good intentions endures to the present day; and lucid discussion of the precise content of responsibility, of the values that compete to judge the consequences of policy, remains a rare commodity.

3

The Idealist
Provocateurs

To move from Weber's world of inexpiable conflicts and tragic ethical dilemmas to the progressive universe of the interwar Anglo-American idealists is like leaving an uninterrupted performance of Wagner's Ring Cycle for a civic meeting punctuated by communal singing of hymns by S. S. Wesley. The unending clash of national cultures gives way to a continually developing international community; a sense of universal moral purpose confidently takes over from Faustian statesmen contracting with the demonic forces of evil. The writers of the idealist school shared a normative vision, and for them, the study of international relations amounted to elaborating this vision as well as convincing recalcitrant national leaders and an ill-informed but well-intentioned public opinion of its higher truth.

The purpose of this brief chapter is to sketch in the main outlines of the idealist approach to international relations in order to understand more fully the context of the realist reaction. Carr, Niebuhr, Morgenthau, and Kennan all wrote in response to what they considered the false assumptions and complacent moralism of such idealist writers as Alfred Zimmern, G. Lowes Dickinson, or James T. Shotwell. I shall not attempt to treat these writers individually because my main point is to demonstrate how, as a school of thought, they provoked writers dissatisfied with their ideas into defining an opposing approach. The chapter, therefore, will treat only the major themes of the idealist hymn to internationalism; and, in the interest of brevity, I shall leave a critical evaluation of their ideas to the realists themselves, as set out in the chapters to follow.

Human Nature

In marked contrast to the dark view of Niebuhr or Morgenthau, idealists reached back to the Enlightenment notion of human perfectibility. No inescapable lust for power, no tragic security-power dilemma, impels men and women to war, and politics need not involve doing evil. In *Causes of International War* (1920) G. Lowes Dickinson asserted firmly that war "is not a fatal product of human nature. It is an effect of that nature when put under certain conditions." He went on to compare the evolution and fate of war to the process by which armed robbery became institutionalized and eventually proscribed in law-abiding societies.[1] Similarly, the classicist Gilbert Murray, active in England's League of Nations Union, wrote in 1929: "The apologists for War ... get their minds badly confused because they continue to speak of war as if it were an element in human nature, like Strife, or Fear, or Ambition. ... The war which is formally renounced in the Pact of Paris and practically guarded against in the Covenant is not an instinct, it is a form of state action. It is not an element in human nature, it is part of a political programme. It is no more an instinct, or an element in human nature, than the adoption of the income tax."[2]

In short, for the idealist school, war stems not from an evil human nature but, rather, from our imperfect political arrangements, domestic or international; and it is a persistent barbarity which gradually evolving civilizations, given the will to do so, can eradicate. As Arnold Toynbee, displaying his unique brand of fire and brimstone, put it in the 1928 *Survey of International Affairs*, "the institution of War [is] the deadly disease and the sin against the Holy Ghost of human societies in process of civilization."[3]

But if human beings are not by nature warlike, they are nevertheless frustratingly stubborn in their attachment to outmoded ideas. Dozens of writers, devoted to the League of Nations and indignant at their national government's perfidy toward it, frequently resorted to exasperated outbursts against inexplicably hidebound human nature: thus Nicholas Murray Butler's lament in 1933 about "how long it takes for even the most practical lessons to sink into the hearts and minds of men," or his schoolmasterly admission a year earlier that "it is difficult to make men see the Supreme power of moral considerations and the overwhelming force of moral influence." Alfred Zimmern, agreeing with Butler, explained this difficulty: "It is not because men are ill-disposed that they cannot be educated into a world social consciousness. It is because they—let us be hon-

1. G. Lowes Dickinson, *Causes of International War* (London, 1920), 16, 22.
2. Gilbert Murray, *The Ordeal of This Generation* (New York, 1929), 29.
3. Arnold J. Toynbee, *Survey of International Affairs: 1928* (London, 1929), 1.

est and say 'we'—are beings of conservative temper and limited intelligence."[4] Zimmern went on to identify the chief obstacle to a genuine internationalism as "muddled thinking."

Thus in the idealist scheme, human nature does not cause war—we are not by nature bellicose—but its limitations and susceptibility to passions and atavistic appeals inhibit the inevitable process by which war is to be abolished. As Dickinson put it, most people "follow passion, not reason, sentiment, not interest, words, not things." For him and for others, the only answer to this unfortunate characteristic was greater education; Zimmern even suggested that an "international lending library," which could make expensive foreign books available to homes "of modest means . . . would do more to lay the basis of an international public opinion than a great deal of more loudly-heralded propaganda."[5]

Rationalism, Faith in Progress, and the Harmony of Interests

As Zimmern's belief in the efficacy of an international lending library suggests, all these writers placed great store in the (eventual) power of lucid argument, and all of them took the task of educating public opinion very seriously. In Britain, the Welsh industrialist David Davies (of whom more later) endowed the first British professorship in international relations at the University College of Wales, Aberystwyth, "for the study of those related problems of law and politics, of ethics and economics, which are raised by the prospect of a League of Nations." The first incumbent of the Woodrow Wilson chair was Alfred Zimmern.[6] Zimmern, Gilbert Murray, and G. Lowes Dickinson were active members of the League of Nations Union, whose avowed purpose was to build public understanding of, and broad support for, the League. In his definition of his fledgling subject, Zimmern insisted that it was not a discipline as such but a "point of view" that stressed the importance of "relations between peoples" and "knowl-

4. Nicholas Murray Butler, *Between Two Worlds: Interpretations of the Age in Which We Live* (New York, 1934), 22, 90; Alfred E. Zimmern, *Neutrality and Collective Security* (Chicago, 1936), 8.

5. Dickinson, *Causes of International War*, 83; Alfred E. Zimmern, *America and Europe and Other Essays* (New York, 1929), 195.

6. Iuean John *et al.*, "International Politics at Aberystwyth, 1919–1969," in Porter (ed.), *Aberystwyth Papers*, 88.

edge of the peoples themselves"; the duty of the scholar was to educate people of all nationalities to a higher notion of internationalism. Politics in this conception was "an idealistic career." In a contribution to the World Committee of the Young Men's Christian Association, Zimmern wrote that "the future of civilization depends on the League of Nations," and he assured his young readers that "there is no finer field for the political idealist than in the day-by-day work" of the technical committees of the League.[7]

In the United States, faith in rational argument and in the need for public education was perhaps even more fervent given the abrupt American refusal to join the League. America had its own League of Nations Association, whose goal was to get the United States to join the League, as well as other organizations devoted to raising the public's consciousness of international affairs. The Foreign Policy Association grew out of meetings between Charles Beard, Herbert Croly, and other liberal writers in 1918–1919. The New York–based Council on Foreign Relations, founded in 1921, gathered influential businessmen, government officials, and academics who were not necessarily committed to the League (or indeed to the idealist conception of international affairs) but believed nevertheless that America had to play a far more active role in the world than the Republican administration in Washington had envisaged.[8]

Prominent among the American idealists were Raymond D. Fosdick, president of the League of Nations Association, Nicholas Murray Butler, the internationalist president of Columbia University, and the indefatigable James T. Shotwell, who taught international relations at Columbia under Butler. Shotwell convinced the Carnegie Endowment to sponsor a massive economic and social history of World War I and assumed the duties of general editor; the project took nearly twenty years to complete and ran to 150 volumes. He acted as consultant to the Council of the League of Nations in Geneva and was instrumental in drafting the famous Geneva Protocol of 1924; later he would give Aristide Briand the idea for the 1928 Pact of Paris. Shotwell believed that the danger facing the world required scholars to take the lead in applying sound academic and scien-

7. Alfred E. Zimmern, *The League of Nations and the Rule of Law, 1918–1935* (London, 1936), 5; see also William C. Olson, "The Growth of a Discipline," in Porter (ed.), *Aberystwyth Papers*, 13; Zimmern, *America and Europe*, 98.

8. See Robert A. Divine, *Second Chance: The Triumph of Internationalism in America During World War II* (New York, 1967), chap. 1.

tific principles to the recurring problems of national and international society.[9]

Common to these idealists on both sides of the Atlantic, then, was a firm belief in the primacy of ideas; hence their untiring efforts to educate a broad mass of people so as to mobilize public opinion on behalf of internationalism. This belief in turn rested on their twin convictions that a continuing progress—given the right ideas, correctly pursued—was well within human capacities and that an underlying harmony of interests existed among all the nations of the world. The highest of these common interests, of course, was peace, and the very creation of the League of Nations was taken by the idealists as evidence that mankind had learned the horrible lesson of the world war and had at last decided to do something about the primitive survival of war.

According to the writings of these often interchangeable authors, the true lesson of the war was the futility of pursuing strictly national interests by means of a balance of power. In Dickinson's history of the ten years up to the outbreak of war, *The International Anarchy*—a book written "consciously and deliberately to point a moral"—he asserted that "all history shows every balance has ended in war." The cause of war, and therefore the chief obstacle to peace, lay in the "international anarchy" prevailing before 1914, and the obvious moral of Dickinson's book is to end this anarchy. "The way to salvation," he wrote in conclusion, "is the development of the League of Nations into a true international organ to control in the interests of peace the policies of all States." He recommended general disarmament, the end of protectionism, "a complete apparatus for the peaceable settlement of all disputes"—in short, the entire, orthodox Wilsonian program. What such traditionalists as Winston Churchill called "the interests, the passions and the destiny of mighty nations" Dickinson renamed "their illusions, their cupidity and their pride."[10]

Similarly, in a book published well after the heady early days of the League, *The League of Nations and the Rule of Law, 1918–1935*, Alfred Zimmern treated the prewar system as a prologue to the more progressive regime of the League. The bulk of the work is devoted to a painstaking

9. James T. Shotwell, *Intelligence and Politics* (New York, 1921), 18–21; see also Harold Josephson, *James T. Shotwell and the Rise of Internationalism in America* (Rutherford, N.J., 1975), esp. chap. 6.

10. G. Lowes Dickinson, *The International Anarchy, 1904–1914* (New York, 1926), 2, 6, 471, 478, 37.

exposition of the "elements of the covenant" and of the "history and working of the League," which even in 1936 Zimmern regarded as the world's best hope for peace. Only the League "as a working machine" could lead the states of the world out of international anarchy, and if states were showing a distressing tendency by 1936 to rely on the methods of the Old Diplomacy, this merely illustrated the extent to which the governments of the world lagged behind the enlightened segments of public opinion within their countries: "The conduct of affairs by the Powers whose peoples were sincere in their desire for a better international system has exhibited all the characteristics of a period of transition."[11]

Other writers echoed Zimmern's attitude toward the League as both a measure of the progress mankind had made in eradicating war and as the primary means for ending the international anarchy and its futile reliance on the balance of power. In a chapter called "From Chaos to Cosmos," Gilbert Murray in *The Ordeal of This Generation* wrote that after the world war, "we seem most conspicuously to have discovered the right method for rebuilding our ordered world. We have invented the League of Nations: before we fight we confer, and when conference gives no immediate answer, we convoke disinterested experts and set them to study the question." Similarly, James T. Shotwell was convinced that "the World War has, after all, taught its full lesson to the generation that has suffered from it. The will to peace is paramount in the civilized world."[12]

This conviction that peace was the common interest of all states and that, as a result, every apparent conflict was subject to rational mediation to everyone's benefit was basic to all the idealists; indeed, it was their constant refrain, expressed in suitably apocalyptic rhetoric. For Murray, "the whole enterprise of the League was a Great Adventure based upon a Great Repentance" and the prospect of averting disaster depended entirely on the depth and sincerity of the repentance. David Davies, the benefactor, in *The Problem of the Twentieth Century*, urged the creation of an international police force to protect and defend the universal common interest in peace. He took 795 pages to explain why this force was necessary, why past systems had failed, and how it would operate in a reordered world. Once man had mastered the difficult task of "the right or moral use of force amongst the nations of this planet," he wrote, "by long and succes-

11. Zimmern, *League of Nations*, 482.
12. Murray, *Ordeal of This Generation*, 221; James T. Shotwell, *War as an Instrument of National Policy* (New York, 1929), vii.

sive states his mentality will gradually become attuned to a Higher Purpose, until at length he attains the perfection of those who inhabit the Kingdom of God." Even so relatively sober a scholar as C. K. Webster, the successor to Zimmern at Aberystwyth, in his inaugural lecture invoked life-or-death terms: "Never, I think, in the whole of history has any generation had so fateful a choice to make as ours. Nothing less than the existence of civilization is at stake. Unless we can find a way to a more sanely ordered system of International Politics, nothing good or beautiful that men erect in the world can be considered safe from destruction."[13]

Of course, apocalyptic rhetoric has long been, and remains today, a staple of idealist approaches to international relations. During and immediately after World War II, scores of Anglo-American authors presented new proposals for a rejuvenated League or an entirely new system of world government. Robert Maynard Hutchins' conclusion that in the atomic era "world government is necessary and therefore possible" was emblematic.[14] Other typical books included Mortimer J. Adler's *How to Think About War and Peace* (1944) and *How New Will the Better World Be?* (1944) by Carl Becker. In his contribution to wartime futurology, *The Great Decision* (1944), James T. Shotwell argued strenuously for the need to build on the example of the League. For all the idealists, the problem remained international anarchy and the system of sovereign states. And as Jonathan Schell has demonstrated recently in *The Fate of the Earth*, this definition of the problem persists.

Schell's identification of "the apparently indissoluble connection between sovereignty and war," his definition of the choice facing the world as "peace on the one hand and annihilation on the other," and his conclusion that "the task is nothing less than to reinvent politics, to reinvent the world" could have been written by any of the interwar idealists but for the emphasis on nuclear destruction; and his call for an aroused public opinion to demand total disarmament reminds one of Murray, Dickinson, or Shotwell.[15] The aspect unique to the interwar idealists was their confidence that, as Davies put it, despite everything "the law of progress still

13. Murray, *Ordeal of This Generation*, 152; David Davies, *The Problem of the Twentieth Century* (London, 1930), 705; Webster quoted in John *et al.* in Porter (ed.), *Aberystwyth Papers*, 89.
14. Robert M. Hutchins, "The Constitutional Foundations for World Order," in Hans Morgenthau and Kenneth W. Thompson (eds.), *Principles and Problems of International Politics* (New York, 1950), 143.
15. Jonathan Schell, *The Fate of the Earth* (New York, 1982), 187, 193, 226.

remains. In all departments of human thought it will reassert itself."[16] Contemporary idealist writers obviously do not share this confidence in progress—far from it. And no facet of interwar idealist thought was more relentlessly criticized than its faith in progress; indeed this criticism, more than anything else, defined the starting point of the entire realist approach.

From Paris to Abyssinia

Perhaps the best way to convey the substance and flavor of the idealists' approach is to examine and compare their response to the 1928 Pact of Paris and the League's reaction to the Italian invasion of Abyssinia (Ethiopia) in 1925. These two events were for the idealists the high and low points of internationalism in the period up to September, 1939, and their treatment of them illustrates vividly the normative character of their analysis, as well as their willingness to engage in direct political action.

The very existence of the Pact of Paris (or the Kellogg-Briand Pact) renouncing war as an instrument of policy was the result of precisely such political action by James T. Shotwell. In 1924, he had been intimately involved with the drafting and diplomacy of the Geneva Protocol, and he proved a tireless promoter of schemes to "associate" the United States with the League of Nations, which would bypass the trauma of ratifying a treaty formally acceding to the League Covenant. In March of 1927 Shotwell called on French Foreign Minister Briand and suggested that France issue a general statement on disarmament to coincide with the tenth anniversary of the American entry into the world war. In the course of his discussion with Briand he broadened the suggestion to include a general renunciation of war. According to his biographer, Shotwell's real goal was to nudge America out of its neutrality and to commit it to the League system of collective security.[17] Briand obviously welcomed this prospect—though his main interest was a bilateral treaty with the Americans—and he also hoped for some reconsideration of France's war debts to the United States.

On April 6, 1927, Briand issued a call for a general conference with the United States which closely reflected a draft Shotwell had submitted to the Quai d'Orsay. But Briand's proposal went unnoticed. Undaunted, Shotwell met with the editor of the New York *Times* and arranged for Nicho-

16. Davies, *Problem of the Twentieth Century*, 704.
17. Josephson, *Shotwell and the Rise of Internationalism*, 161.

las Murray Butler to write a letter to the *Times* calling attention to the offer. Butler's letter "challenged the public opinion of the United States to take up and answer the offer of France," noting that Briand had addressed his proposal to the American public, not just its government, and attesting to the practical cast of Briand's mind.[18] The idea then took off, and with some unofficial encouragement from the American State Department, Shotwell and a Columbia colleague drafted a general treaty that went well beyond Briand's original idea.

The Shotwell draft contained three major sections: a renunciation of war, provisions for arbitration and conciliation, and a process of ratification. Self-defense was defined as resistance to a violated promise not to go to war, "provided that the attacked party shall at once offer to submit the dispute to peaceful settlement or to comply with an arbitral or judicial decision." To meet traditional American concerns, the Monroe Doctrine was excluded, but the signatories undertook not "to aid or abet the treaty-breaking power," thus banning trade with an aggressor.[19] The American government adopted Shotwell's draft as a basis for negotiations, and after a period of diplomatic maneuvering (the details of which need not concern us) the representatives of fifteen states signed the Pact of Paris on August 27, 1928; forty-nine other states had been invited to adhere. By 1930, nearly all states had either ratified the treaty or declared their intention to adhere.[20]

The final treaty bore little resemblance to Shotwell's detailed draft. It contained two operating articles of a sentence each, plus a larger preamble and a detailed article concerning the process of ratification. Signatories agreed "to condemn the recourse to war for the solution of international controversies, and renounce it as an instrument of national policy in their relations with one another" in the first article; in the second they promised simply to settle any disputes "by pacific means" only.[21]

Despite the stripped-down character of the treaty and its obvious resemblance to an undertaking by sinners no longer to sin, idealist writers greeted the treaty as an event just short of the Second Coming. As late as

18. New York *Times*, April 25, 1927, partially reprinted in Shotwell, *War as an Instrument of National Policy*, 43–44. Josephson, *Shotwell and the Rise of Internationalism*, 163, says that Shotwell himself wrote Butler's letter.
19. Text in Shotwell, *War as an Instrument of National Policy*, 271–78; see also Josephson, *Shotwell and the Rise of Internationalism*, 167–76.
20. Toynbee, *Survey, 1928*, 25.
21. Shotwell, *War as an Instrument of National Policy*, 302–303.

1936, Alfred Zimmern called it "the most far-reaching engagement so far entered into by the sovereign states of the world" and "practically speaking, irrevocable." Parties to the treaty "have renounced war: they are not free to *unrenounce* it." Arnold Toynbee saluted the "remarkable" role played by public opinion and otherwise regarded it as a fateful step toward "the unification of Mankind into a single universal society." Gilbert Murray regarded the treaty as evidence of the rising spirit of pacifism, a welcome contrast to "nationalism, the stupidest and most dangerous of public vices." Shotwell, in his history of the diplomacy surrounding the treaty, praised the most constructive aspect of its approach: "Instead of enumerating the duties of law-abiding states, it denies the aggressor the right to calculate on the continuance of friendly relations."[22]

The Paris Treaty seemed to be a triumph of the idealist approach to international relations and was greeted by idealist writers as such. It began as the brainchild of a leading scholar-activist. Its progress was nurtured by the careful management of public opinion operating at first without government sanction. The picture painted was of an aroused internationalist populace demanding that their governments renounce war—rather as though Shotwell and his colleagues had led the world's people in a chorus of Schiller's "Ode to Joy." The success of the treaty seemed to demonstrate the primacy of ideas over tradition, the triumph of the long-term international interest over short-term and parochial national interests.

The sense of victory did not last long, and idealists soon returned to denouncing the stupidity of nationalistic policies and the folly of bypassing the League. The Japanese invasion of Manchuria in 1931 was followed by nearly two years of diplomatic maneuver resulting in the ineffectual League resolution of February, 1934, which succeeded only in causing Japan to withdraw from the League. In October, 1934, Nazi Germany also withdrew. Hard times had fallen on the international rule of law through the League of Nations. But perhaps the gravest blow to the prestige of the Geneva institution came in 1935, when Benito Mussolini's Italy invaded Abyssinia (Ethiopia). After the Manchuria experience, the technical planners of the League had worked out a scheme of economic sanctions ready to be implemented if determined upon by the member states. Still, the League's official response to Abyssinian appeals was cautious: more than

22. Zimmern, *League of Nations*, 392; Toynbee, *Survey, 1928*, 10, 8; Murray, *Ordeal of This Generation*, 201; Shotwell, *War as an Instrument of National Policy*, 221.

eleven months passed between their first approach and the official adoption of economic sanctions against Italy on November 18, 1935.[23]

Caution notwithstanding, League supporters regarded the handling of the crisis through 1935 with satisfaction. In September of that year, the British foreign secretary, Sir Samuel Hoare, made a speech to the League Assembly which emphatically and unambiguously declared that "the League stands, and my country stands with it, for the collective maintenance of the Covenant in its entirety, and particularly for steady and collective resistance to all acts of unprovoked aggression."[24] Earlier in 1935, in response to a house-to-house canvass by the League of Nations Union, more than 11.5 million people expressed overwhelming support for disarmament and collective security, in particular for all sanctions short of war against an aggressor; 6.8 million (versus 2 million against and 2 million abstentions) supported war as the final sanction.[25] Stanley Baldwin's National government in Britain sought and gained reelection in November, 1935, on a platform that emphasized support for the League. Thus through most of 1935 League supporters had reason to feel encouraged.

Then, on December 9, 1935, Paris newspapers published details of a plan worked out between Hoare and the French foreign minister, Pierre Laval—"the Parisian spider," according to Toynbee.[26] In stark contrast to the high-sounding affirmations of the League spoken by both men in September, the plan offered large parts of Abyssinia to Mussolini in exchange for an end to economic sanctions. The resulting "outcry in England against the Hoare-Laval plan was the greatest explosion over foreign affairs for many years, perhaps since the campaign against the 'Bulgarian horrors' in 1876," according to A. J. P. Taylor.[27] Reaction in France was similarly negative, Laval closely surviving two crucial votes in the Chamber of Deputies on December 27–28, 1935.[28] The British and French withdrew the plan but did not change the underlying attitude that inspired it: they were unwilling to apply any sanctions that might lead Mussolini to declare war on them; indeed, they still cherished the hope of enlisting Mussolini's support against Hitler. During 1936, while Mussolini's armies pushed for-

23. Abyssinia first appealed to the League for arbitration on December 9, 1934. For a detailed (virtually day-by-day) chronology, see Arnold Toynbee, *Survey of International Affairs: 1935* (2 vols.; London, 1936), II.
24. Quoted in *ibid.*, 187.
25. A. J. P. Taylor, *English History, 1914–1945* (London, 1965), 381.
26. Toynbee, *Survey, 1935*, II, 291.
27. Taylor, *English History*, 385.
28. Toynbee, *Survey, 1935*, II, 322.

ward (and on March 7, Hitler reoccupied the Rhineland), debate on applying stricter sanctions dragged on. Finally in May, 1936, the Italians defeated the Abyssinian army, and in July the League voted to withdraw sanctions and refused to recognize Italy's annexation.

Idealistic writers denounced the betrayal of the League by their national governments as well as the deterioration of the internationalist "atmosphere of Geneva" into "something that was little better than a miasma of pharisaical hypocrisy." Arnold Toynbee, who devoted an extra volume of the Royal Institute of International Affairs' annual *Survey* to the invasion, was perhaps the fiercest critic. For him, this "tragic episode of international history" was "a tale of sin and nemesis." Mussolini's "deliberate, personal sin" of "positive, strong-willed, aggressive egotism" was matched by "a negative, weak-willed, cowardly egotism" among the politicians of Britain and France. These politicians had "a choice between making the post-war system of law and order genuinely work or else seeing the frail structure relapse into the chaotic anarchy which had begotten not only the war of 1914–18 but one behind another before that." Toynbee's basic explanation of the sorry course of action was "the prevailing lack of a lively faith in ultimate spiritual principles" and the unfortunately still existing "general truth that, in the determination of human action, reason seldom succeeds in asserting itself against Passion and Prejudice." He went on to ask presciently whether England was abdicating "from her eminent and responsible position as arbiter of Europe" to the "two young and lusty nations of Germany and Russia."[29]

Alfred Zimmern, Gilbert Murray, and Lord Robert Cecil similarly deplored the British and French policies at a rally for the League at Manchester University after the Italian victory. Zimmern called the British position "humiliating and shameful," declaring "it was not the League of Nations that had failed, it was ourselves." In his book on the League published during the crisis, he asked whether "force still reigns supreme" in the world and if the "two great democracies of Western Europe" were "united by a bond nobler and more enduring than that of individual self-interest."[30] By June 11, 1936, he had decided, and in a letter to the *Times* put the alternatives facing Britain as either abandoning the League or revitalizing it with strong sanctions and a newly mobilized public opinion. "Both alternatives," he wrote, "involve the risk of a general war," but the

29. *Ibid.*, 490, 1–3, 6, 449, 452, 481–82.
30. Quoted in *ibid.*, 457; Zimmern, *League of Nations*, 445.

risk was "distinctly less" if the active League policy were followed: "We are living in the shadow of a war—of a war which, if and when it breaks out, will not leave us on one side, however much we may crouch to avoid it."[31]

James T. Shotwell was just about the only idealist writer who attempted to put a brave face on the failure in Abyssinia. He acknowledged it to be "serious" with "far-reaching consequences" but compared it to the failure of the American Articles of Confederation—a temporary setback that could conceivably force "the readjustment of nations to a readjusted League." Moreover, the vital part played by public opinion in encouraging sanctions in the first place, in causing the abrupt withdrawal of the Hoare-Laval plan, and in forcing the resignation of Hoare himself was, wrote Shotwell, "of deep significance for those who watch the slow but certain growth of moral issues in international affairs."[32]

Idealists and the Moral Problem of Statecraft

These reactions to the Pact of Paris and the failure of sanctions against Italy illustrate the character of the idealist approach to international relations and in particular their understanding of the ethical dilemmas inherent in foreign policy. For them progress in ending international anarchy consisted of asserting the will and then using reason (usually capitalized) to find the way—hence their promotion of, and loud support for, the Kellogg-Briand treaty. This agreement reasserted—in irrevocable terms—the firm intention of every state to forswear war as an instrument of national policy. That the treaty was vague on definitions (in Shotwell's own glowing account it "define[d] aggression and defense without a definition") did not worry idealist writers because every question was simply referred back to the ready and ever-developing machinery of the League.[33]

The failure of the Western states vigorously to employ this machinery in the case of the Italian invasion called down their wrath against their weak-willed governments in the memorable terms just quoted. On this point at least, the idealists were right. Strict and effective sanctions under the aegis of the League were not employed because Britain and France were ultimately unwilling to risk war on a matter of international princi-

31. Quoted in Toynbee, *Survey, 1935*, II, 462.
32. James T. Shotwell, *On the Rim of the Abyss* (New York, 1936), vii, 191.
33. Shotwell, *War as an Instrument of National Policy*, 218.

ple. Moreover, the warnings by Toynbee and Zimmern about the ultimate consequences of British policy proved apt: clearly there are advantages to holding firm moral beliefs confidently.

But precisely because they held such strong normative beliefs and applied them so surely, the idealists contributed very little to our understanding of the moral problem in statecraft. For them, every question of policy was simple: did it promote the League and the international rule of law? The only areas for discussion lay in devising the most effective machinery. They denounced national interests as parochial and retrograde; nationalism as a stupid superstition long abandoned by men of enlightenment. Thus many of the difficult problems faced by current statesmen were simply dismissed by the idealists as atavisms inhibiting the progress of international civilization. In effect, the problem of morality and foreign policy for them had already been solved: the difficulty lay in getting governments to follow the solution. And that difficulty could be eased by forthright public education, scholarly activism, and widespread organizing at a grass-roots (or at least civic society) level.

Let us now consider how the realists interrupted their internationalist hymn to progress with an unrelenting dirge about power and the national interest.

4

E. H. Carr:
Realism as Relativism

The publication of E. H. Carr's *Twenty Years' Crisis* in November, 1939, launched the realist counterattack against the idealist views we have just considered. Contemporary reviewers unanimously recognized the significance of the book; as Crane Brinton wrote, "when British academic liberals begin to go hardboiled, we are entitled to feel that something is about to happen." The *Times Literary Supplement* called the book "as profound as it is provocative" and praised its "fresh and fearless thinking." In a hostile review, the *New Statesman* nevertheless compared it to Hobbes's *Leviathan*, and even Sir Alfred Zimmern, writing critically and rather condescendingly in *Spectator*, allowed that Carr had "sat in the Foreign Office with an observing eye"—although Zimmern quickly added that "when the ex-foreign officer leaves and the teacher of international relations takes over, his guidance begins to fail us." Thus from its first appearance *The Twenty Years' Crisis* was treated as a challenge to the predominant intellectual approach to international relations, and it is still read today as a classic statement of realism.[1]

The treatment of Carr in this chapter concentrates largely, but not exclusively, on his best-known book. From 1939 to 1951 he wrote frequently on the character and future of international relations; taken together, these works form a distinct period in his overall scholarly output. In treating them distinctly, I follow Carr's own advice in *What Is History?* to consider an author's work by paying close attention to its date of publication and by recognizing "how closely [it] mirrors the society in which he works."[2] The discussion will proceed in six stages: first, Carr's charac-

1. Crane Brinton, "Power and Morality in Foreign Policies," *Saturday Review*, February 17, 1940, p. 19; *Times Literary Supplement*, November 11, 1939, p. 65; Richard Coventry, "The Illusions of Power," *New Statesman*, XVIII (November 25, 1939), 761; Alfred Zimmern in *Spectator*, CLXIII (November 24, 1939), 750.
2. E. H. Carr, *What Is History?* (London, 1961), 51.

terization and theoretical critique of "utopianism"; second, his development of the Weberian theme of the importance and inescapability of power; third, his discussion of the sources and limitations of morality; fourth, the practical policy lessons Carr drew out of his realism, in short, his justification of appeasement; fifth, a brief characterization of Carr's assessment of the postwar character of the state and the international system; finally, some critical remarks on Carr's brand of realism. Carr accepted Weber's ethic of responsibility and his emphasis on power without sharing his nationalist faith. But Carr's own apparent faith in socialism seems to me to be no more successful than Weber's in imparting content to the ethic of responsibility; indeed, his moral relativism may make any effective ethic impossible.

Utopianism Unmasked

Like all good "essays in criticism," *The Twenty Years' Crisis* begins by characterizing the view it seeks to supplant.[3] Carr opens the book with a brief account of the beginnings of the "science of international politics" which emphasizes its normative foundations: "The passionate desire to prevent war determined the whole initial course and direction of the study. Like other infant sciences, the science of international politics has been markedly and frankly utopian." This utopian infancy, Carr asserts, is a stage of development common to all systems of thought: he grounds his discussion in a somewhat crudely teleological sociology of knowledge. He repeats that "the wish is father to the thought" in all fields (citing Plato, the alchemists, and Marx, among others) and argues that a period of "hard ruthless analysis of reality" inevitably follows an initial emphasis on aspiration. In international politics the events of the 1930s revealed the utopian character of the assumptions underlying early work in the field.[4]

Before scrutinizing those assumptions, Carr devotes a chapter to "the fundamental antithesis of utopia and reality," firmly planting a stark contrast in the mind of the reader. A series of dichotomies—rightly described as "breathtaking" by one commentator—is set out.[5] Free will versus determinism, theory versus practice, left versus right, ethics versus politics—all

3. Zimmern's phrase, in *Spectator*, 750.
4. E. H. Carr, *The Twenty Years' Crisis, 1919–1939: An Introduction to the Study of International Relations* (2d ed.; London, 1946), 8, 3, 7.
5. Hedley Bull, "*The Twenty Years' Crisis* Thirty Years On," *International Journal* (Toronto), XXIV (Fall, 1969), 627.

these can ultimately be reduced to utopia versus reality. These dichotomies, artificial and vastly oversimplified to be sure, stand nevertheless for Carr as opposite poles of political thought between which he can steer a sensible-sounding course. "Utopia" and "reality" are not so much ideal types as exaggerated extremes—though the characterizations are slanted obviously in favor of "reality"—whose effects can be traced in virtually all thinking about politics.

In his portrait of utopian thought about international politics, Carr highlights several of the features sketched in the last chapter: faith in reason and in the infallibility of public opinion; a sense of moral rectitude and intellectual superiority; confidence in laissez-faire economics and in an underlying harmony of interests; in short, the view that war is irrational and that the way to end it is through education and the vigorous pursuit of international law and world government in the League of Nations.[6] This characterization of idealist thought—and the reaction against it—is common to virtually all the realists; yet each of them chooses a particular aspect to emphasize and thus each constructs a different foundation for his own realistic alternative. For Weber, as we have seen, the greatest sin of idealists, of those who would make politics more ethical, was their refusal to face and accept the often unpalatable consequences of political actions. The ethical statesman recognized an inevitable admixture of evil in all his actions but accepted this in a profoundly "matter-of-fact" [*sachlich*] way and did what he had to do to serve the higher interests of his state. Thus Weber's critique and alternative rested on the putative irresponsibility of idealists.

Carr's critique, though compatible with Weber's, begins not with a contrast between moral conviction and political responsibility but with a materialist argument about the sociology of knowledge. He challenges the idealist claim to moral universalism on both philosophical and, with respect to the harmony of interests, empirical grounds. Carr's argument on these points deserves careful reconstruction because it forms the basis of his approach.

He begins his realist critique appropriately enough by quoting the famous Chapter 15 of *The Prince* in which Machiavelli proclaims his intention to study things as they are and not as they should be. Carr boldly sums up Machiavelli's conclusions—"morality is the product of power"—and enlists Bodin, Hobbes, and Spinoza as endorsing and elaborating on this

6. Carr, *Twenty Years' Crisis*, 24–25.

claim.[7] These sixteenth- and seventeenth-century thinkers, according to Carr, recognized that coercive power is prior to any effective system of morality; moreover, in asserting that "every man does what he does according to the laws of nature and to the highest right of nature," Spinoza "thus opened [the way] for determinism."[8]

The persuasiveness of Carr's summary of these thinkers need not detain us; he uses them merely as a springboard to his main argument about determinism and the social conditioning of thought. "The outstanding achievement of modern realism," he writes, "has been to reveal, not merely the determinist aspects of the historical process, but the relative and pragmatic character of thought itself." In support of this relativist view Carr cites Bishop John Burnet, A. V. Dicey, Lord Acton, and, above all, Marx; and in a conclusion taken from Karl Mannheim (though not specifically acknowledged) Carr concludes that "the conditioning of thought is necessarily a subconscious process."[9]

As presented by Carr, the argument for the social conditioning of thought and for "the adjustment of thought to purpose" is made to seem virtually self-evident. In the face of representative quotations from a broad range of thinkers, who could deny that social circumstances and pragmatic purposes condition thought? The hard questions about the process of conditioning or determination of thought are left unasked in Carr's gallop to unmask the universalist pretensions of the idealists. Which social circumstances dominate the conditioning of thought? Do they operate equally on all segments of society? Is a class analysis the proper avenue to understanding the divisions of society through which "social circumstances" are filtered and hence thought conditioned? Is class-consciousness historically determinative? What about a Weberian conception of elective affinities between systems of ideas? The closest Carr comes to confronting any of these questions is in a brief criticism of Marx, whose

7. *Ibid.*, 64. Carr's view of these thinkers, especially Machiavelli, does not command universal, or even widespread, agreement. One could interpret Machiavelli as asserting a radical separation of power and morality, as making a factual claim about the negligible effects of moral concerns on the exercise of power. To the extent that his analysis makes any claim about morality, it simply outlines the disadvantages of moral scruples to a glory-seeking prince. Machiavelli nowhere discusses the sources of the actual content of morality; power may *triumph* over morality but it does not necessarily *produce* it. *Cf.* Isaiah Berlin, *Against the Current: Essays in the History of Ideas* (New York, 1980), 25–29; Plamenatz, *Man and Society*, I, 24–31.

8. Carr, *Twenty Years' Crisis*, 65.

9. *Ibid.*, 67–68; 71. Carr mentions his debt to Mannheim in the preface.

materialism is described as "perhaps unduly restrictive" and incorrect in its denial of national interests and "the potency of nationalism as a force conditioning the thought of the individual."[10]

Clearly Carr's argument on this complex issue does not run very deep; indeed, he seems unaware of the problems connected with it. He is content to assert in conclusion on the issue that "theories of social morality are always the product of a dominant group which identifies itself with the community as a whole, and which possesses facilities denied to subordinate groups or individuals for imposing its view of life on the community. Theories of international morality are, for the same reason and in virtue of the same process, the product of dominant nations or groups of nations." The shallowness of Carr's argument on behalf of this conclusion—he goes on to say that "current theories of morality have been designed to perpetuate [the] supremacy of the English-speaking peoples"—reflects his own purpose in making it. Carr wants only to debunk the more sweeping claims to universalism made by idealist writers. He quotes, for example, Arnold Toynbee: "International law and order were in the true interests of the whole of mankind . . . whereas the desire to perpetuate the reign of violence in international affairs was an anti-social desire which was not even in the ultimate interests of the citizens of the handful of states that professed this benighted and anachronistic creed."[11]

Against this assertion, against the identification of the League of Nations with progress, intelligence, and cosmopolitan enlightenment, Carr reminds us that capitalist mineowners and union-bashing employers used the same sweeping terms. It is enough for him to insist that one's own interests exercise a powerful influence on the moral principles one professes to employ. On this basis, he damns advocates of the internationalist ideals of the interwar years for failing to recognize precisely this point: "What matters is that these supposedly absolute and universal principles were not principles at all, but the unconscious reflexions of national interest at a particular time."[12] To score against the assertions of Toynbee *et al.*, Carr's broad argument suffices; as far as it goes, his point is well taken. But, as I shall argue later, when Carr tries to develop his own normative position and when he applies his critique to specific policy, the shallowness of his preferred sociology of knowledge leads him into irresolvable difficulty.

10. *Ibid.*, 69.
11. *Ibid.*, 79, 80, 83.
12. *Ibid.*, 87.

In his attack on the other main pillar of the idealist edifice—the harmony of interests—Carr employs this same argument about the conditioning of thought as well as a more straightforwardly empirical refutation. He asserts first that the laissez-faire doctrines prevalent in nineteenth-century Britain simply reflected British prosperity and predominance in world trade. British statesmen who preached the universal virtues of free trade sincerely believed it; but their belief was the product of concrete British economic interests.

Carr's second argument details instances when a supposed international harmony of interests reflected the specific interests of status-quo powers. To take the simplest example—that nations have a common interest in peace, that "war profits nobody"—Carr points out that, however compelling in 1918 to Anglo-Americans, this proposition would not convince Germans, "who profited largely from the wars of 1866 and 1870 and attributed their more recent sufferings, not to the War of 1914, but to the fact that they had lost it." Thus Britain and America could safely assert that war served no purpose because it *had* served theirs. The Treaty of Versailles embodied the interests of the winners, not those of all mankind. Different nations have different interests; and satisfied powers inevitably couch their particular interests in universal terms. The easy assumption that peace is every nation's interest, writes Carr, enabled Western statesmen and scholars alike "to evade the unpalatable fact of a fundamental divergence between nations desiring the status quo and nations desirous of changing it."[13]

These two arguments against the assumption of a harmony of interests complete Carr's explicit critique of the utopian doctrines. But before he develops his own alternative vision, he pauses to consider the "limitations" of realism. It "often turns out in practice to be just as much conditioned as other modes of thought"; moreover, a consistent realism "fails to provide any ground for purposive or meaningful action." Even realists have to escape their determinist assumptions if they are to be effective leaders; on this point Carr quotes V. I. Lenin: "No situations exist from which there is absolutely no way out." Carr therefore recognizes that pure realism offers no relief from a naked and continuous struggle for power. But his solution is to invoke "the fascination and tragedy of all political life. Politics are made up of two elements—utopia and reality—which can

13. *Ibid.*, 51–53.

never meet." These irreconcilable elements must be combined in political life—but how? At this point in his argument he hints at a cyclical pattern— idealistic aspiration, partial realization, inevitable reduction of the realized ideal to selfish interest, new utopian ideals. But the argument is only suggested.[14] To gain a fuller understanding we need to move on to his theoretical discussion and practical application of the role of power and morality.

Power Rediscovered

Having exposed the philosophical and empirical "bankruptcy" of the idealist approach, Carr turns in Part III of the *Twenty Years' Crisis* to a broad consideration of the place of power in all politics. In this section Carr sounds Weberian themes—but transposed from German assertiveness to English pragmatism. Weber's definition of politics as bound up with the struggle for power, his insistence on the practical inseparability of analytically distinct elements, and his view of the moral compromises inevitable in the pursuit of state interests all find their way into Carr's discussion. But Carr omits Weber's insistence on the need for a strong leader, and he softens the harsh portrayal of national cultures locked in an eternal struggle for dominance. This change in tone helped to establish Carr as an important transitional figure in the development of realist thought on international relations.

Asserting that "politics cannot be divorced from power" Carr argues at the same time that "the illusion that priority can be given to power and that morality will follow is just as dangerous as the illusion that priority can be given to moral authority and that power will follow." His treatment of morality versus power parallels his discussion of utopia versus reality: they operate on completely separate planes yet they can never be divorced. "Since we can neither moralize power nor expel power from politics, we are faced with a dilemma which cannot be completely resolved." On this point Carr explicitly follows Reinhold Niebuhr, and like Niebuhr he dismisses moral stances such as pacifism, anarchism, or Pauline deference to nonmoral worldly powers—all of which amount to a denial of politics. Thus from the beginning Carr rejects views from either a realist or utopian direction which would effect a divorce of power and morality; yet he

14. *Ibid.,* 89, 92, 93.

remains in the somewhat awkward position of insisting that they operate on planes that "never coincide." Even before he undertakes his concrete discussion of power and morality he concludes (with Niebuhr) that our best hope is an "uneasy and tentative" compromise between them.[15]

The examples Carr uses to demonstrate that "politics are, then, in one sense always power politics" are taken from contemporary international politics. Unlike Niebuhr or Morgenthau, he does not produce an argument to explain why this is so or why the international milieu may be worse than the domestic. For him "power politics" is an "obvious fact," an assertion that earlier "would have passed as a platitude." Again, the excesses of "simple-minded spectators of the international game," who failed to recognize the vital, underlying role of power even in the halcyon days of 1920-1931, allow Carr to spare himself the bother of a fully worked-out argument. Instead he divides power into three elements— military, economic, and power over opinion—and gives examples of its use in each of the three categories.[16]

Several interesting aspects of his discussion deserve to be highlighted. First, in each of his categories Carr recognizes that power can be used both as a means and sought as an end in itself, but he draws no analytical lessons from this realization. His point is to emphasize the ubiquity of power, not to explain how and under what circumstances it is used; thus his tendency is simply to examine the "objective," underlying relations of power and regard them as a sufficient explanation for events. In his treatment of the Locarno treaties, for example, he focuses entirely on the change in objective power relations between France and Germany from 1922 to 1925. In 1922, France was strong (indeed, about to invade the Ruhr) and Germany weak; therefore the proposal from Germany for a mutual guarantee (including Great Britain and Belgium) of frontiers "was unceremoniously rejected by Poincaré."[17] In 1925, the French invasion had failed and Germany was stronger; "a treaty which had not been possible two years before, and would not have been possible two years later, was now welcome to both." Ten years after the treaty, "the delicate balance on which it rested had disappeared"; an even stronger Germany "no longer feared anything from France."[18]

15. *Ibid.*, 97, 98, 100.
16. *Ibid.*, 102, 103; for the discussion of types of power see 109-45.
17. E. H. Carr, *International Relations Between the Two World Wars* (London, 1947), 94.
18. Carr, *Twenty Years' Crisis*, 106.

This is not the place to criticize Carr's account of the history of Locarno—"a classic instance of power politics"—but simply to point to its sole reliance on undifferentiated power as an explanatory factor. The change in governments in Britain, France, and Germany and with them a new cast of foreign ministers goes unmentioned. Domestic political pressure in France and Britain for some pacific move after the death of the Geneva protocol also passes without comment. Nor does Carr fully discuss the completely different expectations each country had for the treaty. For him the key explanation is that "the Locarno Treaty was an expression of the power politics of a particular period and locality." Hence he does not even mention that it was Germany's Nazi government which denounced the treaty. Carr's reliance on power as the one key variable becomes virtually determinist in application. Thus not only is power a means toward other ends (whose definition Carr does not discuss), an evil in itself ("the exercise of power always appears to beget the appetite for more power"), but it also acts as a master key for understanding.[19] In short, Carr places enormous weight on a broadly defined conception of power.

Another aspect of Carr's treatment of power illustrates his softening of a Weberian notion. Weber treated economic factors as vital aspects of national power to be harnessed on behalf of the state in its unending competition with other nations. Carr agrees that economic power cannot, and indeed should not, be divorced from politics, that "economic forces are in fact political forces"; but he avoids the exhortative tone of Weber's Inaugural. Instead, he argues coolly against the idealist view that economics are somehow separate from politics and that therefore economic sanctions are morally superior to military sanctions as well as being less dependent on power. Once again Carr responds narrowly to utopian arguments. Consequently, he is content to show, for example, that Zimmern's distinction between states that pursue "welfare" and those that pursue "power" reflects "different degrees of power." "In pursuit of power," he concludes, "military and economic instruments will be used." Note that while criticizing Zimmern, Carr again conflates "economic power" as a means with unspecified "power" as an end.[20]

The last facet of Carr's account of power worthy of emphasis here deals with power over opinion. In this section Carr denies the efficacy of internationalist opinion against those who, like Toynbee or Lord Cecil, cited it as a restraint on aggressors. In addition, in a reprise of his relativist sociology

19. *Ibid.*, 106, 112.
20. *Ibid.*, 116, 120.

of knowledge, he regards all internationalist ideologies—whether on behalf of the League, fascism, or communism—as a mere "cloak for national policy."[21] One of the most important by-products of power, therefore, is the capacity to clothe national ideas in the more respectable regalia of internationalist rhetoric. Supporters of the League did so out of national interest but proclaimed their support in universal terms; a preponderance of power affords one the luxury of defining the terms of international morality. Carr seems to regard this adoption of internationalism as an inevitable effect of gaining relative power and hence of changing from a revisionist power to a "satisfied" power. But he makes no effort to distinguish revisionist states on internal grounds; nor does he recognize any difference in what could be called the degree of cynicism with which particular states portray their national ideas as in the common interest of all states. That there may be some such common interests—even if they are pursued nationally—he does not admit as a possibility. This position has important implications for his views on concrete issues of policy, as I shall suggest below.

Overall, then, Carr's position on the role of power in international politics is straightforward: it is omnipresent and inescapable. Power can be a means, an end, and a vital determining factor: it serves at the same time as the currency of international politics and its most desirable possession. He does not specifically address the question of whether one nation's gain in power inevitably entails another nation's loss, but this conclusion is implicit in most of his discussions. Carr skirts another issue which Weber considered with special urgency: the relation between the survival of national culture and the power predominance of the state. For Weber, culture and national power rose or fell together; Carr is silent on the question. Unlike Weber, Carr draws no direct national lessons from his analysis of power; he makes no call for inspired national leadership. Indeed, the only lesson he seems to insist on is the necessity of recognizing the ubiquity of power and the prudence of accommodating states who have more of it.

Morality Circumscribed

As in his discussion of power, Carr's treatment of morality reflects the degree to which he was writing against the idealist school. His emphases— the personification of the state, the possibility of an international commu-

21. *Ibid.*, 141.

nity, the differences between state and individual morality, the sanctity of
treaties, and the sources of international law—follow, as if in point-by-
point rebuttal, those of antagonists such as Zimmern or Toynbee. He
begins by distinguishing three distinct approaches to morality:

(i)   The moral code of the philosopher, which is the kind of morality most
       rarely practised but most frequently discussed.

(ii)   The moral code of the ordinary man, which is sometimes practised but
       rarely discussed (for the ordinary man seldom examines the moral as-
       sumptions which underlie his actions and his judgments and, if he does, is
       peculiarly liable to self-deception).

(iii) The moral behaviour of the ordinary man, which will stand in fairly close
       relation to (ii), but in hardly any relation at all to (i).[22]

With this idiosyncratic division Carr distances himself from philosophical debate about the foundations and role of morality in international
politics with a Machiavellian maneuver. One could paraphrase Carr's position thus: Philosophers may argue endlessly about what morality ought
to be, but *my* discussion focuses on what *ordinary* people think about
morality and on how these ordinary people actually behave. To the extent
that such an argument has a pedigree in moral philosophy it seems to
correspond to the position usually called "intuitionism"—the notion that
there are certain basic moral principles that most people hold and according to which they make moral judgments. These assumptions exist even if
one cannot explain them—hence the term "intuition." (As we shall see,
Hans Morgenthau espouses roughly the same theory; that he and Carr
disagree on the content of the moral intuitions does not inspire confidence
in it.) But Carr does not want to present just another theory about international morality and rejects approaches he calls "utopian" and "realist,"
which posit that morality is either paramount or irrelevant; this repeats his
opening discussion of power.[23] In eschewing theories, Carr's realism attempts to be *more* realistic, to explain how we really think about and act
upon morality.

Carr's argument has a number of features with implications both for the
future development of the realist approach and for his own specific policy
preferences and analysis of the processes of change in international politics. Specifically important are his delineation of the differences between

22. *Ibid.*, 146.
23. *Ibid.*, 152–54. *Cf.* the discussion on pages 98–101.

what he calls individual and state morality, his discussion of the specific character of the morality of states, and finally, his "ordinary man's" position on the sources and content of international morality and its relation to international law, order, and change. But before taking up these points, Carr's disposal of an issue dear to utopians—the personification of the state—should be mentioned briefly. In their effort to apply a single moral standard to states and individuals, many utopian thinkers (Carr specifically cites the French international lawyer Léon Duguit) took the common practice of referring to states as unitary group persons ("'England' and 'France' agreed yesterday . . .") literally and denounced it as "meaningless anthropomorphism." Carr sensibly replies that "the personification of the state is a tool," a legal fiction necessary for any informed thought and discussion about international politics.[24] He does not consider the extent to which the use of this "convenient fiction" might lead to the oversimplification of the process by which a state defines its interests and policies; his only point is to refute literal-minded idealists.

Carr's discussion of the morality that applies to states rests almost entirely on his characterization of the "ordinary assumptions of the man on the street." "All agree," he writes, "that there is an international moral code binding on states" and that one of its first principles is to avoid the infliction of *unnecessary* death or suffering on other human beings, i.e. death or suffering not necessary for the attainment of some higher purpose which is held, rightly or wrongly, to justify a derogation from the general obligation." Furthermore, obligations from states to states are also "clearly recognized," and violations of treaties are felt to require "special justification." These broad principles express what "most people" think about the way states *ought* to behave; but they nevertheless do not *expect* states to act in this way. In a crucial turn in his sociological account of morality, Carr sharply differentiates between widely accepted moral imperatives on one hand and an equally broad consensus on low moral expectations on the other. "International morality," he argues, "is another category with standards which are in part peculiar to itself."[25]

With this sweeping assertion about people's expectations, Carr shifts the ground of the argument about international morality: the issue be-

24. *Ibid.*, 146, 151.
25. *Ibid.*, 154, 156, 157. Hans Morgenthau directly criticizes this passage; for him the ethical obligation to avoid killing in time of peace is absolute (*Politics Among Nations: The Struggle for Power and Peace* [New York, 1948], 177).

comes why people expect worse moral behavior from states than from themselves as individuals. Rather than building an argument about what would constitute proper standards for international morality, or considering the different issue of whether low expectations simply represented cynicism or despair, Carr simply elaborates on the reasons for lower expectations. This elaboration raises important issues facing any account of international morality but stops well short of developing such an account itself.

Why, then, are states "not ordinarily expected to observe the same standards of morality as individuals"?[26] Carr's answer proceeds in four stages. First, he admits that people often do expect a "group person" or state "to behave generously and compassionately," but, he adds, not "at the cost of any serious sacrifice of its interests." The more secure and wealthy the group or state, the easier it is to behave "altruistically"; thus Anglo-Americans who assume their countries' policies to be "morally more enlightened" reflect the easier circumstances prevailing in both countries. Carr concentrates here on supererogatory acts, on altruistic behavior, rather than on mere obedience to a moral code. This makes his observed expectation of generosity seem more demanding and unreasonable, especially when confronted with "important interests"—which are not defined. In addition, Carr identifies higher moral expectations with greater wealth and security; he does not consider the intrinsic merit of the expectations.

The second stage of the answer effectively negates the first. Even if people (in satisfied countries) occasionally expect generous behavior from states, they more often expect and excuse acts by the state which they "would definitely regard as immoral in the individual." Here Carr adopts the conclusion of Reinhold Niebuhr in *Moral Man and Immoral Society* that groups (powerfully) concentrate and magnify individual egoism. Patriotism and loyalty become "cardinal virtues," and "it becomes a moral duty to promote the welfare and further the interests of the group as a whole." Vices become virtues; Carr, like later realists, quotes Cavour: "'If we were to do for ourselves what we are doing for Italy, we should be great rogues.'" Again, Carr does not probe at the reasons for this attitude or question its rightness or universality; he makes no attempt to reproduce or amend Niebuhr's argument. He simply presents his conclusion as another reason for the prevailing expectations about state behavior.[27]

26. Carr, *Twenty Years' Crisis*, 157.
27. *Ibid.*, 159–60.

Beyond this tendency to magnify and apparently cleanse individual vices, there are other reasons for our low expectations. Not only does "the good of the state come more easily to be regarded as a moral end in itself," but people correctly perceive that there is no authority above states capable of enforcing a higher standard of morality on them. Here, too, in the third stage of his argument, Carr filters a structural characteristic of the international system through his intuitionist account of common expectations.

The final stage of Carr's answer similarly raises fundamental issues of the structure of states. Asserting that any effective morality requires a sense of community, Carr considers whether that community is perceived to exist internationally. Clearly, some sense of world community does exist "for the reason (and for no other) that people talk, and within certain limits behave, as if there were a world community." But that community is severely circumscribed in two basic ways: it observes neither the principle of equality among members nor the postulate that the good of the whole takes precedence over the good of the part.[28]

The evidence Carr cites for these propositions, again, relies on his characterization of common attitudes. Thus concerning the principle of equality he points to the (indisputably) greater sense of obligation and fellow-feeling that prevails among the citizens of a single state as against a putative world community. When Neville Chamberlain exclaimed "how horrible, fantastic, incredible" it was to be at the brink of war "because of a quarrel in a far-away country between people of whom we know nothing," he spoke for the "ordinary Englishman," demonstrating, according to Carr, the "complete negation" of the principle of equality among states at least in the attitude of individuals. When states appeal to the principle of equality, they do so in service of their particular national purpose. The concept is employed inconsistently and self-interestedly: "The constant intrusion, or potential intrusion, of power renders almost meaningless any conception of equality between members of the international community."[29]

Carr cites essentially the same factors to show that the basic principle of priority to the good of the whole is nowhere near acceptance: "Loyalty to a world community is not yet powerful enough to create an international morality which will override vital national interests." One only apparent solution to this split loyalty is to assert (as did Woodrow Wilson or Toyn-

28. *Ibid.*, 160, 162.
29. *Ibid.*, 166.

bee) that one's national interests are in fact universal, or to claim (as did Hitler) to be the "bearers of a higher ethic." Carr equates Wilson (a "neo-liberal") and Hitler (a "neo-Darwinian") in their identification of national with universal interests. His overall point is that no citizens really believe in the priority of the international community over their particular nation-state and that statesmen should not try to paper over conflicts between the two communities. Rather, "a direct appeal to the need of self-sacrifice for a common good might sometimes prove more effective." Given the he-gemony of power in the international order, morality consists of "give-and-take, of self-sacrifice . . . of willingness not to insist on all the preroga-tives of power."[30]

In his treatment of international law and the processes of peaceful change Carr sounds the same themes. He rejects natural law as a source of international law as utopian and "anarchic" because both conservatives and revolutionaries can invoke it in support of their political program. As one would expect, he treats positivism more respectfully but with the caveat that obedience to law involves more than fear of punishment. The main thrust of Carr's discussion of law is to identify it with his treatment of politics as the "meeting place of ethics and power." The main function of law is to help provide some "stability and continuity" in social life. But the real source of the stability is "a pre-legal political agreement. . . . The ultimate authority of law derives from politics." Thus in two more chap-ters devoted to rebutting utopians, Carr denounces *"pacta sunt servanda-ism"* as a confusion of international law and ethics—treaties, like law, reflect a prevailing equilibrium of power—and he dismisses as wholly im-practical a treasured notion of League proponents, the judicial settlement of international disputes. Political issues can be solved only politically; power cannot be whisked away by judicial procedures.[31]

Problems of international politics can therefore be solved neither judi-cially nor legislatively; the model Carr adopts almost by elimination is that of bargaining. Indeed, he explicitly holds up labor-capital relations in nine-teenth-century industrializing countries as a pattern for twentieth-century international relations to follow. The "dissatisfied Powers," like unions, could attempt to redress their grievances peacefully through negotiations ("preceded no doubt in the first instance by threats of force"), and the satisfied powers, like enlightened capitalists, could settle in everyone's best

30. *Ibid.*, 166, 169, 168.
31. *Ibid.*, 178, 180. The general discussion paraphrases chapter 10 of Carr's book.

interests. Though not wishing to push the relevance of the analogy too far, Carr nevertheless finds it apposite because both the elements of power and morality are obviously present—power in the ability to press demands effectively, morality in the mutual decision to do so peacefully.[32]

Carr insists that in both industrial and international relations some uneasy compromise between power and morality is the basis for all peaceful change; but inevitably power holds the upper hand: "Power, used, threatened or silently held in reserve, is an essential factor in international change; and change will, generally speaking, be effected only in the interests of those by whom, or on whose behalf, power can be invoked. 'Yielding to threats of force' is a normal part of the process of peaceful change." Morality enters in the willingness to nurture "the embryonic character of the common feeling between nations" by acting in "a spirit of give-and-take and even of potential self-sacrifice, so that a basis, however imperfect, exists for discussing demands on grounds of justice recognized by both."[33]

To gain a better grasp of Carr's argument here let us consider the example he invoked in the first edition of the *Twenty Years' Crisis*: the 1938 Munich settlement.

Realism as Appeasement

Two passages omitted from the second edition express Carr's analysis of Munich. The first follows soon after the passage on "yielding to threats of force" cited just above: "If the power relations of Europe in 1938 made it inevitable that Czecho-Slovakia should lose part of its territory and eventually her independence, it was preferable (quite apart from any question of justice or injustice) that this should come about as the result of discussions round a table in Munich than as the result either of a war between the Great Powers or of a local war between Germany and Czecho-Slovakia."[34] Carr's conclusion—that it is "hypocritical to deny" the utility of peaceful change thus conceived—is identical in both editions. He does not claim this inevitable bowing to power to be necessarily moral as yet; at this stage he merely points to its "utility."

32. *Ibid.*, 214.
33. *Ibid.*, 218.
34. Carr, *Twenty Years' Crisis* (1st ed., London, 1939), 278. (In the second edition, the deleted passage would have been on page 219, line 17 between "... on the other." and "If we consider ...") Carr's adoption of the post-Munich usage of "Czecho-Slovakia" was retained in the second edition.

Carr addresses the morality of the Munich settlement in the second deleted passage; it follows his discussion of international common feeling as being enhanced by a spirit of give-and-take and potential self-sacrifice:

> The negotiations which led up to the Munich Agreement of September 29, 1938, were the nearest approach in recent years to the settlement of a major international issue by a procedure of peaceful change. The element of power was present. The element of morality was also present in the form of the common recognition by the Powers, who effectively decided the issue, of a criterion applicable to the dispute: the principle of self-determination. The injustice of the incorporation in Czecho-Slovakia of three-and-a-quarter million protesting Germans had been attacked in the past by many British critics, including the Labour Party and Mr. Lloyd George. Nor had the promises made by M. Benes at the Peace Conference regarding their treatment been fully carried out. The change in itself was one which corresponded both to a change in the European equilibrium of forces and to accepted canons of international morality. Other aspects of it were, however, less reassuring. Herr Hitler himself seemed morbidly eager to emphasise the element of force and to minimise that of peaceful negotiation—a trait psychologically understandable as a product of the methods employed by the Allies at Versailles, but none the less inimical to the establishment of a procedure of peaceful change. The principle of self-determination, once accepted, was applied with a ruthlessness which left to Germany the benefit of every doubt and paid a minimum of attention to every Czecho-Slovak susceptibility. There was a complete lack of any German readiness to make the smallest sacrifice for the sake of conciliation. The agreement was violently attacked by a section of British opinion. Recriminations ensued on the German side; and very soon any prospect that the Munich settlement might inaugurate a happier period of international relations in which peaceful change by negotiation would become an effective factor seemed to have disappeared.[35]

In another book published in 1938, Carr was more outspoken in his defense of the British policy of appeasement, praising Chamberlain's "realism" and his intent to pursue a consistent policy of conciliation and concession:

> It is easy to condemn in retrospect the attempts at conciliation and concession made by Britain between 1933 and 1938. But the concessions in fact secured by Germany during this period were such as no serious British statesman could have threatened war to prevent. Broadly speaking, British opinion had long ago recognized that the military restrictions, the demilitarization of the Rhineland and the separation of Austria from Germany could not be maintained indefinitely and that the only issue was the date and manner of their disappearance; and one of the most obvious factors in the crisis of September 1938 was that

35. *Ibid.*, 282. The paragraph that begins "The second example," on page 280 should be compared with the corresponding passage on page 221 in the second edition. Several other references to Germany are excised.

Britain would not fight to maintain a Czechoslovak state which in a population of 14,000,000 contained 3,250,000 Germans and other large and disloyal minorities. It cannot be charged to the policy of conciliation that these concessions were made. The only ground for criticism is that they were not made in other conditions and at an earlier date.[36]

What are we to make of this "brilliant argument for appeasement?"[37] Before answering this question, let us first reconstruct, in paraphrase, the steps by which Carr reached this conclusion to illustrate the operation of his version of realism.

At the end of World War I, the victorious powers of Great Britain, France, and the United States imposed on Germany a treaty injurious to German interests and favorable to their own. This was to be expected: treaties always reflect prevailing relations of power, and the Allies won the war. What was new in the settlement was the insistence by Allied spokesmen, first, on Germany's guilt in causing the war and, second and more important, on the *justice* of settlement. The Versailles Treaty and the League system it created were said to embody universally applicable principles of international morality. Free trade, self-determination, peaceful settlement of international disputes, respect for international law and opinion—all these virtues were widely praised as in the interest of all mankind, and to oppose them was to indulge in stubbornness, stupidity, or wickedness, if not all three.

In fact, these apparently universal interests reflected the particular interests of the satisfied powers. Britain and France promoted these ideas because they sanctified a status quo favorable to them. Notions of morality always reflect underlying material interests. Moreover, states, with no authority above them, accentuate and legitimize the egoistic desires of individuals; the sense of national loyalty vastly outweighs any feeling of international community or abstract justice. That is why people do not hold states to the same moral code as they do individuals.

In any case, the hypocrisy of the Allies' claim to enforce standards of universal morality is demonstrated by their actions toward Germany in the 1920s, while Germany was still weak and they were still strong. Despite a widespread consensus that Versailles was unjust to Germany in many respects (and general agreement even on specific injustices) no real changes

---

36. E. H. Carr, *Britain: A Study of Foreign Policy from the Versailles Treaty to the Outbreak of War* (London, 1939), 175.

37. A. J. P. Taylor's phrase, in the bibliography of *The Origins of the Second World War* (Harmondsworth, 1964).

occurred until Germany was strong enough to demand them. Thus power, not morality, is the motive force behind any change.

The efforts to conciliate Germany in the 1930s made sense for two important reasons. First, power relations had altered in Germany's favor, so some changes were bound to occur anyway: better that they should occur peacefully. Second, Germany's demands were couched in terms of justice, indicating that she did set some store in the continued existence of an international community and in the spirit of compromise which is the essence of international morality. It was not only prudent, but also moral, to encourage this method of pressing demands by entering serious negotiations. Prudence dictated avoiding a war no Western state was prepared for, and morality suggested giving conciliation, compromise, and even self-sacrifice every possible opportunity. As powers become more satisfied, they adopt for themselves the internationalist arguments of the status quo; there was good reason to believe that Germany and Italy would behave in just this way.

This last aspect of Carr's case for appeasement reflects his deterministic view of history and morality. Dissatisfied powers indulge in radical rhetoric and behavior; as their grievances are remedied they become conservative stalwarts of the status quo. In both cases, of course, their claim to universalism is bogus, but the process seems inexorable, as the following passage indicates:

> Since the Munich Agreement, a significant change has occurred in the attitude of the German and Italian dictators. Herr Hitler eagerly depicts Germany as a bulwark of peace menaced by war-mongering democracies. The League of Nations, he declared in his Reichstag speech of April 28, 1938, is a "stirrer up of trouble," and collective security means "continuous danger of war." Signor Mussolini in a recent speech at Turin borrowed the British formula about the possibility of settling all international disputes by peaceful means, and declared that "there are not in Europe at present problems so big and so active as to justify a war which from a European conflict would naturally become universal." It would be a mistake to dismiss such utterances as hypocritical. They are symptoms that Germany and Italy are already looking forward to the time when, as dominant Powers, they will acquire the vested interest in peace recently enjoyed by Great Britain and France, and be able to pillory the democratic countries as enemies of peace.[38]

It is, of course, easy to dismiss this analysis as naive, or even cowardly, and leave it at that. But this is surely too simple. If nothing else, the insis-

38. Carr, *Twenty Years' Crisis*, 1st ed., 107. In the second edition (p. 84) the sentence "It would be a mistake to dismiss such utterances as hypocritical" is omitted.

tence on the importance of power that runs throughout Carr's writing acquits him of naiveté, and accusations of cowardice rarely advance analysis. The questions raised by his argument run deeper—to his entire conception of morality and its relation to power. But before taking up these questions in an explicitly critical way, it will be helpful to consider briefly some of the themes in Carr's other works on international politics so as to present his approach as fairly and completely as possible.

Carr's Guide to the Postwar World

In four main works published between 1942 and 1951 Carr attempted to extend his realism to an analysis of the underlying trends and the future character of the international system. *Conditions of Peace* (1942) was an avowedly speculative exercise in wartime futurology. *Nationalism and After* (1945) was a shorter and more scholarly essay directed to the specific question of the future of the nation-state. *The Soviet Impact on the Western World*, published in 1947 just as the Cold War was setting in permanently, is remarkably free of immediate policy issues and markedly credulous of Soviet achievements in the economic, social, and political spheres. Finally, *The New Society*, which originated as a series of lectures on BBC radio in 1951, is Carr's last survey of world politics; after that he immersed himself in his multivolume history of Soviet Russia to 1929.

Carr advances several important ideas in these books which cluster around three issues: first, the failure of traditional liberal democracy and laissez-faire economics coupled with the inevitable rise of the planned economy and a collectivist state; second, and related to the first, the obsolescence of the nation-state in an increasingly socialized world; finally, his resistance to joining the debate on the causes of the Cold War, indeed his abdication from the Cold War itself. Unlike the American realists, who were obviously caught up in the deterioration of Soviet-American relations, Carr increasingly detached himself from contemporary debates on policy, reflecting both the greatly diminished role of Britain in world affairs and the evolution of his own intellectual interests away from international politics.

Like many Western analysts writing during and immediately after World War II, Carr started by trying to diagnose what went wrong for the victors of World War I in the interwar period. Thus in both *Conditions of Peace* and *The New Society* Carr begins by describing the failures of traditional approaches to new problems. The satisfied powers were uniformly backward-looking in virtually every respect. Militarily they turned the lessons of World War I into dogma and resisted all innovation, with obviously disastrous consequences. Politically, they made no effort to adapt their democratic system to the new conditions prevailing after the war, and in their foreign policy they were inordinately preoccupied with a negative conception of security and the meaningless machinations of the League of Nations. Economically, even the Great Depression did not succeed in dashing "the vain hope of returning to the laissez-faire principles of the pre-war period.[39]

By contrast, the dissatisfied powers of Germany, Soviet Russia, and Italy were dynamic and inventive: "The fact that Soviet Russia and Nazi Germany had virtually eliminated unemployment was slightingly dismissed with the retort that this had been achieved only by methods, and at the cost of sacrifices, which the satisfied countries would never tolerate. The answer was clearly inadequate, so long as the satisfied Powers could find no answer of their own to a problem whose acuteness could not be denied." Militarily and politically the dissatisfied powers were revolutionary; they offered their people something new: "A revolutionary frame of mind confronted an attitude of political complacency and nostalgia for the past."[40]

If the democracies were to emerge from the war with more than a military victory, they would have to reform dramatically. Carr shows himself to be extremely credulous of the achievement of collectivist states such as Soviet Russia or Nazi Germany. Thus he writes in *The Soviet Impact on the Western World* that it was Stalin "who placed democracy in the forefront of allied war aims" and that "the missionary role which had been filled in the first world war by American democracy and Woodrow Wilson had passed in the second world war to Soviet democracy and Marshal Stalin." One looks in vain through the book—with chapters on the social, political, economic, ideological, and international impact of the Soviet state—for some mention of the purges and terror of the 1930s. Instead, Carr holds the Soviet Union up as a harbinger of the future and a positive model in worker management, economic democracy, and "socialization of investment."[41]

39. E. H. Carr, *Conditions of Peace* (London, 1942), xix, Introduction, and chap. 1, *passim; The New Society* (London, 1951), chaps. 2 and 3.
40. Carr, *Conditions of Peace*, xx, xv.
41. E. H. Carr, *The Soviet Impact on the Western World* (London, 1947), 3.

His other works are less keyed to the Soviet Union but make similar points about the need for a planned economy even while sounding Weberian warnings about the growth of bureaucracy. Carr's solution to this problem is to advocate a thoroughgoing "reinterpretation, in predominantly economic terms, of the democratic ideals of 'equality' and 'liberty.'"[42] For Carr the mass unemployment of the 1930s "drove the last nail into the coffin of laissez-faire capitalism and provoked massive state intervention in every function of the economy." In all these works Carr reveals himself to be an orthodox English socialist along the lines of Harold Laski and perhaps—at least in his treatment of the Soviet Union—Sidney and Beatrice Webb. The point is that he regards the growth of the state to be an inevitable historical development with important consequences for the future character of international politics. And unlike the American realists, who (apart from Niebuhr's brief Marxist phase) all tend to social conservatism, Carr welcomes this change from "individualist democracy of a privileged class" to at least the hope of "a new mass democracy of the principle of government of all and by all and for all."[43]

Carr's analysis of the inevitable growth of the economic functions of the state provides the foundation for his predictions about the fate of nationalism and the traditional nation-state in the postwar world. As citizens' demands on the state to guarantee economic well-being as well as physical security grow, the irrationality and obsolescence of the traditional unit of the nation-state will become ever more apparent. For not only have individual states "ceased to be convenient, or even tolerable, units" for the purpose of social and economic planning, but changes in modern warfare have meant that they can no longer guarantee the military security of their citizens. He therefore concludes forthrightly: "National self-determination can hardly hope to survive so long as it is interpreted in a way which nullifies security and limits economic well-being and economic opportunity." More specifically, he asserts that "we shall not again see a Europe of twenty, and a world of more than sixty 'independent sovereign states' . . . nor shall we see in our time a single world authority as the final repository of power."[44]

This, of course, stands as one of the more famous wrong predictions in the literature and deserves some explanation. Carr was not arguing from a strictly functionalist point of view as, say, David Mitrany was; he contin-

42. Carr, *Conditions of Peace*, 27, 29.
43. Carr, *New Society*, 27, 78, 111.
44. E. H. Carr, *Nationalism and After* (London, 1945), 47, 59, 51–52.

ued to pay considerable attention to power. His concern was precisely that the state could not guarantee security and economic growth while locked into traditional national boundaries and political practices; thus he foresaw not a dramatic end to the nation-state but a steady evolution of new forms of sovereignty: "The existence of multi-national units of military and economic organization does not stand in the way of the maintenance, or indeed of the further extension, of national administrative and cultural units, thus encouraging a system of overlapping and interlocking loyalties which is in the last resort the sole alternative to sheer totalitarianism."

Carr's idea was to have security organized in a "series of international general staffs for different regions"; his description sounds rather like what eventually occurred in the North Atlantic Treaty Organization (NATO) and Warsaw Pact countries, although there has obviously been no formal change in the conception of national sovereignty. Thus though the letter of Carr's prediction has clearly not happened, to some extent the substance has. The world is largely "dominated by new concentrations of power in great groups of nations, but crossed with strands of common social and economic policy and woven loosely together in a system of pooled security"; but the main reason for this was the postwar division into two rival blocs, not the demand for multinational social welfare and security.[45]

On the reasons and effects of this postwar division Carr is curiously silent. Indeed, his detachment from the issue is the last striking feature, the hound that does not bark, in his general writings on international relations. In the few times he does address the issue, he treats the two superpowers as equally affected by an inexorable logic of power. Neither really intends to forge an alliance; neither is really at fault. Hence in a 1949 paper given at the University of Colorado he writes:

> Both Americans and Russians are in the same situation. The countries within their respective orbits alternately grumble at them as intruders and woo them as sugar-daddies. What happens is simple enough. In each country, the need is felt to court the patronage and aid of the most accessible great power; in each country the group of men most sympathetic to that power, most acceptable to it and therefore most likely to extract the largest favors from it, rises to positions of influence and molds the policy and institutions of the country in the shape most calculated to support the appeal. Power in international relations is commonly thought of as a bludgeon working by methods of compulsion and

45. *Ibid.*, 59, 71.

oppression; the better analogy is sometimes a magnet working by involuntary attraction.[46]

Regardless of one's position on the origins of the Cold War, one may doubt whether Poland, Romania, or Czechoslovakia was "bludgeoned" or "magnetized"; in any case Carr's equation of the two superpowers is clear.

Carr treats the two superpowers in *The New Society* similarly: each heads a power bloc in which smaller countries have only limited freedom of action. In line with his general position on the bankruptcy of traditional liberalism, he treats the social and ideological challenge from the Soviet Union as fundamental, but he does not question the need to resist the advance of Soviet power. Like many other Europeans, however, he worries that Americans are concerned "with the question how a third world war is to be won" rather than "with the question how it is to be avoided," and he urges that less emphasis be placed on military defense. Moreover, he deplores the tendency to blame the Russians for all the problems in the West.[47]

Beyond these brief passages, Carr adds little on the vital issue of the Cold War. Unlike the American realists writing at the same time, he makes no effort either to interpret Soviet goals or to analyze the specific means of their postwar policy. Why not? The basic reason lies in Carr's overall approach. Morally, neither side has a "better case" because both are struggling to be the primary definers of "international" morality. Thus he never even considers an Achesonian argument about Russian perfidy. In pure power terms, some sort of struggle was inevitable given the outcome of World War II; small powers are "involuntarily attracted" to larger ones. Thus he does not find very much of interest to say about the pure power struggle either—a curious position given his insistence on the determining influence of power.

Fundamentally, Carr sees the struggle as social and ideological: the important issue for him is how the West will respond to the Soviet challenge to its outdated individualist notions of politics and discredited conception of economics. The crucial factor is the character of our social and economic response. As he puts it in the conclusion of *The Soviet Impact on*

46. Carr, "The Moral Foundations for World Order," in *Foundations for World Order* (Denver, 1949), 65, 66. Internal evidence in the essay shows that Carr gave the paper in early 1949. (He refers to the outcome of the 1948 election, p. 73.)
47. Carr, *New Society*, 98, and chap. 5, *passim*.

the Western World, "the fate of the western world will turn on its ability to meet the Soviet challenge by a successful search for new forms of social and economic action in which what is valid in individualism and democratic tradition can be applied to the problems of mass civilization." Thus what is crucial in the process and outcome of the Cold War is the internal character of Western societies, not the relations of external power between the two blocs.[48]

Quite apart from its assumptions about the far-reaching nature of the Soviet ideological challenge, this view represents quite a change from the argument of *The Twenty Years' Crisis,* in which broadly defined power seemed to determine everything. By contrast, Carr's writings on the postwar character of international politics stress the necessity for states to develop in a collectivist direction internally and to adapt their conception of sovereignty externally so as to permit wider and overlapping focuses of loyalty. Although cast as empirical analysis, these recommendations are in fact normative in a way that the Carr of 1939 would have described as utopian. They reflect Carr's basic conviction that traditional liberal democracy must give way to some species of socialism and his apparent faith that a world reformed along socialist lines would represent an "uneasy compromise" between power and morality superior to those of the past. In this sense Carr looks forward in a way unique among the realists; but unfortunately he never explains the normative basis of his faith or the reasons for his confidence that it points to a better way out of the fundamental dilemmas of politics.

Reasoned Realist or "Utopian of Power"?

In Carr's version of realism, the basic and unending problem of all politics is the confrontation of power and morality, and his analysis of these two concepts forms the foundation of his entire enterprise. Against the idealistic hopes of internationalist writers who thought power had been domesticated in the League of Nations, Carr rediscovered Weber's insistence that power was the common currency—and fundamental end—of all nations. To the moralizing proponents of "international morality" and world public opinion, Carr pointed at the individual and national interests that lay behind their claims of universality. In their underestimation of

48. Carr, *Soviet Impact,* 113.

power and their false claim to morality, Carr asserted, idealist writers misrepresented the realities of international politics.

But Carr's own picture of these realities is itself flawed. As we have seen, his analysis of power is debilitatingly inclusive, and his discussion of morality rests on an oversimple sociology of knowledge and a questionable characterization of common moral intuitions. These premises led Carr to a justification of appeasement notable for its selective blind spots and to predictions about the postwar world which paradoxically undervalued the importance of external power relations. Let us take up these points in turn.

Like Weber, Carr treats all politics as power politics, at least "in one sense," but he fails to distinguish the senses in which politics is not about power.[49] Nor does he explain why politics always involves power, an explanation vital to any attempt to channel the exercise of power along lines compatible with an ordered social existence. Is a lust for power basic to human nature—the view of Niebuhr and Morgenthau—and hence controllable only by meeting power with power? Is it the result of a security dilemma basic to all individuals? This explanation is somewhat more optimistic than one based on a version of original sin and has different prescriptive implications.[50] Or is the inescapability of power primarily the result of the anarchic character of the international milieu? Carr's works have passages that could support all of these views, but nowhere does he explicitly choose among them. He simply adopts Weber's conclusion about power as a way to argue against the idealist position, without adequately considering its implications.

For example, Carr does not share Weber's concern about leadership or his worry about the survival of national culture. What enables Carr to soften Weber's harsh vision? We are given no clue and are left only to speculate about differences in time and temperament. Less worry over leadership may reflect greater satisfaction with British leaders—though Carr's discussion of the failures of the interwar democracies in *Conditions of Peace* hardly constitutes a paean to the likes of Ramsay MacDonald and Stanley Baldwin. Carr clearly presents a less Gothic portrayal of the international competition than Weber, but given his agreement that all politics is power politics, it is hard to understand why. As a result, the flaws in Weber's position remain flaws in Carr's: distinctions between the kind and

49. Carr, *Twenty Years' Crisis*, 2d ed., 102.
50. This is the approach taken by John Herz, *Political Realism and Political Idealism* (Chicago, 1951).

level of force employed are ignored, and an analysis of the circumstances most likely to lead to different kinds of force is completely absent. Politics may be a struggle for power, but that struggle can obviously take many different forms.

Far from making distinctions about kinds of power and struggle, Carr offers a concept of power that is extraordinarily broad and undifferentiated. Power can be an end or it can be a means. As a means it can take political, military, economic, or ideological ("power over opinion") forms; how and under what conditions a nation uses which kind of power are problems Carr does not consider. As an end, power can be either intermediate, ultimate, or self-sustaining ("power can lead to the desire for more power"), but again, Carr offers no answers to the questions why, where, and when this is true. Clearly it makes a difference whether power is a means or an end, and if it is an end, how it is defined. Carr tells us nothing about the process by which a state decides upon the purposes of its foreign policy—not even to the extent of positing the primacy of the national interest, as Morgenthau does. Instead, he simply asserts that the element of power is present in every political decision, indeed almost always determining its outcome. But without a much more refined concept of power, this conclusion amounts to an unhelpful platitude.

In the scheme of *The Twenty Years' Crisis*, morality is the yin to power's yang. It offers the only way out of a vicious circle of power-seeking, yet the most morality can achieve is a temporary and uneasy compromise with power. But the basis and content of that compromise remain as elusive as ever: Carr's only conclusion is to recommend a spirit of self-sacrifice to nations apparently more secure. This provides even less concrete guidance than Weber's ethic of responsibility, which at least insisted that the individual leader accept the consequences of his acts. In his treatment, Carr implicitly adopts Weber's definition of the moral problem in statecraft, but his rebuttal of the ethic of conviction is far more radical. Weber accepted the sincerity of believers in this ethic as well as the integrity of the conception itself; his quarrel was with the refusal of a would-be statesman-saint to bear the responsibility for the worldly consequences of his principles of leadership. *Fiat justitia pereat mundi* fundamentally negates politics in Weber's view; the responsible statesman recognizes that to deal in politics is to contract with the forces of evil.

By contrast, Carr questioned both the sincerity of his utopian antagonists and the integrity of their beliefs. His attack on the internationalist writers of the 1920s focused not on their unwillingness to accept responsibility but on their claim to enunciate universal moral principles; these principles, at best, were "unconscious reflections" of specific national interests. But in challenging the utopians' claim to universalism, Carr goes well beyond their particular views. He argues that all thought reflects underlying economic and social conditions, seemingly denying any autonomy for the realm of thought—a position Weber obviously rejected. One can hardly deny that thought is in some way "socially conditioned." The difficult questions arrive in detailing the process, mechanism, and extent of this conditioning; and as I have suggested, Carr addresses virtually none of these thorny problems. The result, as Carr himself later acknowledges, is a thoroughly destructive relativism that can be "pursued to the point where the debunker is himself debunked."[51] Carr's own position on morality in general, and appeasement in particular, could easily be shown to reflect the interests and views of the British Foreign Office in the late 1930s.

With his intuitionist "morality of the ordinary man" Carr sought to avoid such criticism. Even if socially conditioned, his account of morality could at least claim to represent what people actually thought. But his problem here is common to all moral philosophies based on intuitionism: another writer can always claim that *his* version is the correct one. Jeremy Bentham's refutation of natural law comes to mind: a dozen people assigned to list the ten most important provisions of the natural law will come up with a dozen different lists. Although Carr shares Bentham's distaste for natural law, he nevertheless adopts a moral philosophy that shares its weakness—agreement on basic moral intuitions is far from universal.

Not only does Carr's morality of the common man appear vulnerable to competing alternatives, it fails to provide any underlying explanation of its principles. Carr writes that ordinary people think that states ought to respect treaties and avoid unnecessary deaths, but that in general they do not expect states to observe these norms. These putative expectations then become the basis for Carr's discussion of the morality of states, which he argues differs fundamentally from the morality of individuals. At this point Carr adopts Niebuhr's conclusion about the cumulation of egoism in states but not his supporting account of original sin; *Moral Man and Immoral Society* is employed only to explain why people do not expect

51. Carr, *Soviet Impact*, 92.

states to follow the usual moral standards. Thus the expectations of apparently immoral behavior by states become the foundation of a separate morality for states; Carr therefore has no independent standard of morality at all.

This fundamental weakness explains how Carr could make a case for appeasement on grounds of realism *and* morality. The Germans' claim on the Sudetenland was as "moral" as arguments employed against it—all moral arguments reflect prevailing relations of power. As a powerful revisionist state with some claim to justice, Germany couched its national goal in the terms of the international norm of self-determination, just as Czechoslovakia cast its interest as exemplary of the principle of the inviolability of sovereignty. The German claim prevailed because of greater German power. What made Munich "moral" was the spirit of give-and-take and self-sacrifice that informed the agreement; an inevitable change was made peacefully, instead of by force.

Quite apart from the obvious point that all the "give" was on one side and all the "take" on the other, Carr's position illustrates vividly the pitfalls of his radical moral skepticism. His view of morality permits no genuine conception of the moral interest of the international community. Based on material conditions and unexplained expectations, Carr's morality of states leaves no room for any international norms by which German demands could be judged. For him, such international norms would always act as disguises for national power goals; they could have no validity on their own. Indeed *no* moral argument possesses real integrity: inevitably it reflects particular circumstances and interests.[52]

Significantly, this moral relativism deprived Carr of even a "realist" case against Munich. One could have argued that so transparent an attack on the principles of international order, however cloaked in claims of self-determination, represented a threat to the power interests of the other states. Therefore German claims should be resisted to preserve the stability of the international system and the power position of the "status quo" states. This argument (roughly that of Churchill) assumes first, that one can justifiably appeal to international norms as supportive of "realistic" arrangements, and second, that it is possible to distinguish among kinds of revisionism and to make judgments about the validity of supposedly just demands for change. Carr's position denies both these assumptions: without an overarching standard one moral claim is as good as another.

---

52. *Cf.* Bull, *"The Twenty Years' Crisis* Thirty Years On."

Moreover, Carr's own assumption that a state's tendency to employ internationalist arguments grew with the satisfaction of its demands blinded him to the uniquely malign character of fascist Germany and Italy. Germany especially was no ordinary revisionist state; it was not a simple "have-not" nation that would become a pillar of the international order once granted "the privileges of membership" in it. Yet Carr was remarkably credulous of Hitler and Mussolini and, even as late as 1943, quite taken with their revolutionary consequences. I am not suggesting in any way that he was a fascist sympathizer. But without a moral compass it is easy, as Hans Morgenthau put it in an essay about Carr, to "surrender to the immanence of power."[53]

Morgenthau criticized Carr sharply for adopting "a dual standard of morality," but, as I shall argue later, Morgenthau himself fails to recognize the extent to which the harmony of interest lurks behind his own conception of the "moral dignity of the national interest." Carr does not adopt this easy way out, and it is possible to sympathize with his difficulties in solving formidable problems of metaethics. But his oversimple relativism led to a paralysis of judgment: surely it would have been possible to outline some moral principles as truly reflecting the international interest. He could even have attached these principles to his moral code of the ordinary man. Instead he clung to a notion of morality which recommended and approved a settlement that placed no more than a thin veneer of international respectability over a blatant venture in national aggrandizement. Thus one is left with a morality that urges a reasonable and timely acquiescence to demands backed by power, in the hope that the peaceful achievement of such demands will lead to a new attitude of satisfied internationalism on the part of the heretofore revisionist state. Indeed, morality seems to be defined by precisely this acquiescence.

Carr's conception of morality leads nowhere because it rests upon a crudely materialist sociology of knowledge and an ill-conceived moral philosophy of intuitionism. Ironically, his postwar predictions went awry for virtually the opposite reason: Carr allowed his own (socially conditioned?) moral and political convictions to sway his empirical analysis even as he denied the relevance and autonomy of such convictions. His positions on the end of the traditional nation-state, the inevitability of collectivism, and the internal character of the Soviet challenge all stem from his own belief in socialism. The nation-state in its traditionally autonomous

53. Carr, *Twenty Years' Crisis*, 2d ed., 155; Hans Morgenthau, "The Political Science of E. H. Carr," *World Politics*, I (October, 1948), 134.

form is unequal to the postwar tasks of security and economic growth; the planned economy has clearly replaced laissez-faire and the only issues are about the most successful forms of planning; the real threat from the Russians is not military but political and economic—all these views express variations of a world-view that places not power but mass social welfare at its center. And without judging the merit of Carr's view, there can be no doubt that it is normative, even utopian.

Hans Morgenthau has written that Carr was a "utopian of power," a "Machiavelli without *virtù*."[54] Perhaps this overstates. Carr does have a vision that extends beyond the relativist critique of *The Twenty Years' Crisis* because he manifestly cares about social and economic reform in ways that extend well beyond a mere apotheosis of power. But his Marxian approach to morality and "systems of thought" requires that moral conviction be expressed as scientific analysis—Marxism is supposed to be a science, not a faith—and as a result Carr never explains or justifies the basis of his values. Moreover, to the extent that Carr's values embody faith in reason they serve to unify all of his work. For behind his rediscovery of power lies the hope that a reasoned appreciation of its force can lead, if not to its domestication, then at least to a better understanding of the workings of history.

In the end, Carr the realist gives way to Carr the rational yet deeply skeptical student of history whose "constant preoccupation with the pace and direction of the historical process represent[s] a protest against the profoundly unhistorical view which elevates the values of a comparatively recent Western European past into an absolute standard, a touchstone by which the values of the present and the future—not to mention those of a remoter past—are to be assessed and judged."[55] But an understanding of the past need not preclude making informed moral judgments about it from a contemporary perspective. We can understand the system of values that led, say, to the Inquisition (or to Stalin's Great Purge in the 1930s) without surrendering our right to judge these acts morally or indeed even politically. Carr's conception of history seems to give up this possibility of judgment. And surely such judgment and understanding are essential if we are to learn anything at all from history. Morgenthau's assessment may be harsh and unsympathetic, but it has at least a grain of truth: in the hands of E. H. Carr realism ultimately becomes an agnostic relativism of power.

54. Morgenthau, "Political Science of E. H. Carr," 134.
55. E. H. Carr, *From Napoleon to Stalin and Other Essays* (London, 1980), viii–ix.

5

The Prophetic Realism of Reinhold Niebuhr

E. H. Carr was only the first of the Anglo-American realists to adopt some aspect of Reinhold Niebuhr's thought: its range, depth, and complexity make Niebuhr without question the most profound thinker of the modern realist school. George Kennan's well-known comment that Niebuhr "is the father of us all" fits very well as long as one remembers that his progeny have proven to be an extraordinarily diverse lot. Not only Kennan and Hans Morgenthau have claimed filial ties, but Jimmy Carter, David Stockman, Ernest Lefever, and Paul Ramsey, among many others, have acknowledged an important debt to Niebuhr; indeed, Ramsey and Lefever both invoked his spirit in their opposing testimony at the latter's Senate confirmation hearings.[1] As the editors of *Reinhold Niebuhr on Politics* have written, Niebuhr's thought is "full of dialectical cantilevers" open to a variety of interpretations. His aphoristic style invites ambiguous quotation, and perhaps for this reason he has been a touchstone for writers seeking to add moral and intellectual legitimacy to their own positions. In a debate with Niebuhr on the Vietnam War, Ramsey was once reported to have remarked that Niebuhr seemed not to have read Niebuhr.[2]

Niebuhr's legacy remains ambiguous partly because of his longevity and his willingness to change his mind. It is not hard to quote Niebuhr against Niebuhr, though such a sterile exercise is obviated by taking account of the historical context of a particular work. In any case there were no major changes in the essentials of Niebuhr's thought after the publication of his *magnum opus*, the two-volume Gifford Lectures published as *The Nature and Destiny of Man* in 1941 and 1943. In this chapter I shall pay particular attention to the Christian conception of human nature and

1. See John C. Bennett, "Niebuhr's Ethic: The Later Years," *Christianity and Crisis,* XLII (April 12, 1982), 92.
2. Harry R. Davis and Robert C. Good (eds.), *Reinhold Niebuhr on Politics* (New York, 1960), 10; and Bennett, "Niebuhr's Ethic," 92.

its implications for social life which Niebuhr develops in this work. Then, to facilitate comparison with his contemporary realists Morgenthau and Kennan, Niebuhr's account of the post–World War II slide into the Cold War and his justification of the American policy of containment will be considered. More than anything else, the pressing problem of how to define America's role in the postwar world inspired a characteristic response from these men which identified them as realists.

Niebuhr's primary concern was to demonstrate the continuing relevance of his prophetic vision of human nature and politics and thus to offer a sounder basis for American policy in a time of crisis. He by no means confined himself to the pulpit or the study: throughout his life he was a political activist, from the 1930s, when he worked for the Socialist party, until the late 1960s, when he joined antiwar teach-ins. In the meantime he had founded the journal *Christianity and Crisis*, served on the *Nation's* editorial board, was among the founding members of the Americans for Democratic Action, and throughout the 1940s and 1950s participated in countless governmental or quasi-governmental bodies.[3] Niebuhr was a theologian, but his voluminous writings had a tremendous impact on the evolution of realism as an approach to international politics. To assess that impact, one must first explicate his views as carefully as possible, particularly since they are frequently less than straightforward. Once this groundwork is established, it will be possible to evaluate Niebuhr's contribution, at least in a preliminary way.

Creature and Spirit: Niebuhr's Doctrine of Man

"Man has always been his own most vexing problem. How shall he think of himself?" With this question Niebuhr opened his 1939 Gifford Lectures at Edinburgh University; in developing his answer his most consistent concern was to establish the preeminence of a Christian view. This concern runs through all of Niebuhr's works: again and again he insists that only the Christian conception of human nature points the way to true understanding of the uniqueness of man.

3. Biographical details can be found in June C. Bingham, *Courage to Change: An Introduction to the Life and Thought of Reinhold Niebuhr* (New York, 1961); Ronald H. Stone, *Reinhold Niebuhr: Prophet to Politicians* (Nashville, 1972); Richard Wightman Fox, *Reinhold Niebuhr: A Biography* (New York, 1985).

To arrive at this Christian conception, Niebuhr tries to combine a broad cultural and historical analysis of the "traditional views of human nature which have informed western culture" with the insights of a "religion of revelation."[4] Neither approach, on its own, can convey the richness of the human condition. The cultural view fails because it is too narrow. Theologians such as Karl Barth, who concentrate solely on the transcendent elements in Christianity and who believe that the function of theology is solely to interpret revelation, however, fail to recognize that revelation is crucially related to human culture and knowledge. They deny the very idea Niebuhr sets at the center of his thought—"the relevance of the Christian conception of man as a possible source of light for the confusion of modernity" (I, 25). Moreover, such theologies "threaten to destroy all relative moral judgments by their exclusive emphasis upon the ultimate religious fact of the sinfulness of man, [and] are rightly suspected of imperilling relative moral achievements of history" (I, 220). This stricture is worth remembering: Niebuhr believes that prophetic religion has a duty to guide men in their relative moral judgments, and to fulfill this duty it must maintain and develop its "points of contact" with human history.[5]

The first four chapters of *Nature and Destiny* present competing modern explanations of human nature. Rationalism, romanticism, renaissance and bourgeois individualism, naturalism, and idealism are all considered and found wanting in various ways. The common element that unites these faulty conceptions is the "easy conscience of modern man: No cumulation of contradictory evidence seems to disturb modern man's good opinion of himself" (I, 94). All these conflicting theories converge in their "stubborn resistance" to the idea that man is himself sinful: Niebuhr approvingly cites Martin Luther's dictum that the final sin of man is his

4. Reinhold Niebuhr, *The Nature and Destiny of Man: A Christian Interpretation* (2 vols.; New York, 1941, 1943), I, 5. For the sake of continuity, subsequent quotations from this work will be cited in the text. Indirect citations, paraphrases, and references to other works will be noted as usual.

5. Niebuhr makes several negative references to Barth, of which the following is typical: "The theological movement initiated by Karl Barth has affected the thought of the church profoundly but only negatively; and it has not challenged the thought outside the church at all" (*Nature and Destiny*, II, 159; see also I, 158, 220, 283; II, 66–67).

Reference to the duty of prophetic religion comes explicitly in Niebuhr, *Beyond Tragedy: Essays on the Christian Interpretation of History* (New York, 1937), 235–36. On these points see John Macquarrie, *Twentieth Century Religious Thought* (London, 1963), 235–36; and William John Wolf, "Reinhold Niebuhr's Doctrine of Man," in Kegley and Bretall (eds.), *Niebuhr*, esp. 232–33.

unwillingness to concede that he is a sinner. Against these theories Niebuhr argues:

> Both the majesty and the tragedy of human life exceed the dimension within which modern culture seeks to comprehend human existence. The human spirit cannot be held within the bounds of either natural necessity or rational prudence. In its yearning toward the infinite lies the source of both human creativity and human sin. . . . The fact that man can transcend himself in infinite regression and cannot find the end of life except in God is the mark of his creativity and uniqueness; closely related to this capacity is his inclination to transmute his partial and finite self and his partial and finite values into the infinite good. Therein lies his sin. (I, 122)

Here we come to the heart of Niebuhr's Christian doctrine of human nature: man is an "organic unity" of a spirit capable of self-transcendence and a creature that sins inevitably. "In its purest form the Christian view of man regards man as a unity of God-likeness and creatureliness in which he remains a creature even in the highest spiritual dimension of his existence and may reveal elements of the image of God even in the lowliest aspects of his natural life" (I, 150). In his capacity for self-transcendence man defies the restraints of both reason and nature; this capacity is the source of man's creativity as well as his sin and is based on the Christian doctrine of man as "Image of God." Theories that try to explain man solely in terms of reason or nature therefore fail to comprehend man in his entirety. Niebuhr argues that man's continued seeking for meaning in an eternal universe proves that in some sense he stands outside that universe. He knows that his relation to his eternal environment cannot be grasped by "the mere logical ordering of his experience." Thus, argues Niebuhr, man cannot "comprehend himself in his full stature of freedom without a principle of comprehension which is beyond his comprehension" (I, 125).

What is this principle? What can Niebuhr mean by self-transcendence? Clearly these are problematic notions even to other theologians.[6] Niebuhr answers by propounding his twofold conception of revelation: "a personal-individual revelation, and a revelation in the context of social-historical experience" (I, 127). Only through these complementary forms of revelation can man's capacity for self-transcendence find fulfillment. Introspective evidence leads man to private revelation, which is the experience of God, "the 'wholly other' at the edge of human consciousness" (I, 131). Historical revelation, in which man discovers, through faith,

6. See Wolf, "Niebuhr's Doctrine of Man," in Kegley and Brettall (eds.), *Niebuhr*, on this and the following points.

God's self-disclosure in history, confirms the personal experience and gives "meaning and tragedy" to human history.[7]

But the other side of self-transcendence is the sinful creatureliness of man; man the spirit is organically united with man the sinner. For Niebuhr, sin is basically pride. Man's very capacity to reach beyond himself, to participate in revelation, makes him unwilling to accept his dependence, finiteness, and insecurity.[8] Man's greatest achievements and his worst sins have the same source—"the ambiguity of his position, as standing in and yet above nature."

> Man is insecure and involved in natural contingency; he seeks to overcome his insecurity by a will-to-power which overreaches the limits of human creatureliness. Man is ignorant and involved in the limitations of a finite mind; but he pretends that he is not limited. He assumes that he can gradually transcend finite limitation until his mind becomes identical with the universal mind. All of his intellectual and cultural pursuits, therefore, become infected with the sin of pride. Man's pride and will-to-power disturb the harmony of creation. (I, 178–79)

These ideas must be considered in turn, for Niebuhr's doctrine of sin is the most frequently cited—and perhaps most misunderstood—aspect of his thought.

Niebuhr begins his analysis of sin with a description of temptation. For reasons that will become clear, it is important for him to establish the groundwork for his notion of original sin—the idea that man's sin is inevitable but not necessary. First, let us examine the character of temptation, symbolized in the myth of the Fall. In the biblical story, the serpent tempts man to "break and transcend the limits which God has set for him." Yet in yielding to the temptation to defy these limits, man is not simply making an error. He knows that he is weak and dependent but willfully seeks to assert his independence: "His sin is never the mere ignorance of his ignorance. It is always partly an effort to obscure his blindness by overestimating the degree of his sight and to obscure his insecurity by stretching his power beyond its limits" (I, 180, 181).

Man is free, yet bound; limitless, yet limited. This position, "at the juncture of nature and spirit," leads to anxiety, which is the "internal

---

7. *Nature and Destiny*, II, *passim*, but especially chaps. 3 and 10. See also *Faith and History: A Comparison of Christian and Modern Views of History* (New York, 1940), in which Niebuhr elaborates the ideas he sets out in the second volume of *Nature and Destiny*. An analysis of Niebuhr's philosophy of history lies outside the scope of this essay.

8. *Nature and Destiny*, I, 150.

description of temptation." Anxiety is not sin itself but is its precondition as well as being one basis of creativity. It is the manifestation of man's recognition of his contingent position: "Man may, in the same moment, be anxious because he has not become what he ought to be; and also anxious lest he cease to be at all" (I, 182, 184). Thus a single action may reveal a creative effort to transcend natural limitation and a sinful attempt unconditionally to deny that limitation. The destructive aspects of anxiety are inseparable from its creative elements.[9]

"When anxiety has conceived, it brings forth pride" (I, 186). The sin of pride consists in denying the contingent nature of one's existence, in raising that contingency "to unconditioned significance." Pride expresses itself in observable human behavior in three distinguishable but not fully distinct ways: in pride of power, pride of knowledge, and pride of virtue or self-righteousness.

Pride of power manifests itself in attempts to achieve self-sufficiency, to guarantee security. Man seeks proudly to be the author of his own existence, the master of his destiny. Regardless of whether they are more or less apparently secure, men try to obscure or overcome their insecurity by arrogating excessive power to themselves. Since the insecurity results not only from man's contingent relation to nature but also from the uncertainties of society and history, this "lust for power" expresses itself in vain attempts to dominate nature and other men. The desire for power, therefore, is much more than a survival instinct that could be satisfied in a truly cooperative society. The will-to-power reflects a desire for "security beyond the limits of human finiteness"; thus it is "both a direct form and an indirect instrument of the pride which Christianity regards as sin in its quintessential form" (I, 192). This quest for security can never be satisfied: the more power we accrue in the attempt to guarantee our security, the more we fear losing all power and security.

It is important to recognize that for Niebuhr the quest for security stems from man's sinful pride and that the source of this pride—the capacity for self-transcendence—is equally the source of man's greatest achievements. The will-to-power is only one aspect of the sin of pride. To be sure, this aspect is crucial for Niebuhr's later analysis of collective behavior, but it remains a single factor among a multitude of others. An account of Niebuhr's view of sin which isolates it and posits a primordial "security-power dilemma" in my opinion skews his overall conception of sin toward

9. *Ibid.*, 186.

power. To characterize Niebuhr's view by saying, "The human predica-
ment has roots primarily in the security-power dilemma," is to magnify
inordinately the security aspect of pride.[10]

Intellectual pride leads man to ignore the contingent nature of his
knowledge. Because of their intellectual pride, the great philosophers have
all made the mistake of imagining themselves "the final thinker." Even
Marx, who rightly identified "the ideological taint of all culture," nonetheless failed to recognize the same element within himself, and Marxism
"therefore ends in a pitiful display of the same sin" (I, 197). Any philosophical system that imagines itself able to transcend history, to apprehend
truth from a higher, final perspective, manifests intellectual pride; the case
of Marxism is the more striking because it relentlessly exposes the corruption of other systems even as it exhibits the selfsame sin. This point should
be emphasized, for in later works Niebuhr extends this argument by asserting that Marxism is the most dangerous expression of intellectual pride
because fanaticism springs from its blindness.[11]

Moral pride, or self-righteousness, is defined by Niebuhr as "the pre-
tension of finite man that his highly conditioned virtue is the final righteousness and that his very relative moral standards are absolute" (I, 199).
This notion leads to a general spiritual pride, a pride of unconditioned
claims for one's philosophical position, one's ideology, one's religion.
Niebuhr concludes: "Religion, by whatever name, is the inevitable fruit of
the spiritual stature of man; and religious intolerance and pride is the final
expression of his sinfulness. A religion of revelation is grounded in the
faith that God speaks to man from beyond the highest pinnacle of the
human spirit; and that this voice of God will discover man's highest not
only to be short of the highest but involved in the dishonesty of claiming
that it is the highest" (I, 203).

The last aspect of Niebuhr's doctrine of sin has mainly theological
interest and is probably better left to the theologians; but it has wider
significance in that it allows Niebuhr to admit the ideal possibility that man
can appreciate his own limits and act on that appreciation. For Niebuhr,
original sin is inevitable but not necessary: "Sin is natural for a man in the

10. Kenneth W. Thompson, "The Political Philosophy of Reinhold Niebuhr," in Kegley
and Bretall (eds.), *Niebuhr*, 166. *Cf.* Thompson's "Beyond National Interest: A Critical
Evaluation of Reinhold Niebuhr's Theory of International Politics," in *Review of Politics*,
XVII (April, 1955), 167–89. I am grateful to Thompson for several enlightening discussions
about Niebuhr in general and specifically about this issue, on which we have cordially agreed
to differ.

11. This position is already implicit in *Nature and Destiny*, I, 197.

sense that it is universal but not in the sense that it is necessary" (I, 242). This sounds contradictory, as Niebuhr admits; but he argues that, in discovering the inevitability of his sin while recognizing that the sin is not *necessary*—in other words, that he is responsible for his sin—man reaches his greatest freedom: "Man is most free in the discovery that he is not free" (I, 260). This paradox stands beyond rationality, "unless the paradox be accepted as a rational understanding of the limits of rationality and as an expression of faith that a rationally irresolvable contradiction may point to a truth which logic cannot contain." Thus original sin is for Niebuhr a "dialectical truth" which asserts that man sins inevitably, "but not in such a way as to fit into the category of natural necessity" (I, 262–63).

Man in Collectivities

How does man's membership in collectivities affect his nature? Niebuhr has given several answers to this question during his career, but the view he outlines in *Nature and Destiny* and elaborates in *The Children of Light and the Children of Darkness* represents his mature position; these works are the definitive sources.[12]

In his earlier works, particularly *Moral Man and Immoral Society* (1932), Niebuhr was reacting against the Social Gospel school of theology. Briefly, this school argued that man is essentially mild and reasonable; injustice is caused by ignorance; and as civilization advances and education is extended, compromise and accommodation will lead the way to social justice.[13] *Moral Man* is a polemic against this view. It argues that a radical antinomy exists between individual and collective behavior. Individual men are capable of moral acts from disinterested motives; such "achievements are more difficult, if not impossible, for human societies and social groups." Man's sinful tendencies—and at this stage in Niebuhr's thought his doctrine of sin was tentative—are magnified and projected on a national scale. Even individual unselfishness feeds "national egoism," which is subject to no restraints, religious or rational.[14]

Moreover, the basis of man's efforts to justify his collective behavior is that "individuals have a moral code which makes the actions of collective

12. See Niebuhr's new prefaces to each of these works (*Nature and Destiny*, 1964; *Children of Light*, 1960). See also his "Intellectual Autobiography" in Kegley and Bretall (eds.), *Niebuhr*, 1–24.
13. I follow Niebuhr's own characterization here, from *Moral Man and Immoral Society: A Study in Ethics and Politics* (New York, 1932), xix.
14. Niebuhr, *Moral Man*, xi, 94, 9.

man an outrage to their conscience"; man therefore seeks to obscure the true character of his collective behavior. In 1933, Niebuhr summarized the relation of man to society: "Society . . . merely cumulates the egoism of individuals and transmutes their individual altruism into collective egoism so that the egoism of the group has a double force. For this reason no group acts from purely unselfish or even mutual intent and politics is therefore bound to be a contest of power."[15]

Niebuhr explicitly modified his position in *The Nature and Destiny of Man* to accord with his more developed view of human nature. Gone are the notions that society "merely cumulates" individual egoism and "transmutes" individual selfishness. The radical antinomy of *Moral Man* collapses into a need to make only "some distinctions between the collective behavior of men and their individual attitudes" (I, 208). There is no longer a qualitative difference between the way man acts individually and in groups; rather, the difference is essentially one of degree.

Just as man's sinful pride expresses itself in his individual behavior, it does so in his collective activities; the result in the latter instance is group pride. The force of group pride on the individual differs from his own inherent pride and is stronger because the group achieves some authority over the individual and therefore invests the group pride with greater intensity. The group, especially when it obtains all the trappings of a state, "seems to the individual to have become an independent center of moral life" (I, 208). The individual therefore will be inclined to bow to the demands of the state even if those demands violate his own moral scruples. In addition, the pretensions of a collective far exceed those of an individual; the group is more hypocritical, ruthless, and arrogant. Tension between individual and group morality results. Here, like Carr, Niebuhr quotes Cavour: "If we did for ourselves what we do for our country, what rascals we would be!"[16]

The pride of nations, like the pride of individuals, has spiritual and creaturely dimensions. Spiritual pride is expressed in the "self-deification" of nations and in "their unconditioned claims for their conditioned values"; equally, the basic feeling of insecurity leads nations to claim that any struggle is a fight for survival. Both claims—and the ambivalence felt between them—reflect an attempt to "break all bounds of finiteness": the

15. Niebuhr, "Human Nature and Social Change," *Christian Century*, L (1933), 363, quoted by Thompson, "Political Philosophy," in Kegley and Bretall (eds.), *Niebuhr*, 168.
16. Morgenthau quotes the same remark—a favorite of realists—in *Scientific Man vs. Power Politics* (Chicago, 1946), 179.

nation is either the carrier of higher values or is itself the ultimate value: "The nation pretends to be God" (I, 212). The sin of collective pride is the same as the sin of individual pride—it denies the contingent and determinate character of its own existence. It differs in the degree of plausibility attached to its pretensions; because of this, "collective egotism and group pride are a more pregnant source of injustice than purely individual pride."[17]

All nations, like all individuals, exhibit the sin of pride, but this does not mean that all nations are equally evil: "Relative distinctions must always be made in history" (I, 214). Such distinctions rest on the degree to which "nations are still receptive to prophetic words of judgment spoken against the nation." Even if "only a prophetic minority feels this judgment keenly," one can still morally distinguish "between nations which do not officially destroy the religious-prophetic judgment against the nation and those which do" (I, 219). In this important passage, Niebuhr emphasizes that although all nations are guilty of the sin of pride, critical differences in their degree of pride and self-will remain. Niebuhr makes moral distinctions between nations on this basis. The final sin for a nation, as for an individual, "is the unwillingness to hear the word of judgment spoken against our sin." On this criterion Niebuhr condemns the "daemonic" national self-assertion of modern fascist nations; later he would apply it to Marxist Russia.

But man's collective life reflects more than his sinful pride. In "organic relation with his fellow men," man has sought justice as an aspect of his capacity for self-transcendence; in man's continuing struggle for justice, Niebuhr sees "historical revelation" (II, 244). In his analysis of that historical revelation, which of course includes biblical history, Niebuhr identifies Christ's perfection—the essence of which is pure, sacrificial love—as the ultimate norm of human nature.[18] But Christ's sacrificial love *transcends* history; it is totally beyond human achievement and therefore cannot provide the basis of human ethics. The source of historical human ethics is the "law of mutual love," which Niebuhr calls, paradoxically, "history's 'impossible impossibility'" (II, 69, 76). By these words he seems to mean that man never fully achieves that ideal, but he never ceases—and should never cease—to try.

17. *Nature and Destiny*, I, 213; also in *The Children of Light and the Children of Darkness: A Vindication of Democracy and a Critique of Its Traditional Defense* (New York, 1944), 20–21.
18. *Nature and Destiny*, II, 68. This is obviously a bald summary; a careful reconstruction of the way Niebuhr reaches these assertions cannot be attempted here.

From the law of mutual love Niebuhr derives brotherhood as the fundamental requirement of man's social existence. Man's attempt to achieve brotherhood in his communities again reflects his dual nature: his greatest achievements are attended by equally great elements of corruption. Because of this ever-present possibility of corruption, "structures of justice" (states) need to take care that the "political instruments" basic to any community—a central, organizing power and a balance of power among the elements of the community—do not degenerate into either tyranny or anarchy. These instruments are themselves morally ambiguous; but they make "approximations of justice" possible.

Concerning international politics, Niebuhr writes that "we face all the old problems of political organizations on the new level of a potential international community." The central organizing principle would be an "implied hegemony of the great powers"; its attendant danger is imperialism. To guard against such imperialism, all nations should be armed "with constitutional power to resist the exactions of dominant power. The principle of balance of power is implied in the idea of constitutional justice." Without a sufficiently strong central principle, the political equilibrium achieved by carefully managing the two forces degenerates to a disorganized balance of power, which is potential anarchy. The dangers are therefore those of a domestic political structure—tyranny or anarchy. Niebuhr concludes: "The new world must be built by resolute men . . . who will neither seek premature escape from the guilt of history, nor yet call the evil, which taints all their achievements, good."[19]

Some Implications of Niebuhr's View of Man

The approach in the previous section has been straightforwardly, and doubtless somewhat laboriously, exegetic. Such an approach is justifiable because Niebuhr's view of man is often presented in caricature, with many of its facets distorted or entirely left out; my concern has been to present Niebuhr's view, in his own terms, as clearly and completely as possible.[20] It will now be useful to point to some of the issues raised by these views in light of their significance for his later specific writings on American foreign policy.

19. *Ibid.*, 284–86.
20. Following Niebuhr's advice, I have relied on *Nature and Destiny*. He and his critics agree that it is the definitive source. See the essays by Brunner, Bennett, Wolf, and Burtt in Kegley and Bretall (eds.), *Niebuhr*.

Although I am not concerned to evaluate his view of human nature, it should be pointed out that realism notwithstanding, it rests wholly on faith. On the basis of the Christian doctrine of man as image of God, Niebuhr asserts that man is a spirit and a creature who defies natural and rational limitations. Naturalist or rationalist philosophies (among many others) that try to explain man's nature fail to apprehend him in his totality. Only a Christian conception does full justice to his spiritual and creaturely aspects. But suppose one rejects his initial assertion? He can only appeal to us to accept it on faith. To be sure, he tries valiantly to demonstrate the relevance of the Christian view throughout his work, indeed throughout his life's work, to some effect; but to the skeptic who questions his first assertions his only reply would be that these are mysteries beyond human reason.[21] Similar objections can be made to his notion of self-transcendence, which is defined in terms of religious revelation, to his doctrine of original sin, with its necessary-inevitable paradox, and to his idea that brotherhood is history's "impossible possibility." Niebuhr will not attract the skeptically minded.

Nonetheless, an interesting consequence of Niebuhr's dual man is that it allows him an escape hatch from the totally pessimistic view that man is unremittingly sinful. Such a view, as we shall see in the next chapter, makes it very difficult to find a source for relative moral distinctions. Niebuhr also avoids making morally ambiguous instruments like the balance of power wholly normative; they are only instruments, and man is capable of achieving some justice. Indeed, according to Niebuhr, he has a responsibility to do so—man must strive for justice, and paradoxically, by realizing that he can never fully achieve it, he comes closer to doing so. Man is most free when he recognizes the limits of his freedom.

To bring about this recognition is the duty of prophetic religion. Religion opens the way to the revelation that comprises genuine self-transcendence. Through religion we recognize our sin and our high potential; we learn to be aware of our pride and to try, through faith, to temper it. Prophetic religion also has the duty to deliver "prophetic judgments against the nation," to inveigh against the nation's inordinate pride, to push it toward a greater recognition of its own limitations. Indeed, it is on the basis of a nation's openness to these prophetic judgments that Niebuhr

21. See Leslie J. Stevenson, *Seven Theories of Human Nature* (Oxford, 1974). He observes, "The trouble with this kind of statement is that it can appeal only to those already disposed to believe, it can do nothing to answer the genuine difficulties of the sceptic" (43).

makes moral distinctions between nations. This point cannot be made too strongly.

But the effect of prophetic religion on the nation depends on the existence of a "prophetic minority" sensitive to its judgments. The spokesman of prophetic religion—and Niebuhr himself was one—must activate such a group. I believe that this desire to awaken a sensitive prophetic minority can explain Niebuhr's lifelong preoccupation with American liberals and with liberalism in general. Of course, a large element of his consistent "exposure of illusions" is simply an important intellectual disagreement with the liberals. But there is more to it; Niebuhr wrote for the quintessentially liberal *Nation* frequently from 1940 and was a member of its editorial board; he chaired the meeting that organized the Americans for Democratic Action; almost all of his articles from 1944 to 1951 are addressed to liberals. He saw the liberals as potentially becoming the "prophetic minority" if only they would shed their sentimental illusions. Led by an aware and active group of men attuned to the insights of prophetic religion, America could achieve a better approximation of justice.

How exactly did Niebuhr appeal to this potential minority? In what way did he hope to put America's policy on better moral ground?

From Light to Irony: Niebuhr's Program for Postwar America

Niebuhr opened his appeal in 1944 with the publication of *The Children of Light and the Children of Darkness*, which has been described by one theologian as "his only systematic study of social ethics."[22] In the book Niebuhr "vindicates" democracy by basing it on a "more realistic" Christian view of human nature; he states in a compressed and theoretical way all the themes that inform his prescriptive writings up to 1952.

The children of light "seek to bring self-interest under the discipline of a more universal law and in harmony with a more universal good." The children of darkness are "moral cynics": they "know no law beyond their will and interest." "Foolish" children of light have built modern, democratic civilization, but because they have failed to recognize the true facts of human nature, their civilization has "come close to complete collapse" under the attacks of the children of darkness. If they are to preserve what they have achieved, Niebuhr writes, "the children of light must be armed

22. John C. Bennett, "Reinhold Niebuhr's Social Ethics," in Kegley and Bretall (eds.), *Niebuhr*, 48.

with the wisdom of the children of darkness but remain free from their malice. They must know the power of self-interest in human society without giving it moral justification. They must have this wisdom in order that they may beguile, deflect, harness and restrain self-interest, individual and collective, for the sake of the community."[23]

The last sentence points to the book's main argument: that democracy, properly understood, is the best form of government because it provides a method to cope with the basic problems of community. Democracy balances the central organizing power of the community against the equilibrium of the particular powers within the community. Human nature makes it impossible to move beyond these fundamental instruments of rule; by carefully maintaining them, and by constantly reexamining the balance between them, however, it is possible to achieve approximations of justice. Niebuhr rejects "dogmas" like individualist liberalism and Marxism because they purport to have a final solution to what in reality is a never-ending problem; these dogmas are advanced by the worldly wisdom of the children of darkness.[24]

Niebuhr identifies the same pattern in international relations. The duality of human nature expresses itself in formidable national pride; such national pride is most dangerous in the attractive guise of universalist doctrine because it appeals to sentimental children of light. Oblivious to national pride, especially when it is their own, these children of light believe they can construct a genuine world community according to formulas of international law or world government. Americans are particularly prone to this illusion, it seems, because many have plausibly—but wrongly—attributed the success of the American republic to its ingenious Constitution.

But communities can be established only by the "organic processes of history" in combination with the prudent management of the basic instruments of rule.[25] According to Niebuhr in January, 1944, the only possibility for even a modicum of world community lay in a "stable accord between the great powers"; further, some way must be found to implicate them in "careful plans reaching beyond their immediate interests." A straightforward agreement to divide the world into spheres of influence

23. Niebuhr, *Children of Light*, chap. 1, esp. 9–11, 41.
24. *Ibid.*, chaps. 3 and 4; esp. 77–78 and 150–52.
25. *Ibid.*, 166. For an example of the view Niebuhr here criticizes see Frank Tannenbaum, "The Balance of Power vs. the Co-ordinate State," *Political Science Quarterly*, LXVII (June, 1952), 31–50.

would "only slightly delay ultimate conflict" because no such agreement could "apply to all areas of the continents or give tolerable health to their economic and political life." This position led Niebuhr to distinguish his view from that held by such early realists as Nicholas Spykman. These writers believe that the balance of power is the highest possible achievement in world politics; they ignore the spiritual aspects of man's nature. A balance of power is often a necessary but never a sufficient condition for world order: lacking a central organizing principle, the balance of power is a "potential anarchy which becomes actual anarchy in the long run." Niebuhr's answer sounded very much like an advance brief for the United Nations Organization as it emerged from Dumbarton Oaks in late 1944. Order would be guaranteed by an agreement among the great powers; "moral and constitutional checks" placed on such a working alliance would prevent it from becoming imperialistic.[26]

Chief among the enormous obstacles to the application of such checks was national pride. Niebuhr thought that national will-to-power could be tempered, but only through rigorous self-criticism. For this reason, Soviet Russia was the least likely of the great powers to overcome its pride; not only is it governed by "pretentious" Marxism, but it also lacks the "democratic institutions through which, in other nations, sensitive minorities may act as the conscience of the nation and subject its actions and pretensions to criticism." Thus the Russians possessed no internal means to check their collective, national pride; for Niebuhr, they entered the postwar period, as it were, on probation. America, too, had problems: its illusions and its immaturity cause it to swing from moods of complete irresponsibility, in which it stays "uncorrupted" by power, to moods of cynicism, in which it "displays an adolescent pride of power." Necessity provided the best and perhaps only hope for both nations to overcome their pride: "A stable order is not possible without introducing instruments of justice into the agreements which are to provide for order."[27]

Thus Niebuhr's message in *Children of Light* was to guard against the faults of the children of darkness, the moral cynics, and the children of light, the naive utopians, by confronting the reality of human nature. Man can reach for the heights of justice, but his every attempt contains proportionate elements of corruption. Neither sentimental idealism nor cynical realism does full justice to the range of man's capabilities.

26. Niebuhr, *Children of Light*, 177–79, 180, 174, 178.
27. *Ibid.*, 183–85, 181.

In the more than one hundred prescriptive essays he wrote between 1945 and 1952, Niebuhr moved from this balanced message—castigating liberal illusions, warning against realist cynicism, and promoting great power collaboration—to a justification of America's position at the head of a Western world "containing" the Soviet Union. The explanation for the change lies in Niebuhr's different assessment of the national pride exhibited by the great powers; by 1947 he believed that Russia's could be stopped only by an active policy of containment. This view forms the first half of Niebuhr's justification of containment; the second was expressed in 1952 in *The Irony of American History*. In this book Niebuhr argues that despite the sentimental illusions of America's dominant dogmas, "we have builded better than we knew"—hence the irony.

Niebuhr's prescriptive essays exhibit a distinctive pattern, and through all of them he seems to be addressing a prospective "prophetic minority." A typical essay begins by identifying a particular problem facing American policy makers, for example, what to do about Germany, and follows with a denunciation of liberal illusions that hinder its genuine solution. Niebuhr then presents his own analysis and recommendations, and the essay ends by warning against the excessive pride of the nation and the danger of cynicism that lurks behind realism.

An article published in January, 1945, illustrates this pattern. Niebuhr began by outlining the problems of the coming peace, particularly that of Poland. Liberals were not "playing a creative role" in the solution of these problems: either they promoted world government or they urged the adoption of a spheres-of-influence policy because they trusted Russia. Niebuhr exhorted them to recognize "hidden realities of international politics"; agreed-upon spheres of influence were no solution because the Russians could "extend their ideological sphere" beyond any agreed boundary. At the same time, the Americans should not allow problems over Poland to block a broader, substantive agreement with the Russians: for better or worse, America "washed its hands" of any genuine interest in Poland at Teheran. The main imperative was European recovery without domination by either Russia or the West. If liberals realized this, they would stop "playing into the hands of the moral cynics."[28]

Throughout 1945 Niebuhr repeated his misgivings about the ultimate objectives of the Soviet Union, but he continued to advocate collaboration with the Russians to build a central organizing principle of power that

28. Niebuhr, "Will America Back Out? Our Stake in Europe's Future," *Nation*, CLX (January 13, 1945), 42–43.

could combat international anarchy. On April 7, 1945, he wrote that "Russia is not driven by the mania of world conquest, though it obviously has residual fears of the Western world. Shall we seek to quiet those fears by efforts to achieve a mutual security system, or shall we play upon those fears and make another war inevitable?"[29] The naively universalist plans of liberals did just this: "The theory is: 'let us set up a real world government and if the Russians fail to adhere, so much the worse for them.'" Niebuhr presumably had in mind Clarence Streit's proposal for a federal union of Western democracies, Emery Reves's plan for an Anglo-American federation that would compel other nations to give up their sovereignty, and Supreme Court Justice Owen Roberts' scheme for binding, "supra-national law." All such plans, Niebuhr wrote, are based on the illusion of a basically benevolent human nature and ignore the force of group pride present even among the proposers. In these passages Niebuhr sounds very much like E. H. Carr on Alfred Zimmern *et al.*[30]

Niebuhr did not spare those liberals he regarded as explicitly pro-Russian. In their eagerness to work "constitutional magic" on the Russians by signing them up in world government, they yield to Russia at every opportunity: "Any responsible analyst of world affairs knows that we must find a basis for a stable accord with Russia. But it is stupid to imagine that we can find one only by accepting the policy of the Soviet Union as unwaveringly virtuous." These liberals ignore the tragic realities of world politics: that nations are proud and that they will not submit to constitutional engineering that abandons the essential political instruments. Even if by some miracle nations did surrender their sovereignty, such engineering would be doomed. The duality of human nature dictates the prudent application and management of power. He concluded with what became a standard indictment of a recalcitrant prophetic minority: "American liberalism has failed to exercise the kind of restraint upon the pride of powerful and victorious nations which it is the traditional function of liberal intelligence to exercise."[31]

Niebuhr's critique of the liberal program, which he tended to identify with plans for world government, had two sides which coincided with his dual conception of human nature. Negatively, he decried liberal naiveté

29. Niebuhr, "Is This 'Peace in Our Time'?" *Nation*, CLX (April 7, 1945), 383.
30. Niebuhr, "The Myth of World Government," *Nation*, CLXI (February 16, 1946), 312–13. See also Clarence Streit, *Union Now* (New York, 1939), and Emery Reves, *A Democratic Manifesto* (New York, 1942). For a general account of the internationalist movement see Divine, *Second Chance*, esp. 38–39, 57–59, 119–29.
31. Niebuhr, "A Lecture to Liberals," *Nation*, CLXI (November 10, 1945), 493.

and self-righteousness. Intellectual pride in their rational plans blinded liberals not only to the nationalist element in their own plans but also to the dangerous combination of nationalist ambition and universalist goals present in Soviet Russia—a combination all the more threatening because it was not tempered by the internal criticism of a prophetic minority. Thus, reviewing Frederick L. Schuman's *Soviet Politics at Home and Abroad* in February, 1946, Niebuhr dissented from Schuman's contention that "the Soviet leaders are realists in their foreign policy" and have no desire to expand. Their Marxist creed, Niebuhr argued, causes them to be ambivalent at best; this is why Western policy should avoid both outright hostility and craven acquiescence to all Russian initiatives. Either policy would confirm their ideological suspicions, fuel their inherently universalist tendencies, and lead, ultimately, to a new international anarchy.[32]

The other aspect of Niebuhr's critique pointed to the failure of liberals to propose creative policies that could serve as a realistic foundation for world order. As early as January, 1945, Niebuhr explicitly advocated a comprehensive American program for the political and economic recovery of the war-ravaged areas of Europe and the world. He continued to promote this policy because it would tap America's spiritual resources and provide a way for it to develop the political "points of contact" to match its unquestionable economic power. A policy of economic aid would serve as the means to implicate justice in the search for order. Prescriptions for agreed-upon spheres of influence, apart from all their other problems, fail to include precisely this implication of justice and therefore offer no escape from international anarchy. Such prescriptions borrow too much wisdom from the children of darkness; they ignore the spiritual capacity of human nature.

In the autumn of 1946, Niebuhr was in Europe as a delegate to a meeting of the World Council of Churches. He traveled extensively through Germany and later became a member of the United States educational mission there. His interest in Germany was enduring; in 1947 he chaired a group called the American Association for a Democratic Germany. Niebuhr's stay in Europe influenced his views on American policy toward Russia, especially concerning Germany. While still in Europe, he wrote reports of his impressions for several journals.

32. Niebuhr, "The Russian Adventure," *Nation*, CLXII (February 23, 1946). That Schuman was widely considered a liberal realist is used by Niebuhr to show that even sophisticated liberals miss this essential point.

The first of these reports appeared in the *Nation* on September 14, 1946. Niebuhr found European attitudes, on the whole, "superior to the American approach." First, Europeans were skeptical about the United Nations but were willing to cooperate in its operation. Second, there was fear, but not hysteria, about the policies of Soviet Russia—Europeans, according to Niebuhr, regarded Russian motives as rooted in their fear about security, and they were afraid that an American misunderstanding of this situation would lead to war. Niebuhr therefore counseled a patient strategy that would "stop futile efforts to change what cannot be changed in Eastern Europe." Such a policy might disturb liberal consciences and conservative prejudices, but America had no other choice; besides, by leaving Russia alone, the Americans were more likely to help the indigenous, noncommunist forces within Eastern European countries. As for Western Europe, Niebuhr repeated his call for comprehensive economic aid: "The way to save Western Europe is to give it a sound economic base for a sound political life."[33]

In his second report, "Will Germany Go Communist?" Niebuhr began by praising "the vigor with which the Germans have rejected Communism." He then sounded the same theme: "Sooner or later we shall have to decide how to restore a measure of economic health to Western Germany and Europe without waiting on Russia. We have learned the lesson of strategically resisting Russian penetration into Western Europe. But unless we support our political policy with an adequate economic policy, Soviet ideology will cross our strategic barrier. If anyone thinks peace can be secured by such a development, he has read the history of past decades in vain." Here, in linking his proposal for economic aid with his references to a strategic barrier, Niebuhr anticipated President Harry S. Truman's description of the Truman Doctrine and the Marshall Plan as "two halves of the same walnut."[34] When General George C. Marshall at the 1947 Harvard Commencement announced the plan for European economic recovery developed largely by George Kennan, Niebuhr praised it as "a kind of turning point in postwar history."[35]

33. Niebuhr, "Europe, Russia and America," *Nation*, CLXIII (September 14, 1946), 288–89.

34. Niebuhr, "Will Germany Go Communist?" *Nation*, CLXIII (October 5, 1946); on Truman, see Walter LaFeber, *America, Russia and the Cold War* (New York, 1967), 53.

35. Editorial notes in *Christianity and Crisis*, VII (August 4, 1947), 2, quoted in Gordon Harland, *The Thought of Reinhold Niebuhr: An Introduction* (New York, 1960), 198.

While Niebuhr was writing these reports on his European experience, the Truman administration was suffering its most severe internal challenge. On September 12, 1946, former Vice-President and then Secretary of Commerce Henry A. Wallace addressed a rally at Madison Square Garden; his speech, or more precisely the reaction to his speech after President Truman carelessly announced that it had his "full approval," caused an uproar. By September 20, acceding to demands from his secretary of state, Truman demanded and received Wallace's resignation. In the speech, Wallace warned that "British balance-of-power manipulations" and an "anti-Russian press" could lead to war: "The tougher we get, the tougher the Russians will get." He advocated a $4 billion American investment in "underdeveloped areas" and argued that "we should recognize that we have no more business in the political affairs of Eastern Europe than Russia has in the political affairs of Latin America, Western Europe, and the United States."[36] After Truman sacked him, Wallace announced that he would continue his "fight for peace," and together with some former New Dealers, notably Harold Ickes and Henry Morgenthau, Jr., he formed a new political group called the Progressive Citizens of America.

Liberal reaction to this episode was mixed. The editors of *Nation* (who included I. F. Stone) noted in an editorial on September 21, 1946, that Wallace's speech had "many interesting parallels with the ideas expressed by Dr. Niebuhr on September 14." James Reston, in the New York *Times*, drew attention to the inconsistency of Wallace's opposition to a balance of power at the same time he proposed leaving Russia alone in Eastern Europe.[37] Niebuhr himself chose the popular journal *Life* as the place to clarify his view. The article marks an important turning point in Niebuhr's postwar position.

Far from tracing the "interesting parallels" between his own position and Wallace's, Niebuhr challenged the rationale of Wallace's policy: "The confusion in America's liberalism, of which Wallace's speech is the symbol, must be regarded as catastrophic in the light of European realities." Wallace's line of criticism is based on the same illusions as those held by the interwar appeasers of Hitler. Drawing heavily on the Munich analogy, Niebuhr warned against future appeasement: "Russian truculence cannot be mitigated by further concessions. Russia hopes to conquer the whole of Europe strategically and ideologically. . . . Russia's policy is much too

36. New York *Times*, September 13, 1946, p. 3.
37. *Ibid.*, September 19, 1946, p. 3.

hard-boiled and has too many prospects of success to be diverted by soft-ness on our part." Such illusions spring partly from the usual liberal easy conscience, but "they are partly the synthetic product of Communist influ-ence within Liberal movements."[38]

Rather than appeasing the Russians, Niebuhr wrote, America should hold to a policy of "strategic firmness and affirmative economic recon-struction." He advocated Western acceptance of a divided Germany—a position opposite to Kennan's but in tune with future American policy; indeed, Niebuhr frequently anticipated the policy eventually adopted by the Truman administration. After noting the refusal of liberals "to con-template the tragic aspects of human existence honestly," Niebuhr con-cluded typically: "Since the new tyranny we face is not only unscrupulous, but possesses the guile to exploit our moral and political weaknesses, it must be the business of a genuine liberalism not to relax our outer defenses but to make our political and economic life more worthy of our faith and therefore more impregnable. War with Russia is neither imminent nor inevitable if we have a creative policy. Let us therefore avoid hysteria even while we abjure sentimental illusions."[39]

Wallace's speech obviously aroused Niebuhr into writing this stinging and often intemperate article; certainly it is the shrillest in tone of all of Niebuhr's postwar writings. He saw in Wallace the embodiment of all the dangerous illusions he had been trying to dispel; Wallace was a siren to liberals. His position demanded a serious counterattack, and Niebuhr did not rest after writing a few articles. On January 4, 1947, he chaired the meeting that organized the Americans for Democratic Action; the group proclaimed as its immediate objective the "reconstruction of a liberal movement free of totalitarian influence from either the Left or the Right."[40] On these grounds, communists were excluded. Niebuhr obvi-ously regarded Wallace as a threat to his careful efforts to build a prophetic minority within the liberal community and sought therefore to "lay the basis of a robust, pragmatic opposition" to the "older liberalism" which Wallace represented.[41]

The Wallace affair, as well as his experience in Germany, pushed Nie-buhr in the *Life* article into adopting a harsher assessment of Soviet inten-

38. Niebuhr, "The Fight for Germany," *Life*, XXI (October 21, 1946), 65–72.
39. *Ibid.*
40. "130 Liberals Form a Group on Right," New York *Times*, January 5, 1947, p. 19.
41. Niebuhr, "The Sickness of American Culture," *Nation*, CLXVI (March 6, 1948), 267.

tions than he had expressed only five weeks earlier. On September 14, 1946, he argued that Soviet intentions primarily reflected their security fears; on October 21, they hoped to conquer the whole of Europe. Of course, Niebuhr had all along regarded the Russians as potentially danger- ous; at the end of 1946 he dropped the qualifying "potentially." Russian "truculence" could no longer be assuaged by conciliatory policies; a firm American line was required.

After 1946 Niebuhr adapted his dual critique of liberalism to fit this darker view of the Soviet Union. Thus, what had been a blanket injunction to guard against sinful national pride because it hindered attempts at genu- ine collaboration turned in 1947 into a warning that "without the humility and imagination to think beyond the characteristic prejudices of American life we cannot win the ideological battle against Communism." When he attacked liberals, it was because Soviet Russia had become "a fixed point of international virtue" for them; because they had failed to see through the false attractiveness of Marxist utopianism; or because they had not made it clearer that "we stand for freedom and justice and not for preser- vation of privilege."[42]

After Congress adopted the Marshall Plan in April, 1948, Niebuhr was generally satisfied with the administration's foreign policy; the plan sup- plemented military and strategic firmness with an imaginative program for West European economic and political recovery. When the North Atlan- tic Treaty was signed in 1949, Niebuhr called it the "logical capstone" of American postwar foreign policy and asserted that it linked America's new sense of responsibility for world community with her position as head of the Western world. Niebuhr had anticipated the dual pillars of America's containment policy in 1946 and consistently defended that policy after 1947. In his view, Russian behavior made this policy necessary; America was justified in adopting it.[43]

Niebuhr avoided the typical realist justification of "national interest," stressing instead the necessity to contain the Soviet Union so that Western democracies at least could continue to pursue their "approximations of justice." He worried that a too consistent national interest realism would produce avoidable confrontations—especially in Asia—and might even lead to preventive war with the Russians. In a 1950 essay called "A Protest

42. Speech to the New York *Herald Tribune* "Forum," reported in New York *Times*, October 22, 1947, p. 25.
43. "The North Atlantic Pact," *Christianity and Crisis*, IX (May 30, 1949), 3.

Against a Dilemma's Two Horns" he compared the advance of Russia's "fanatic creed" with Mohammedism: Marxism, too, would subside. In the meantime he argued, "It is important to resist counsels of desperation on our side which would tempt us to confront communism in Asia primarily in military terms and thus play into the hands of the communist political propaganda by which it would expand still further into Asia. . . . Idealists must learn that nothing but a preponderance of power in the noncommunist world can preserve the peace. Realists must learn that power consists of the unity of the moral and economic health of our world."[44]

Thus Niebuhr's changed perception of the Soviet threat did not lead him to embrace the national interest doctrines of other realists without qualification; he continued to exhort against national pride, but he regarded this as subsidiary to awakening liberals to the danger from Russia. Repeatedly, he reminded his readers or listeners that because Soviet Marxism professed the ideals of equality and justice—because the Russians masqueraded as children of light—they were more attractive to the dispossessed of the world than rich Americans were. The Soviets "had the advantage of a political religion, scattered beyond its borders, the tenets of which could persuade gullible men to regard its most tortuous and cynical power politics as proofs of its virtues and good intentions."[45] American liberals were gullible enough to be persuaded; American conservatives lacked the imagination to see how anyone could be. Conservatives therefore saw the confrontation with communism in too exclusively military terms and opposed the political and economic programs that could "eliminate the social conditions and resentments that are exploited by Communism."[46] But Niebuhr did not outline the content of such programs beyond expressing support for Truman's foreign aid proposals.

As Niebuhr's disquiet over the Soviet threat deepened, his satisfaction with the achievements of American society seemed to grow correspondingly. In 1944 Niebuhr agreed that some socialization of property could aid justice: democratic socialism was healthy. But by late 1949, he had concluded that democratic socialism was as encumbered with "confusing dogmas" as plutocracy. The best way for a democracy—which he defined

44. Niebuhr, "A Protest Against a Dilemma's Two Horns," *World Politics*, II (April, 1950), 344.
45. Niebuhr, "The Conditions of Our Survival," *Virginia Quarterly Review*, XXVI (Autumn, 1950), 482.
46. Niebuhr, "American Conservatism and the World Crisis: A Study in Vacillation," *Yale Review*, XL (March, 1951), 386–92.

as "a method of finding proximate solutions for insoluble problems"—to approximate justice was through "pragmatic, whirligig reform."[47]

Niebuhr presented a full statement of his revised position in *The Irony of American History*, published in 1952. The thesis of the book states that America is involved in a double irony: "If the experiences of America as a world power, its responsibilities and concomitant guilt, its frustrations and its discovery of the limits of power, constitute an ironic refutation of some of the most cherished illusions of a liberal age, its experiences in domestic politics represent an ironic form of success. Our success in establishing justice and insuring domestic tranquility has exceeded the characteristic insights of a bourgeois culture."[48]

America's involvement in the confrontation with the "monstrous evils of communism" had forced it to abandon its liberal notions of human nature, of inevitable progress, and of the possibility for world government; only by abandoning these "cherished illusions" could America preserve its way of life in the face of the communist threat. That communism should bring this about is itself ironic, for communism is a "noxious elaboration" of some of the same illusions. American history, Niebuhr wrote, has proven to be the "triumph of experience over dogma: We have equilibrated power. We have attained a certain equilibrium in economic society itself by setting organized power against organized power. When that did not suffice we used the more broadly based political power to redress disproportions and disbalances in economic society." America has developed "social policies which are wiser than its social creed." Niebuhr in these passages sounds what would, in the 1950s, become a familiar theme: the celebration of America's pragmatic pluralism—power balances power, and social justice results.[49]

Thus in *The Irony of American History*, Niebuhr explicitly accepted the American solution of the problem of justice: "The unarticulated wisdom embodied in the actual experience of American life has created forms of justice considerably higher than our more articulate unwisdom suggests."[50] Herein lies Niebuhr's final justification for the policy of containment—America's achievement of relative justice.

47. Niebuhr, *Children of Light*, chap. 3; see esp. 115–18. The definition of democracy is on page 118; the final quote is from "Plutocracy and World Responsibilities," *Christianity and Society*, XIV (Autumn, 1949), 4.
48. Niebuhr, *The Irony of American History* (New York, 1952), 89.
49. *Ibid.*, 165, 101.
50. *Ibid.*, 105.

Yet Niebuhr still left open a path of criticism. He warned that pragmatism must not succumb to opportunism; the "perplexities" of global responsibilities must not "betray us into a complacent acceptance of national loyalty as the final moral possibility of history." This is why Niebuhr rejects the "national interest" as the sole and reliable guide to foreign policy. In a brief consideration of George Kennan's *American Diplomacy: 1900–1950*, which urges a policy of national interest in place of an oversimple "legal moralistic" approach, Niebuhr writes that "the cure for a pretentious idealism, which claims to know more about the future and about other men than is given mortal man to know, is not egotism. It is concern for both the self and the other in which the self, whether individual or collective, preserves a 'decent respect for the opinions of mankind,' derived from a modest awareness of the limits of its own knowledge and power."[51] This concern can be developed only within the context of prophetic religion; Niebuhr thus concludes with a theologian's affirmation of faith.

The Later Niebuhr: Variations on a Theme

An examination of Niebuhr's writings from 1953 until his death in 1971 reveals no major change in his thought comparable to his abandonment of Marxism in the late 1930s, but a number of interesting developments. Especially in the 1960s, Niebuhr reshaded the emphases of his basic ideas: their primary characteristics remained readily recognizable, but some different features stood out. His animating concern was still to apply the insights of prophetic religion to contemporary problems, but as his reading of those problems evolved so did his advice. In particular, he moved gradually from stressing the danger of moralism and simplistic idealism to underlining the limits of power and the pitfalls of a too consistent realism. His earlier works had regularly identified both dangers, but his view of which was the more deleterious to American foreign policy changed in the years from Korea to Vietnam. In addition, Niebuhr continued to elaborate his ideological reading of the Cold War; like Carr—but for different reasons—he took the ideological challenge of Soviet communism seriously. Here he differed from Morgenthau and Kennan, who tended to emphasize the purely power-political aspect of the struggle while at the same time chafing against its bipolar inflexibility.

51. *Ibid.*, 144, 149.

During the Eisenhower-Dulles years Niebuhr still regarded the major problem of American diplomacy to be an underlying moralism, which expressed itself in several ways, leading to errors of both excessive idealism and excessive realism. Foremost among the former was John Foster Dulles' inability to treat communism as a potent ideological force, especially in emerging Asian and African countries, because he was so utterly convinced that it was evil. It may have been enough for Dulles to have "defined the issues between ourselves and the communists as a contest between those who believe in the 'moral law' and those who do not," but such a definition betrayed woeful ignorance of the difficulties of establishing "our democratic alternative [in the] nations of Asia and Africa."[52]

Niebuhr thought that the West had "not fully appreciated as yet how great the ideological advantages of the communist imperialism are," not least because of our certainty of the "moral superiority of liberal democracy." Of course, he shared this belief, but he argued that it was a mistake both tactically and morally to base our foreign policy on it. Such a policy of exerting power explicitly in the name of superior democratic and moral virtue was bound to fail: "We are not a sanctified nation and we must not assume that all our actions are dictated by conditions of disinterested justice. If we fall into this error the natural resentments against our power on the part of the weaker nations will be compounded with resentments against our pretensions of superior virtue."[53]

Dulles' moralism led him to err in the realist direction as well, according to Niebuhr, in his indiscriminate policy of seeking military pacts on the model of NATO throughout the developing world. These pacts, which "enraged our neutralist 'allies,'" reflected a fundamental misreading of the character of the communist challenge in Asia and Africa. This challenge was not military, as in Europe, but resulted from "the plausibility of the communist creed to the two 'colored continents.'" Marxism's account of class struggle and its promise of technical competence and economic justice, though false and oversimplified, nevertheless had greater relevance to the "social facts" obtaining in the new countries than any sermons on the superior morality of Western democracy from Secretary Dulles. The combination of these sermons and inappropriate military alliances led Niebuhr to "expect many a defeat in Asia and Africa before the tragic facts [of

52. Niebuhr, "A Qualified Faith," *New Republic*, CXXXIV (February 13, 1956), 14–15.
53. Niebuhr, *The Structure of Nations and Empires: A Study of the Recurring Patterns and Problems of the Political Order in the Nuclear Age* (New York, 1958), 28–29.

communist tyranny], gradually disclosed to the Western world in these past decades of experience, are gradually disclosed to these new nations."[54] Niebuhr believed that the power of the West to affect the course of revolutionary change in the Third World was limited, but he took comfort in his conviction that ultimately time was on our side. Thus his advice was to renounce Dulles' "self-righteousness" and "moral complacency" and instead "try to find the point of concurrence between the parochial and the general interest, between the national and the international common good."[55]

As the Cold War proceeded, Niebuhr continued to sound this theme of avoiding the extremes of a policy based on a too selfishly defined national interest on one hand and a policy of moralistic certainty on the other. Dwight D. Eisenhower's abandonment of Britain and France during the Suez crisis fell into the latter category, but increasingly Niebuhr stressed that "the national interest when conceived only from the standpoint of the self-interest of the nation is bound to be defined too narrowly and therefore to be self-defeating" and that what was really needed was a creative "combination of idealism and realism." For Niebuhr this combination was possible only in the context of "Biblical faith," but beyond a reaffirmation of religion, the precise character of the synthesis he sought remains obscure. Carr's solution of national self-sacrifice was rejected by Niebuhr as impossible for the statesman who must bear the responsibility for his acts on behalf of the entire collectivity, not just himself; hence the self-sacrifice conceivable for the individual goes "beyond the realm of moral possibilities for the nation."[56] Thus although Niebuhr was acutely aware of the limits of the national interest, his specifically political ethic does not go much beyond Weber's ethic of responsibility—to which he imparts a religious tone of tragedy and possibility.

Perhaps oddly, Niebuhr's most systematic treatment of international relations, *The Structure of Nations and Empires* (1958), does not explicitly address the moral problem in statecraft. Instead, the book has the ambitious goal of "distinguishing the contingent and the novel from the permanent and the perennial in history." Niebuhr attempts to accomplish this goal by developing the concept of empire in history, treating the

54. Niebuhr, "Qualified Faith," 15.
55. Niebuhr, "Our Moral and Spiritual Resources for International Cooperation," *Social Action*, XXII (February, 1956), 19; also in Davis and Good (eds.), *Niebuhr on Politics*, 333.
56. *Ibid.*, in Davis and Good (eds.), *Niebuhr on Politics*, 335.

United States and the Soviet Union as two imperial nations. In broad survey, the book attempts to draw lessons from empires ranging from ancient Rome to nineteenth-century Britain, finding that "the desire for power and glory is a constant factor in imperialism" and that the "imperial enterprise" is invariably characterized by "a certain moral ambiguity."[57]

More interesting conclusions express Niebuhr's conviction that "the sovereignty of the nation [has become] a fixed norm of international morality" and his exhortation to Americans: "The task of managing to share the world without bringing on a common civilization must include, on our part, a less rigid and self-righteous attitude toward the power realities of the world and a more hopeful attitude toward the possibilities of internal developments in the Russian despotism." In his hope for change within the Soviet Union, Niebuhr here echoes George Kennan's similarly phrased hope for the "break up or gradual mellowing" of Soviet power in his famous "X article"; both realists based a good part of their practical advice on a hope whose prospects of fulfillment seem as distant as ever.[58]

Despite its avowed concentration on international politics, *The Structure of Nations and Empires* does not stand out among Niebuhr's many books. Its concept of empire is too broad and inclusive, and its attempt to separate ephemera from permanent factors in the history of states and empires unfortunately results in more or less qualified platitudes.[59] In a shorter book of essays published in 1965, *Man's Nature and His Communities*, he returned more successfully to familiar themes in a way that illustrates his gradual change in emphasis.

In *The Nature and Destiny of Man*, and again more explicitly in a 1953 essay, "Augustine's Political Realism," Niebuhr stressed the importance and continuing relevance of Augustine's thought. Augustine, Niebuhr wrote, reminded us of our original sin and lust for power, yet his realism did not become cynical or nihilistic because it recognized that "the corrup-

57. Niebuhr, *Structure of Nations and Empires*, 3, 215.
58. *Ibid.*, 199, 282.
59. For example, "The variations in the pattern of international community vary endlessly. But the fixed pattern in all these variations is a combination of dominion and community above the level of the nation and below the level of mankind. It is safe to predict that no future history will annul this pattern though it may produce hitherto unknown variations in the pattern" (*ibid.*, 200).
   Niebuhr's sympathetic biographer reports him saying, "I've never worried so much about a book before," and attributes his worry to his general exhaustion (he was recovering from a series of small strokes and only gradually regained his energy) and to "the boldness of his generalizations" (Bingham, *Courage to Change*, 377). Also see Fox, *Niebuhr*, 269–70.

tion of human freedom may make a behavior pattern universal without making it normative. Good and evil are not determined by some fixed structure of human existence." Both aspects of Niebuhr's doctrine of man, his sinfulness and his spirituality, appear in his reading of Augustine; but in his earlier works Niebuhr emphasized the account of sin, affirming to Christians Augustine's "immense superiority both over those who preceded him and who came after him." To secular political theorists as well, Niebuhr recommended him as "a more reliable guide than any known thinker."[60]

In his 1965 book Niebuhr reconsidered: "An analysis of Augustine's and Luther's dualism and consequent 'realism' affecting political communities must yield the negative conclusion that the realism was too consistent to give a true picture of either human nature or the human community, even before the advent of free governments, and was certainly irrelevant to modern democratic governments."[61] In the same essay Niebuhr restates his discomfort with a normative national interest, especially as recommended by Hans Morgenthau, tracing his disagreement on this point to Morgenthau's reduction of the impulse of love simply to another goad for power. For Niebuhr, the impulse of love always retained "residual force": "The statesman's will-to-power is not [as Morgenthau thinks] a substitute for, but a corruption of, his desire to serve his community."[62] Thus in this book, written, as Niebuhr put it, "in my old age" (he was seventy-three), he revised the emphasis of his dual conception of human nature and the dual problems it created, pleading once more for a balance between realism and idealism.

Perhaps the event most influential in changing Niebuhr's mind in his final years was the Vietnam War. His criticism of American involvement did not come as early as Hans Morgenthau's, nor was it as consistent. In 1962 he expressed ambivalence over the prospects of South Vietnam's president, Ngo Dinh Diem, but ended by quoting Franklin Roosevelt on dubious allies: "They may be bastards but at least they are our bastards."[63]

60. Niebuhr, "Augustine's Political Realism," in *Christian Realism and Political Problems* (New York, 1953), 130, 145–46.

61. Niebuhr, *Man's Nature and His Communities* (New York, 1965), 46. Ronald H. Stone also points to this contrast, arguing that "the resources of liberalism penetrated more deeply into Niebuhr's mind" as he grew older (*Niebuhr*, 164–66).

62. Niebuhr, *Man's Nature*, 75–76.

63. Niebuhr, "Can Democracy Work?" *New Leader*, XLV (May 28, 1962), 9, quoted in Stone, *Niebuhr*, 193.

And as late as 1965 he continued to hope that administration policy was wisely based on information it could not make public.[64] In 1967, however, he wrote in a preface to a collection of addresses on the war delivered at the Riverside Church: "My illness prevented me from attending the meeting, but I am deeply persuaded by its concern about our bloody, costly and essentially futile involvement in a civil war in Vietnam. Some of our citizens regard our involvement as an expression of our responsibility, but we are among those who regard it as an example of the illusion of American omnipotence."[65]

Similarly, in a remarkable 1969 article published in *Christian Century* as part of its series "How My Mind Has Changed," Niebuhr, after repeating his earlier admission that he failed "to recognize that Augustine's Pauline realism was, like all realism, excessively consistent," condemned the Vietnam involvement as "the most pointless, costly and bloody war in our history." The article is striking in both its vigor and its expression of past errors: Niebuhr retracts his criticism of Karl Barth for his neutralism, writing, "I must admit that our wealth makes our religious anti-communism particularly odious. Perhaps there is not much to choose between communist and anti-communist fanaticism."[66] Niebuhr could never be considered an anticommunist fanatic, but his profound theology did provide a moral basis for the American policy of containment, which its less religious proponents eagerly welcomed.

In the same article—one of Niebuhr's last—he advised disarmingly: "One must be suspicious of all these theologians, whether Barth, Niebuhr or someone else. The reader must therefore be particularly careful in judging these religiously inspired opinions, particularly when we forget Paul's reservation 'Thus say I, and not the Lord.'"[67] In this spirit, let us consider critically Niebuhr's overall contribution to the developing idea of realism.

Niebuhr as Prophet: An Assessment

Basic to Niebuhr's "realistic" approach is his dual conception of human nature: man is a transcendent spirit and a creaturely sinner. His dual nature

64. Niebuhr, "The Fateful Triangle?" *New Leader*, XLVIII (January 4, 1965), 18–20, quoted in Stone, *Niebuhr*, 193.
65. Quoted in Bennett, "Niebuhr's Ethic," 93.
66. Niebuhr, "Toward New Intra-Christian Endeavors," *Christian Century*, LXXXVI (December 31, 1969), 1663.
67. *Ibid.*, 1662.

expresses itself in his collectivities, and nations exhibit group pride and will-to-power even as they seek approximations of justice. The possibility of corruption is ever-present; doctrines seeking the full achievement of justice and the end of conflict rest on the illusory notion of the perfectibility of man. More than anything else, Niebuhr's rejection of man's perfectibility accounts for his reputation as a realist.

In the immediate postwar period Niebuhr applied his view of man to an analysis of international issues, focusing on the relation between America and the Soviet Union. Unwilling to apply the instruments of rule, lacking a critical prophetic minority, and ruled by a pretentious ideology, the Soviet Union proved unable to temper its national pride: it sought to conquer the whole of Europe. America was handicapped in its foreign relations by sentimental illusions about power and the possibility of world government; these illusions led it to misread the real motives of the Russians. As a realistic spokesman of prophetic religion, Niebuhr sought to alert Americans to the excessive will-to-power manifested by the Russians; only firm resistance would stop them. The "creaturely" justification of containment was that only power can stop power.

Beyond this, however, lay the spiritual justification. America had achieved a fair approximation of justice; for this reason it was justified in protecting itself against the threat to its achievement and was obliged continually to temper its own national pride and keep the implication of justice in its own policy. This last stricture prevented Niebuhr from recommending a policy based solely on national interest. Thus Niebuhr justified containment because the Soviet Union was relatively more proud and sinful and the United States was relatively more just. Moreover, as a pluralistic society America had within it independent centers of power that tempered its group pride and aided its pursuit of justice. In 1965 Niebuhr described the Marxism that ruled the Soviet Union as "a jealous creed which scorns the pluralism of the West and intends to annihilate all cultural and scientific and religious interests and groups which do not subscribe to its dogma."[68]

In evaluating Niebuhr's realism, the first point to remember is that it is religious and self-consciously prophetic. Niebuhr was a theologian with a social conscience who sought to demonstrate the relevance of Christianity to the great social questions facing the modern world. All of his views stem from his Christian view of human nature and can properly be grasped only

68. Niebuhr, *Man's Nature and His Communities*, 77.

by understanding that. Attempts to adopt Niebuhr's ideas minus their Christian content and then to apply them to other problems result in over-simplification. Niebuhr cannot be taken on without all of his Christianity.

Yet this is precisely what Carr, Morgenthau, and to a limited extent, Kennan did: they adopted the pessimistic side of Niebuhr's view of human nature, applied it to their conception of international politics, and concluded, if they considered it at all, that the spiritual aspects had relevance only in church. Certainly, Niebuhr was best known for his doctrine of sin, and even that was disseminated in caricature. But Niebuhr himself holds some responsibility for this distortion. Throughout his career, he was always more sensitive to the pitfalls of liberalism than to the dangers of realist pessimism. His prescriptive policy essays rarely considered the spiritual capacities of men, and then only vaguely; but there were many memorable scorings of liberal illusions. Niebuhr understandably was known as a pessimistic theologian of sin.

Niebuhr's practice of indicting "liberals" and "liberalism" in broad and sweeping terms also contributed to his reputation for sternness. Almost never—Henry Wallace is the notable exception—does one know exactly whom Niebuhr was criticizing. "Liberalism" often became a catch-all for any position, theological or political, Niebuhr disagreed with. He later admitted that "many of my broadsides at liberalism were indiscriminate."[69]

In these "broadsides," Niebuhr seemed to be unaware of the wider prescriptive implications of his analysis. His characterization of the Russian menace was so vivid that it was easy to forget his occasional qualification that the Russians, too, had their problems. He condemned moralistic illusions so convincingly that one could not easily tell that the words came from a theologian whose object was to promote Christian brotherhood. Niebuhr cannot be blamed for the later application and misapplication of his ideas; in my view he would blanch at being claimed by contemporary neoconservatives. It can be ironic to observe the ways his analyses have been used to justify the very universalist policies he so thoroughly rejected. *Pace* Irving Kristol, one cannot imagine Niebuhr approving the American invasion of Grenada and the national self-righteousness it occasioned.[70] Perhaps more than anything else, the Vietnam War demonstrated to Nie-

69. Quoted in Bingham, *Courage to Change*, 342.
70. Irving Kristol, "Towards a Moral Foreign Policy," *Wall Street Journal*, November 15, 1983, p. 8.

buhr the dangerous potential of an apparently tough-minded realism wedded to a zealously idealistic determination to defeat communism wherever it arose with every means at our disposal. The self-righteousness of Wilson combined with the cynicism of Cavour leads to moral and political disaster.

Beyond these suspect uses of his ideas, there remain some substantive difficulties with Niebuhr's analysis. Even if one accepts his view of human nature on its own terms, the crucial notion of collective pride remains problematic. Niebuhr's formulation of the idea can only be described as woolly—he describes the building of community as an "organic process," but there is no systematic account of precisely how and at what stage group pride, and then national pride, enter into this process. Niebuhr would presumably answer that group pride takes part in the process all along, but this raises the question of exactly how group pride expresses itself. When does a statesman reflect national pride and when does he act independently of it? Can he be independent of it? Can he mold the national pride to suit his purposes?

Perhaps these are questions ultimately to be answered by social psychologists rather than theologians; but Niebuhr's failure to consider them explicitly raises important problems for the way he makes moral distinctions between nations. As we have seen, these distinctions are based on the openness of a nation to prophetic words of judgment spoken against it; such judgments can temper excessive manifestations of group pride. That the Soviet Union combined a pretentious ideology with the absence of a sensitive prophetic minority led it to just such excessive manifestations— or so Niebuhr argued. But if the notion of group pride rests on shaky ground, so does Niebuhr's moral condemnation of the Soviet Union—at least in the way he goes about it. Of course, this is hardly to say that the Soviet Union is in any sense "moral"—but it is striking that in his last years, Niebuhr moved back to the position of *Children of Light*, condemning national pride and self-righteousness in both communist and noncommunist states with almost equal vigor.

Similarly, Niebuhr's positive justification for containment, America's achievement of relative social justice, was surely premature and, as one commentator has suggested, had strong overtones of complacency.[71] Still, the operative word is "relative": even at the height of the Cold War, Nie-

71. Paul Merkley, *Reinhold Niebuhr: A Political Account* (Montreal, 1975), 177–78.

buhr regarded America's achievements as qualified and even "precarious." Admirers of Niebuhr have also pointed out that he was a strong supporter of the civil rights movement and was keenly aware of the evil of racial injustice.[72] Nevertheless, in his early postwar writings Niebuhr did provide for the policy of containment a moral sanction that lent it perhaps greater durability than he had intended.

Neither of Niebuhr's justifications for containment was advanced as such by any other realist. Indeed, Niebuhr's hesitancy to adopt the national interest as the ultimate standard for foreign policy always set him somewhat apart from his fellow realists. Like them, Niebuhr insisted on the importance of power and the futility of legalistic schemes based on goodwill. But he never drew the seemingly natural conclusion of urging a policy of national interest based on power; here the Christian theologian took precedence over the realist. Niebuhr resisted giving moral sanction to the balance of power because it failed in itself to involve justice. He was convinced that without some "approximation of justice," a mere balance would necessarily break down and lead to war or international anarchy. Carr, Morgenthau, and Kennan, in their different ways, accepted the balance of power and believed that it would produce moderation; Kissinger, of course, had an ambitious scheme of his own which was supposed to construct a "stable structure of peace."

To my mind, the most suggestive aspect of Niebuhr's analysis lay in his attempt to find a way between the moralistic illusions of world government and the blind alley of a normative balance of power. Niebuhr relentlessly exposed the shortcomings of legalistic pipe dreams, and he saw that "realism" easily becomes morally pretentious and celebrates its moral superiority to other conceptions of foreign policy. Niebuhr rejected both the relativism of E. H. Carr and his somewhat plaintive call for national self-sacrifice, and despite general agreement with Hans Morgenthau on specific issues, he could not share Morgenthau's confidence in the moral dignity of the national interest. Thus Niebuhr clearly recognized the necessity for a third approach ("A Protest Against a Dilemma's Two Horns"), but it cannot be said that in all his writings throughout the postwar period he succeeded in defining what that third approach would be.

Niebuhr provided to the idea of realism a deep theological account of human nature and its implications for social life; in this sense he was in-

72. *Cf.* Bennett's account in "Niebuhr's Ethic," 94–95.

deed the "father" of all the realists who followed him. But all too often the substance of his political and moral advice amounted only to an injunction to avoid the extremes of credulous idealism and cynical realism—wise counsel, to be sure, but not very specific, as the range of self-professed Niebuhrians and the wide disagreements among them demonstrate. In the end, perhaps Niebuhr's most distinctive contribution to the idea of realism in the theory of international relations was to fashion a religious foundation for Weber's ethic of responsibility. Unfortunately, this foundation proved no more helpful than Weber's nationalism, or Carr's socialism, in defining its precise content.

6

Hans Morgenthau: Power and the National Interest

In describing his intellectual relationship with Reinhold Niebuhr, Hans Morgenthau once remarked that "Reinie and I come out about the same on politics, but I do not need all his metaphysics to get where we both get."[1] The differences between the two writers do indeed reflect those between theology and political science: Niebuhr was concerned to reassert the relevance of a Christian approach to man and society, whereas Morgenthau, trained in political theory and international law, sought to incorporate Niebuhr's insights (in the process, of course, secularizing them) into a general theory of international politics. As Kenneth Thompson has written, Morgenthau "in the broadest intellectual sense, helped to lay the foundation for international politics," and Niebuhr himself has called Morgenthau "the most brilliant and authoritative political realist."[2] Morgenthau's project was to turn realism from a critique of utopianism and a characteristic approach to man and politics into a comprehensive theory that would explain the underlying essence of relations among states, illuminate the moral problem in statecraft, and provide a sound basis for evaluating specific, contemporary problems of national policy.

My task in this chapter is to explicate the key aspects of this formidable project, to compare it with the approaches of other realists, and to scrutinize its claims on its own terms. Morgenthau's writings are so voluminous that some abbreviation and selectivity are essential. Although later writings are considered, I have chosen to emphasize three works written between 1946 and 1951 which express the essence of Morgenthau's position. In particular, I consider the basis of his moral position, his elaboration of power politics—which owes much to Carr—and his development of the

1. Quoted by Martin E. Marty, "The Lost Worlds of Reinhold Niebuhr," *American Scholar*, XLV (Summer, 1976), 569.
2. Kenneth W. Thompson, *Political Realism and the Crisis of World Politics* (Princeton, 1960), 32–33; Niebuhr, *Man's Nature and His Communities*, 71.

key concept of the national interest. In his notion of the national interest Morgenthau claimed to define an approach to policy that would lead to both political success and ethical moderation. This claim, I shall argue, fails on both analytical and normative grounds: Morgenthau's realism may provide a way to structure the political and moral dilemmas of foreign policy, but it does not prove to be an especially reliable guide to empirical success or automatic morality.

Foundations of Politics and Morality

In 1946 Morgenthau presented the first and in many ways most basic statement of his philosophy in *Scientific Man vs. Power Politics*. The book is a broad polemic against what he calls "dogmatic scientism," a wrongheaded philosophy rooted in modern rationalism and liberalism. Its thesis fits well with Niebuhr's main position: it argues that the currently dominant rationalist philosophy is based on illusions and fails to explain the basis of the moral and political problems facing modern man. Of course, as a Christian theologian, Niebuhr directs his greatest attention to the failure to understand man himself; his political ideas flow from his analysis of that failure and from his argument that only the Christian perspective can apprehend man in his totality. Morgenthau, as a professor of political science, concentrates on the inadequacy of "scientism" as an approach to politics. For most of the book he criticizes a general tendency to adopt "a scientific theory of society where politics has, at best, a place as the evil finally overcome," arguing first that the model of science employed is mistaken and second that "politics is an art and not a science" anyway.[3] Still, although Morgenthau is less explicitly concerned with doctrines of human nature than Niebuhr, *Scientific Man* does in its last two chapters offer a view of human nature which is vital to Morgenthau's account of the moral issue in international politics. For this reason, as well as for convenience of comparison with Niebuhr, it seems sensible to begin with this view, even though this is not the way Morgenthau himself proceeds.

Morgenthau places selfishness and lust for power at the center of his picture of human nature. All of one's acts and intentions emanate from and refer back to one's self, and all action bears either positively or negatively on others: "The connectedness of the self with others through his

3. Hans J. Morgenthau, *Scientific Man vs. Power Politics* (Chicago, 1946), 32, 10. Subsequent page references to this work are given in the text.

action is inevitable." Selfishness, for Morgenthau, is a basic and inescapable fact of human nature; he goes on to argue that the impossibility of pure unselfishness—even an act intended unselfishly "can never completely transcend the selfishness to which it owes its existence"—necessarily "leads to the paradox of the ethical obligation to be selfish in order to be able to satisfy the moral obligation of unselfishness at least to a certain extent" (p. 192). Since Morgenthau nowhere explains the source of the moral obligation, this formulation of the ethical issue is problematic; but the main point here is that in Morgenthau's conception, man is inevitably selfish.[4]

The second aspect of Morgenthau's version of human nature is the universal desire for power. This desire has two sources: the first reflects a Hobbesian logic of competition; the second, a universal *animus dominandi*, is rooted in man's nature. In Morgenthau's account, the second source tends to subsume the first. An essential and universal human lust for power as an end in itself that knows no limits—one's "lust for power would be satisfied only if the last man became the object of his domination"—becomes, in Morgenthau's treatment, more compelling an explanation for conflict and competition than scarcity and the absence of a supreme arbiter.[5] Men seek power because of some evil born in them, and that evil is inevitable, at least as far as acts are concerned: "As soon as we leave the realm of our thoughts and aspirations we are inevitably involved in sin and guilt" (p. 188). And the necessity of selfishness, in turn, makes even a pure intention impossible.

Morgenthau presents here a form of original sin which, unlike Niebuhr's, is both necessary and inevitable. Morgenthau has split the "organic unity" of creature and spirit that Niebuhr identified and, with only slight changes, adopted the creature: Morgenthau's man is necessarily evil. The change is that man can recognize his own evil and adopt an ethical norm against his lust for power even though he cannot realize that norm. Morgenthau regards himself as returning to an older Western tradition in which "the sinfulness of man is conceived . . . not as an accidental disturbance of the order of the world sure to be overcome by a gradual develop-

4. A statement early in the book, "The dominance of a philosophy over its age and its fecundity for the future are not determined by the standards of a seminar in logic or metaphysics but by its relation to the life experiences of the common man" (7), suggests an intuitionist position. (See also 208–209 for support of this view.) I consider this question below.

5. *Scientific Man*, 193. See Kenneth N. Waltz, *Man, the State and War* (New York, 1959), 34–36, on this point.

ment toward the good but as an inescapable necessity which gives meaning to the existence of man and which only an act of grace or salvation in another world is able to overcome" (p. 204). Morgenthau, therefore, has taken on the pessimistic side of Niebuhr's Christian view and rejected the aspect of self-transcendence; the most man can do is recognize his own evil and try to minimize it. For Morgenthau, the will-to-power is the starting point of his analysis; for Niebuhr, it is an aspect of the sin of pride which itself is part of a larger analysis. This difference has important consequences for their judgment of the possibility of building a just international order. Despite the overall similarity of their political views, Morgenthau is consistently more pessimistic on this point. The pessimism stems from Morgenthau's darker view of man.

Since the lust for power is universal—"there is no escape from the evil of power, regardless of what one does"—it follows for Morgenthau that politics is an unending struggle for power and that "political ethics is indeed the ethics of doing evil" (pp. 201–204). Morgenthau's notion that "international politics, like all politics, is a struggle for power" is the most familiar aspect of his thought and needs no emphasis here; the point to remember is that he bases these ideas on his pessimistic view of human nature. In *Politics Among Nations* he writes of "the ubiquity of the struggle for power in all social relations" and asserts that "the desire to dominate is a constituent element of all human associations."[6] Only in *Scientific Man* does he explain why this is so.

Morgenthau's position on political morality also stems from his belief in a universal *animus dominandi*: "The evil that corrupts political action is the same evil that corrupts all action, but the corruption of political action is indeed the paradigm and prototype of all possible corruption. The distinction between private and political action is not one between innocence and guilt, morality and immorality, goodness and evil, but lies in the degree alone in which the two types of action deviate from the ethical norm" (p. 195).

Morgenthau here takes a Niebuhrian stance: the difference between political and private morality is one of degree, not of essence. Questions of political morality are more difficult because states make greater, and seemingly more plausible, demands on the individual citizen than other individuals do. "The state," Morgenthau writes, "has indeed become a 'mortal God,' and for an age that believes no longer in an immortal God, the state

6. Morgenthau, *Politics Among Nations*, 13, 17–18.

becomes the only God there is" (p. 197). This statement directly echoes Niebuhr's remark that "the nation pretends to be God."[7] Moreover, we are apt to accede willingly to such demands because our individual desires for domination find vicarious, collective fulfillment in the state: "In the end the individual comes to believe that there is less evil in the aspiration for state power than there is in the lust for individual dominance" (p. 199).

Not everyone, of course, will "experience such a complete reversal of ethical valuation." Those who resist the state and still entertain "moral misgivings" about some of its demands characteristically assuage their consciences by condemning power politics in general. To Morgenthau this amounts to "a formidable perversion of the moral sense itself" (p. 199). People who issue a general condemnation of power politics do not recognize "the ubiquity of the lust for power and of its evilness" (p. 200). There is no choice between wanting and renouncing power; the "sham battle against power politics" constitutes an evasion of "one of the great tragic antinomies of human existence," the insoluble "contradiction between political power and ethics" (p. 201).

Morgenthau argues strenuously that the various attempts to bridge this antinomy all fail basically because they shrink from its implications. Either they deny the lust for power itself—which is to deny "the very conditions of human existence"—or they renounce the ethical stricture against the lust for power—which is to renounce "the human nature of man" (p. 201). Thus Morgenthau eliminates as ethical solutions all of the following: utilitarianism; perfectionism; Machiavellism, that is, the view that posits the amorality of state action; what he calls the "philosophy of the dual standard," which argues that there are separate standards of ethics for the political and private spheres (Carr's position); and finally, the justification of means by ends, which is a particular example of the dual standard. He insists especially on the error of the dual standard, arguing that "no civilization can be satisfied with such a dual morality; for through it the domain of politics is not only made morally inferior to the private sphere but this inferiority is recognized as legitimate and made respectable by a particular system of political ethics" (p. 179). More broadly, the dual standard—together with all these explanations—reflects "an optimistic belief in the intrinsic goodness of the rational individual and the pessimistic conviction that politics is the seat of all irrationality and evil" (p. 187). Morgenthau

---

7. Morgenthau explicitly acknowledges his agreement with Niebuhr on this point in *Scientific Man*, 236.

therefore rejects Carr's formulation of the moral problem as totally unacceptable.

What, then, is Morgenthau's solution? He begins with a disclaimer, wishing "to leave the production of neat and rational solutions to those who believe in the philosophy against which this book is written" (p. 10). Nonetheless he presents a view that he himself characterizes as the ethics of the lesser evil. Like his definition of the problem, Morgenthau's answer is strikingly reminiscent of Weber: "We have no choice between power and the common good. To act successfully, that is, according to the rules of the political art, is political wisdom. To know with despair that the political act is inevitably evil and to act nevertheless, is moral courage. To choose among several expedient actions the least evil one is moral judgment. In the combination of political wisdom, moral courage, and moral judgment, man reconciles his political nature with his moral destiny" (p. 203).

This passage has a number of interesting implications. Since political wisdom requires knowledge of the rules of the political art, it follows that the task of the scholar is to illuminate those rules and thus influence the determination of policy. In *Politics Among Nations* Morgenthau states this as his avowed purpose.[8] Furthermore, like Weber, Morgenthau places great emphasis on the quality and character of statesmen; indeed, he writes that the statesman is "the prototype of social man himself," that he "creates a new society out of his knowledge of the nature of man" (p. 221). He argues that the modern attempt to reduce the wisdom of the statesman to rational formulas is futile, quotes Edmund Burke for support, and even suggests that "reliance on factual knowledge" has "actually contributed to the decadence of the art of politics" (p. 213). Statesmen need to know the constant rules of the political art, not mundane facts.

Morgenthau asserts in the passage that the best solution to the ethical problem inherent in all political action is for the individual statesman to exert the moral and political judgment to choose, at the same time, the most effective and least evil of several actions. This amounts to a restatement of the ethic of responsibility. But Morgenthau tries, at least implicitly, to go beyond Weber's characterization of this ethic by giving some clue to the source of his nonperfectionist ethic of the lesser evil. Surprisingly, he seems to adopt an intuitionist position, just as Carr did. To restate, that position (this time in the words of John Rawls) argues that

8. Morgenthau, *Politics Among Nations*, 1–8.

"there is an irreducible family of first principles which have to be weighed against one another by asking ourselves which balance, in our considered judgment, is the most just."[9] Thus we confront particular moral dilemmas with our considered "intuitions"; these intuitions are taken to be shared by the entire community. In this sense, intuitionism is the formal theory behind Carr's "morality of the ordinary man." When Morgenthau writes that "the ethical standards which men feel actually bound to follow conform by no means to the rational calculus of utility, but, on the contrary, endeavor to satisfy non-utilitarian aspirations" and "the non-utilitarian ethical standards of Western civilization have their roots in the tragic conditions of human life," he too seems to express an intuitionist view (p. 209).

Of course, Morgenthau's version of intuitionism contrasts sharply with Carr's. Carr argued for a different, less demanding standard of morality to govern the behavior of states; Morgenthau rejects this notion as an illegitimate evasion of the central conflict between power and morality. Yet both base their position on a nonperfectionist, nonutilitarian ethic supposedly shared by everyone; their differences on the actual content of this ethic illustrate vividly the pitfalls of an intuitionist moral philosophy. Thus, although Morgenthau elaborates on Weber's ethic of responsibility to the extent of providing for it an intuitionist foundation, this foundation does not turn out to be very helpful. In the end, the possibilities for moral behavior in international politics depend almost entirely on the quality of statesmen—the extent of their moral and political wisdom—at a given time, for it is individual statesmen who confront the "tragic antinomies of political life" armed only with their understanding of what is both necessary and effective on one hand and their judgment as to what constitutes the least evil alternative on the other. Hence in his characterization of the moral problem, Morgenthau does not take us further than Weber in providing concrete standards by which to define the ethic of responsibility. Moreover, in his definition of what is necessary in world politics—in other words, in his vision of politics as an unending struggle for power and domination—he leaves precious little room for maneuver for even the wisest and most moral statesman.

Nevertheless, Morgenthau does move beyond Weber in the explicit attention he gives to understanding the underlying logic of politics among nations. In his attempt to provide an enduring theory of international

9. John Rawls, *A Theory of Justice* (Cambridge, Mass., 1971), 34.

relations, Morgenthau seeks no less than to define the content of political wisdom, at least in the realm of foreign policy. His theory is nothing if not ambitious: he tries to explain the timeless essence of interstate relations, to impart principles by which concrete policy can be formulated, and in accomplishing these tasks, to provide criteria for judging the political—and ultimately the moral—quality of statesmen and their policy. This is the formidable agenda Morgenthau sets for himself, an agenda which he organizes according to the key concepts of power and the national interest. Power is the central theme of *Politics Among Nations*, and the national interest is developed as an integral part of Morgenthau's position on America's interests in the early Cold War, as set forth in his book *In Defense of the National Interest*.

Continuity and Power

Perhaps the most striking impression left on the reader of *Politics Among Nations* is that of continuity. Although Morgenthau pays passing obeisance to important innovations in technology and, in subsequent editions of the book, brings his account of United Nations procedures up to date, the main message of the book is that the crucial features of the international landscape have remained remarkably constant over history. Illustrations of characteristic behavior are taken from every period of history, and these illustrations have remained intact through each of the book's six editions.[10] For example, in a section on the Russian national character Morgenthau quotes passages from Bismarck and *Time* magazine to demonstrate the "elementary force and persistence" of that character. Similarly, his examples of the three basic types of policy ("to keep power, to increase power, or to demonstrate power") range from the Macedonian empire to the Good Neighbor Policy. The basic datum of all politics is power, and "the struggle for power is universal in time and space and is an undeniable fact of experience."[11]

Given this "fact," which is explained in *Scientific Man* and reasserted in the opening chapters of his textbook—like Carr and Niebuhr, Morgen-

10. *Cf.* especially the sections on the "elements of national power" (chapter 7 in the 1948 edition, chapter 9 in the 1967 edition), on diplomacy (Part Ten in all editions), and on the operation of the balance of power (Part Four). The sixth edition (edited and revised by Kenneth W. Thompson, 1985) contains some interesting new material on the "power of oil" (133–36).

11. Morgenthau, *Politics Among Nations* (1948), 97–98, 21, and chaps. 2–4; 16–17.

thau devotes much effort to refuting utopian illusions—the task of a theory of international relations is to understand and illuminate this struggle for power. Morgenthau's method, as one critic has pointed out, is to build an elaborate ideal type out of the historical international relations of the eighteenth and nineteenth centuries.[12] The familiarity of Morgenthau's model in *Politics Among Nations* makes a detailed exposition here unnecessary; instead I shall highlight his elaboration upon the struggle for power and his effort to define the right principles for successful policy and moral judgment.

After asserting the timeless ubiquity of power politics, in good Weberian fashion Morgenthau proceeds to outline three ideal types of policy and the ideologies that correspond to them. The types are essentially three different attitudes toward power: the policy of the status quo concentrates on maintaining power; imperialism obviously seeks to acquire more power; and the policy of prestige demonstrates power either for its own sake or "much more frequently . . . in support of a policy of the status quo or of imperialism." The third type therefore can be subsumed under the first two; it is an adjunct of the perennial attempt either to hold onto or to increase power. Morgenthau's assertion that "all political phenomena can be reduced to one of three basic types" thus reduces to two. While defining the types, Morgenthau offers advice on "how to detect and counter an imperialistic policy," explains methods of pursuing the policies, and uncovers corrupt versions of them. For example, "appeasement" is an inappropriate response to imperialistic policy, but as "compromise," it would be the right way to deal with a country consolidating its position within a policy of the status quo.[13]

Ideologies, in Morgenthau's austere world, are actually "manifestations of the struggle for power," but as a doctor might put it, they do not present that way: they are used by statesmen to explain and justify particular policies whose real goal is power. Morgenthau is unclear about whether ideologies can define "ultimate goals of political action" or whether they are mere "pretexts and false fronts" for the usual policies of power. He resolves the problem by dismissing ultimate goals as a concern of his theory—surely a problematic position—and asserting that power is *always* the intermediate, and usually the only important, goal of politics.

12. Stanley Hoffmann, "International Relations: The Long Road to Theory," *World Politics*, XI (April, 1959), 348.
13. Morgenthau, *Politics Among Nations*, 55, 21, 43.

Thus he attaches particular ideologies to his ideal-type policies, as it were unmasking the real purpose behind their apparent content. Indeed, penetrating these ideological disguises is "one of the more important and most difficult tasks" of the statesman and student of international politics, and once again Morgenthau provides general guidance on how to do so.[14] In these passages Morgenthau echoes and elaborates *The Twenty Years' Crisis*.

This mixture of ideal-typical definition and frankly practical advice bears emphasis not only because it is a hallmark of the book but also because it strains against Weber's injunctions on the limits of social science.[15] Morgenthau frequently seems to offer a practical handbook—a how-to for realist statesmen—in addition to a disinterested exploration of likely consequences from particular policies. He stops short of claiming theoretical or "scientific" validity for preferred policies in *Politics Among Nations*, but it is nevertheless true that he sees his theory as a foundation for wise and effective policy and therefore does not hesitate to invoke it to criticize particular positions.[16] There is some tension in trying to write a general theory and, at many points, a tactical handbook at the same time; but virtually all the realists share this characteristic, suggesting a common tendency to blend empirical and normative analysis.

After defining the ideal types of policy and their corresponding ideologies—without considering the issue of the independent motive force of ideology—Morgenthau goes on to list the eight major elements of power, to elucidate the problems connected with evaluating national power, and to summarize the principles and operation of the balance of power.[17] In these chapters lie the keys to successful policy because the appreciation and management of power define the essence of politics. Morgenthau's list of the constituents of power mixes objective (*e.g.*, geography, natural resources) and subjective (*e.g.*, national character, quality of diplomacy) factors; it is the job of the statesman to maximize his own factors as well as to judge correctly the standing of other nations. But even the wisest and best-informed statesman is at the mercy of "the contingencies of history and of

14. *Ibid.*, 61, 68.
15. See Max Weber, "'Objectivity' in Social Science and Social Policy," in Shils and Finch (eds.), *Methodology of the Social Sciences*, 50–113.
16. See in particular his discussion of the weaknesses of American diplomacy (107–108 and 429ff.) and of corruptions of the policy of prestige (58–60).
17. *Politics Among Nations* (1948), chaps. 7–8. In later editions the number of factors grew to nine.

nature," and "the assumed perfection in intellect and information is never available." He concludes therefore that "the task of assessing the relative power of nations for the present and for the future resolves itself into a series of hunches" that may be right or wrong. These hunches clearly cannot be taught—some leaders are just more gifted than others—but certain typical errors can be avoided. Of these Morgenthau singles out the following: assuming power to be absolute, not relative; treating one's power position as permanent, not contingent; and relying on the fallacy of a single factor, such as geopolitics.[18]

The discussion in these chapters remains general, and in treating the typical errors, Morgenthau strikes another Weberian chord in describing the virtues of real leadership. Morgenthau's ideal leader possesses "a creative imagination capable of that supreme intellectual achievement which consists in detecting under the surface of present power relations the germinal developments of the future, in combining the knowledge of what is with the hunch as to what might be, and in condensing all these facts, symptoms and unknowns into a chart of probable future trends which is not too much at variance with what actually will happen."[19] This almost lyrical description of leadership echoes Weber's hopes for a responsible, plebiscitarian statesman and anticipates some similarly expressed passages from Henry Kissinger. But it cannot be said that overall, Morgenthau provides very much in the way of concrete analysis of how one detects the "germinal developments of the future" lurking so pregnantly under the surface of present power relations. And considering Morgenthau's stress on the continuity of the struggle for power, it is hard to see what form the new developments would take.

The chief mechanism in Morgenthau's model of international politics is the balance of power, and the proper way to manage this mechanism is through a developed and sophisticated diplomacy. In his power-centered scheme "the balance of power and policies aiming at its preservation are not only inevitable, but an essential stabilizing factor in a society of sovereign nations." Only power can restrain power. Two basic patterns of the balance of power—"direct opposition" and "competition"—are set out and illustrated with the famous diagrams of opposing billiard balls representing the competing states. Morgenthau also runs through the different methods of the balance of power, including alliances, compensations, and

18. *Ibid.*, 111–12.
19. *Ibid.*, 116.

preventive wars, and he stresses the "moral and political unity of Europe," which provided the foundation for its successful operation.[20]

The demise of this moral consensus, which on Morgenthau's account existed from 1648 to 1772 and 1815 to 1933, in favor of the "new moral force of nationalistic universalism" has made the new "two bloc" balance of power prevailing after World War II more difficult to operate; nevertheless "the new balance of power is a mechanism which contains in itself potentialities for unheard-of good as well as for unprecedented evil." The key to its successful operation lies in a revived diplomacy characterized by the "sensitive, flexible and versatile mind of the diplomat" instead of the "rigid, relentless and one-track mind of the military." Morgenthau reaffirms the value of diplomacy after devoting long chapters to the weaknesses of international law, morality, organization, and disarmament as alternative paths to moderation. Each of these alternatives lacks a requisite appreciation of power: "Sovereign nations are moved to action by what they regard as their national interests rather than by the allegiance to a common good which, as a common standard of justice, does not exist in the society of nations."[21] Under these circumstances, a skilled and flexible diplomacy in service of a stable balance of power is far more likely to lead to international moderation.

Thus the main political lesson imparted by Morgenthau's theory is to learn how to assess and seek power by means of the balance of power, and statesmen are presumably to be judged according to how well they do this. If this standard seems a bit general, the criteria for moral judgment are even less clear. In his chapters on international morality Morgenthau underlines its weakness as a restraint on power and insists, as he does in *Defense of the National Interest* (see below), that morality has meaning only in national societies. He also asserts that the personal accountability of individual statesmen "is a precondition for the existence of an effective system of international ethics," and in the absence of an international mechanism to enforce "what is morally required in international affairs . . . international morality as an effective system of restraints becomes impossible."[22]

Does a moral consensus on international behavior exist, and if so, how does it operate? Considering Morgenthau's intuitionist position in *Scien-*

20. *Ibid.*, 125, 130, 161. The patterns would now be called bipolar and multipolar.
21. *Ibid.*, 285, 430, 460.
22. *Ibid.*, 189.

tific Man and his argument against Carr's "dual standard of morality," one would expect him to say yes, with an account of why the single standard is so difficult to apply to international relations. Instead, he asserts that the "fragmentation of a formerly cohesive international society into a multiplicity of morally self-sufficient national communities, which have ceased to operate within a common framework of moral precepts," has irretrievably weakened universal, supranational morality and "has finally endowed, in the minds and aspirations of individual nations, their particular national systems of ethics with universal validity." This statement seems to contradict his earlier insistence on a single universal standard of morality in its account of "a multiplicity of particular moral systems claiming, and competing for, universality." Indeed, Morgenthau explains the process by which the individual, troubled by an "uneasy conscience" over the obvious weakness of universal ethics, "pours . . . the contents of his national morality into the now almost empty bottle of universal ethics." This process results in a struggle of unprecedented "ferociousness and intensity" because each nation fights convinced "that it fulfills a sacred mission ordained by providence, however defined."[23]

In these passages Morgenthau seems to adopt willy-nilly the relativist position for which he criticizes Carr so severely. But in fact he refrains from endorsing these competing nationalistic claims, which "meet under an empty sky from which the gods have departed." A transcendent morality *does* exist—"the actions of states are subject to universal moral principles"—but it cannot serve as an effective restraint on their behavior.[24] Morgenthau saves himself from relativism by reserving the right of moral judgment, but at the cost of rendering the judgment *post hoc* and treating the conception of morality as essentially irrelevant to practical problems of policy. Indeed, in later editions of *Politics Among Nations* he asserts that "ethics in abstract judges action by its conformity with the moral law; political ethics judges action by its political consequences."[25] This position acquits Morgenthau of relativism *per se*, but it seems nevertheless that he introduces a dual scheme of judgment through the back door: moral judgment applies transcendent standards, whereas "political ethics" judges political consequences.

23. *Ibid.*, 191, 195, 193, 196.
24. *Ibid.*, 196; Morgenthau, "The Problem of the National Interest," in *The Decline of Democratic Politics* (Chicago, 1962), 106; originally published in the *American Political Science Review*, XLVI (December, 1952), 959–85.
25. Morgenthau, *Politics Among Nations*, 4th ed. (1967), 10.

Morgenthau's apparent way out of this dilemma is to appeal to the concept of "national interest defined in terms of power," a concept that "saves us from both . . . moral excess and political folly." If all states pursue "their respective interests defined in terms of power, we are able to do justice to all of them . . . moderation in policy cannot fail to reflect the moderation of moral judgment."[26] Thus Morgenthau's answer to the moral problem in statecraft is to refer it back to the problem of political judgment of power and interest. To understand how he applies this apparent solution we need to look beyond the vague and general strictures of *Politics Among Nations* to his more specific treatment of concrete issues. In a work published in 1951, Morgenthau explicitly tried to apply his general principles of international politics to the immediate issues facing American foreign policy; his account of the "moral dignity of the national interest" is embedded in this critique.

American Foreign Policy and the Moral National Interest

In Defense of the National Interest identifies four general and persistent flaws plaguing American foreign policy—utopianism, legalism, sentimentalism, and neoisolationism—which Morgenthau illustrates by citing specific failures of policy and attitude. Americans manifested the naive error of utopianism in their hopes for a permanent postwar settlement based on principle. Throughout the war, Americans believed that the Grand Alliance could continue after its conclusion and that it would be possible to transcend power politics and enjoy permanent peace. But "in the life of nations," Morgenthau writes, "peace is only respite from trouble—or the permanent peace of extinction."[27] In their failure to recognize this basic truth, in clinging to their utopian illusions of a postwar millennium, the Americans made foolish concessions to the Soviet Union at Teheran and Yalta: it did not "occur to the framers of American policy that the Soviet Union might be destined to succeed Germany and Japan as a threat to the balance of power in Europe and Asia, and hence to the security of the United States" (p. 96). American utopians such as Cordell Hull thought that the United Nations could act as a substitute for power politics rather

26. *Ibid.*, 11.
27. Morgenthau, *In Defense of the National Interest: A Critical Examination of American Foreign Policy* (New York, 1951), 92. Subsequent page references to this work will be given in the text.

than as simply another forum for it. Moreover, American leaders over-looked the power-political aspects of their own behavior: "The United States flatters itself that in its dealings with other countries it seeks no selfish advantages but is inspired by universal moral principles" (p. 93). Morgenthau spared no opportunity to remind his readers that the struggle for power was the basis of all politics.

The flaw of legalism turned up in America's attitude toward the United Nations as a legal body "before which the peace-loving, law-abiding nations summon the criminal aggressors" and in its naive faith in the efficacy of treaties (p. 102). "No other event in the recent history of Russo-American relations has had so lasting and profound an effect on the American mind as the violations of the Yalta agreement by the Soviet Union" (p. 111). The United States was profoundly disillusioned by these violations and later regarded them as the "symbol both of Russian perfidy and of American gullibility and humiliation" (p. 111). But the disillusionment and indignation were misplaced for two reasons: first, states adhere to treaties only when it suits them, and second, the issue of political control over Eastern Europe had already been settled by the time of the Yalta agreements.[28] The United States' legalism led it to believe that a formal, legal agreement could change a power-political reality.

Americans could have avoided all this disillusionment over the outcome of Yalta—and the domestic recriminations that followed—had they recognized the reality of the Russian presence and negotiated accordingly. Still, the breakdown of Yalta did at least teach Americans "that in international affairs power is as indispensable to the righteous as it is to the wicked" (p. 112), but its real lesson remained unlearned. Instead of realizing the permanent necessity of power, they attempted to justify their military buildup "by making it appear a means to an end of our utopian ideals" (p. 113). Morgenthau's larger point is that the four flaws he identifies feed into one another; only a wholesale reform of thought can cut through the mistakes.

The Truman Doctrine stood for Morgenthau as the prime example of America's third basic error, sentimentalism. This 1947 statement of policy cast what was a wise and necessary response to events in Greece and Tur-

28. He writes later, "From that iron law of international politics, that legal obligations must yield to the national interest, no nation has ever been completely immune" (144). As Robert W. Tucker pointed out in 1952, this is an odd way to describe an "iron law" ("Professor Morgenthau's Theory of Political Realism," *American Political Science Review*, XLVI [March, 1952], 219).

key in the inflated terms of a universalist doctrine: "The Truman Doctrine transformed a concrete interest of the United States in a geographically defined part of the world into a moral principle of worldwide validity, to be applied regardless of the limits of American interest and power" (p. 116). He castigates the doctrine's failure to discriminate between local conditions and broad principles and between "what is desirable and what is possible" (p. 117).

According to Morgenthau, the Truman Doctrine's sentimentalist devotion to absolute moral principle robbed American foreign policy of the ability to make these crucial distinctions. Their inability had, for the time being, no terrible effects in Europe, "where the defense of democracy is indeed an intricate part of the defense against Russian imperialism." But in the "fundamentally different" situation in Asia, "the Truman Doctrine has caused great confusion in thought and action" (p. 119). Morgenthau's critique here is both sharp and specific. Twenty years later he would apply the same principles to oppose the Vietnam War. In dealing with China after the fall of Chiang Kai-shek, the Truman administration had no choice but to throw "the moral principle of the Truman Doctrine overboard," all the while insisting "for purposes of domestic propaganda" that it still applied. As a result, it was blamed for the "loss" of China when events were beyond American control. Ironically, Morgenthau praises Dean Acheson for the 1950 National Press Club speech in which South Korea was excluded from the American "defense perimeter"; the statement, Morgenthau asserts, "cut down—at least in words—the Truman Doctrine to the size of the national interest of the United States" (p. 120). Nonetheless, although Acheson understood the "realistic requirements of American foreign policy," the policy for which he was responsible more often reflected sentimental illusions than the realities of power politics (p. 121).

The last general error Morgenthau considers is neoisolationism, of which there are two main manifestations—the belief in American omnipotence and the disparagement of the traditional methods of diplomacy. The neoisolationist turns traditional isolationism inside out and says, "We shall deal with the world, but only on our terms" (p. 129). His crusading spirit and contempt for diplomacy spring from his confidence that America is strong enough to reform the world. The neoisolationist therefore underestimates the strength of the enemy—Morgenthau asserts that American policy makers consistently underrate Russian strength—and has an "implacable hostility to the idea that diplomatic negotiations are the only alternative to war" (pp. 135–36). The importance of traditional diplomacy is a recurrent theme for Morgenthau. In *Politics Among Nations*, as we have seen, he asserts that diplomacy is the only true means toward international conciliation and sets out eight rules for the conduct of successful and professional diplomacy. Detractors of traditional diplomacy, he argues, betray an ignorance of the fundamental realities of international politics that is born of their sentimental and isolationist illusions about power.

In addition to these general aspects of America's "defective intellectual equipment" in making foreign policy, Morgenthau identifies two specific "failures of judgment"—in Europe and in Asia (p. 159). Common to both areas is America's failure to maintain a proper balance of power. In Europe, Morgenthau writes, the American success is only apparent and accidental: "Furthermore, its supreme test has not yet come" (p. 160). In any case, a true restoration of the balance of power in Europe would require a retreat of the Red Army from "central and much of eastern Europe." The only way to achieve such a withdrawal would be for America "to bring overwhelming power to bear upon the Soviet Union, power so great as to make likely the defeat of the Soviet Union in war" (p. 178).

Yet in the face of this imperative, America has consistently underestimated Soviet strength on the Continent. Morgenthau is at pains to show that the Russian explosion of an atomic bomb in 1949 "shattered American foreign policy as it had evolved since 1945" (p. 178) and that, as a result, America needed fundamentally to reformulate her policy because the chief block to Soviet expansion in Europe in the immediate postwar years had been the American monopoly of the atomic bomb. With this monopoly ended, the balance of power in Europe—even the tenuous one prevailing in 1951—was threatened.

To meet this threat, Morgenthau urges that America embark on a crash program of rearmament as a "matter not of political necessity but of national survival" (p. 233). European and West German rearmament should follow. The point of such rearmament is not directly to oppose the Red Army: "It is a profound misunderstanding of the policy of containment to think that the Soviet Union could be, or has ever been, contained by the rearmament of those countries at its periphery which seem to be threatened by Russian aggression" (p. 182). The purpose of all rearmament is to deter a Soviet attack; European and West German rearmament in a European framework merely strengthens that deterrent: "It is not a matter of holding a line at the Elbe, at the Rhine, or at any other particular place" (p. 185).

Morgenthau here anticipates what later strategic writers would call active deterrence, a strategy designed to deter an enemy from attacking one's geographically distant allies. He dismisses the idea that the Soviet Union, with its enormous frontier, was ever "contained" by American divisions, bases, or military aid: "The real deterrent has been the certainty that any step taken by any unit of the Red Army beyond a line of demarcation of 1945 would call forth an atomic attack upon the Soviet Union, against which it was unable either to protect itself or to retaliate effectively" (p. 183).

Thus Morgenthau argues that America's apparent success in Europe stemmed from the implicit threat of massive atomic retaliation; after America lost its nuclear monopoly this threat lost its force. Its superior military position would soon enable the Soviet Union to dictate to the West. Therefore, "frantic speed" in American rearmament was imperative: "Once the deterrent of your atomic superiority is gone, a rearmament will likewise lose its deterrent effect and will tend, to the extent that it approaches Russian strength, to invite war rather than prevent it" (p. 180). Presumably, this is because once "the Soviet Union has acquired a stockpile of atomic bombs sufficient for a devastating attack on the West" (p. 193), it would be unlikely to postpone fulfillment of its imperialist desires until the West had rearmed on land; it would press hardest while it still possessed an advantage. The result could well be a third world war.

America's inability to distinguish Russian imperialism in Europe from genuine revolution in Asia constitutes its second main failure of judgment. This failure stems from confusion between Russian imperialism and communist revolutionary ideology. In Europe, "Communist revolutions" have not succeeded in any country (but Russia itself) "except as a by-product of conquest by the Red Army and as an instrument for perpetuating Russian power. . . . In the West, then, the opposition to Communism is an integral part of the resistance to Russian imperialism, and to oppose Russian imperialism is tantamount to opposing Communist revolution" (p. 79). Here Morgenthau regards the main problem to be Russian imperialism, of which communist ideology is merely another instrument.

In Asia, however, a revolutionary situation exists for reasons independent of communist ideology. Asian revolutions are the result of the decline

of Western power and, more especially, of the moral and political princi-
ples which the West carried with it in the wake of its imperial conquests.
"It is these principles of national self-determination and social justice
which Asia today hurls against the West, condemning and revolting against
Western political and economic standards" (p. 64). Later in the book,
Morgenthau writes that "in Europe we face Russian imperialism, but in
Asia we face genuine revolution" (p. 201). For this reason, "the clamor for
consistency in dealing with the different revolutions sailing under the flag
of Communism is the result of that confusion which does not see that the
real issue is Russian imperialism, and Communist revolution only in so far
as it is an instrument of that imperialism" (p. 80). This passage is an obvious
criticism of Senator Robert A. Taft and others who were arguing that
America ought to apply the same standards in Asia as it did in Europe.
Morgenthau also criticizes the Truman administration's Asian policy for
its vacillation, especially in China, where the halfhearted and quixotic
support for the Nationalists resulted in a triumph for both communist
ideology and Russian imperialism. Revolutions in Asia, he writes, "cannot
be suppressed by military means"; the real struggle is "for the minds of
men" (p. 209). He goes on to set out some "principles of ideological warfare" whose main point is that America ought not to allow the genuine
revolutionary conditions in Asia to be exploited by Russian imperialism.

In general Morgenthau held to this conservative view of the Soviet
Union: its ideology was the servant of its imperialism and had no real
motive force of its own. He was fond of asking rhetorically whether the
United States would be facing the same problems if Russia were still ruled
by the tsars.[29] But Morgenthau was not consistent in this traditional power
interpretation; at times he presented the conflict between the superpowers
as ideological: "Washington and Moscow are not only the main centers of
power, they are also the seats of hostile and competing political philosophies. The two super-powers fight for political and military advantage
with potential world dominion as the ultimate prize, but parallel to this
political and military contest there runs a conflict between two kinds of
moral principles, two types of moral conduct, two ways of life" (p. 62). In
a succeeding passage, he writes that Bolshevism, "of which the Soviet
government makes itself not only the spokesman but also the executor . . .
is not a political philosophy among others but a political religion" (p. 63).

29. Morgenthau, *In Defense*, 77, and in a review of George Kennan's *American Diplomacy* in *New Republic*, CXXV (October 22, 1951), 17–20.

At the same time, he could write unequivocally (about the "struggle for the minds of men," which makes it all the more striking) that "this is not a struggle between good and evil, truth and falsehood, but of power" (p. 219). Other statements are ambiguous: "This is not a contest between virtue and vice, defined in the terms of a lawyer's code of conduct, but of a clash between the foreign policies of two great powers pursuing apparently incompatible objectives" (p. 146).

Moreover, Morgenthau sometimes treated communist ideology as a disadvantage to the foreign policy goals of the Soviet Union. Driven by the "Bolshevist nightmare of encircling coalition" and "its general conception of human nature, politics and morality . . . the foreign policy of the Soviet Union is limited to a much more narrow choice of means than the foreign policies of other nations."[30] Thus although Morgenthau usually emphasized the traditional power goals of Russia as the right way to understand the Soviet Union, his overall view in these early years can only be described as ambiguous.[31]

Despite this ambiguity, Morgenthau's most specific recommendation to American statesmen—to initiate "with frantic speed" a program of rearmament—stemmed from his concern about Soviet military power (p. 179). His emphasis on the Soviet acquisition of the atomic bomb and the resultant need for massive conventional rearmament betrays a common tendency among analysts to equate Soviet capability with intention. This assumption, of course, was one of the pillars of the policy of containment; Morgenthau seems to have accepted it wholeheartedly. Even as he criticized the universalism of containment, he shared its approach to the Soviet Union—its inclination to see everything in terms of military power and then to assume that the possession of such power necessarily included the intention to use it. Indeed, Morgenthau's argument that the United States—no less than to ensure its political survival—had to rearm conventionally before the Soviets achieved even a minimum capacity for nuclear war rests on this same assumption. Nothing but superior military power would restrain the Russians: if they had equality or local superiority they would not hesitate to use it.

Apart from this specific call to rearmament, Morgenthau's prescription for a successful American foreign policy was, in his view at least, straightforward: the policy should be based on the national interest "restrictively

---

30. Morgenthau, "Problem of the National Interest," 107–108.
31. I follow Tucker, "Morgenthau's 'Realism,'" 220–24, here.

and rationally defined" rather than on moralistic illusions.[32] In 1951 Morgenthau defined the American national interest as the restoration and maintenance of a genuine balance of power involving "stable lines of demarcation" between the two superpowers. He regarded arguments against spheres of influence on moral grounds as fatuous and naive: the issue for him was where to draw the line. Accordingly, he favored continuing negotiations with the Russians even while the West rearmed; he disdained the Achesonian belief in the efficacy of building "situations of strength": "If American foreign policy consisted of nothing but the accumulation of strength at the points of conflict with the Soviet Union, Mr. Acheson's principle would be no more than a rationalization of the cold war, of the continuation of the armaments race in the hope that time was on our side and that we would eventually be able to impose a settlement favorable to ourselves upon the Soviet Union. Such a policy would fall short of constructive statesmanship" (pp. 149–50). For Morgenthau diplomacy was a continuing process—"the refusal to negotiate in the false conviction that conflicting interests are irreconcilable is to court a needless war." Nevertheless, "concessions born of the false belief that conflicting interests are actually compatible is appeasement" (p. 149); the task of the statesman is to determine which was true. Despite his call for "frantic speed" in conventional rearmament and his insistence that Americans underestimated Soviet power, Morgenthau did not believe that the Soviet-American rivalry had to result in war. If both powers would allow diplomacy a chance and negotiate on the basis of their national interests, a working arrangement—but not a United Nations love-feast—could be established.

But how was the national interest to be defined? Morgenthau's view on this question is not as simplistic as is frequently asserted. He recognized that groups representing "sub-national, other-national and supra-national interests" all compete to determine the national interest. Capitalists, ethnic minorities, and ideologues of all stripes seek to identify their particular interests as the national interest; the latter is not simply an obvious objective datum. Nevertheless, Morgenthau significantly calls the efforts of these other groups "attempts to usurp" the national interest. He insists that the "rational core of the national interest" can be ascertained by objective analysis. Groups may succeed temporarily in grasping the national interest; foolish statesmen may misjudge it; certain of its elements are undeniably variable. But Morgenthau believes that "scientific analysis"

32. Morgenthau, "Problem of the National Interest," 100.

has the "urgent task" of defending the true national interest, of "pruning down over-weening ambitions to available resources," of exposing "the nefarious consequences of false philosophies and wrong ways of think-ing."[33] The national interest can always be defined rationally even if that rational definition does not always prevail in concrete foreign policy.

When the "rational core" does prevail against the attempts by various groups and false ideas to usurp it, the national interest provides the foun-dation for a wise and prudent foreign policy. Indeed, against moralistic critics Morgenthau insists on the "moral dignity of the national interest." Because of its centrality in his approach, his argument on this issue bears careful reconstruction. As set out in *Defense of the National Interest*, the first line of reasoning concerns success: "A foreign policy guided by moral abstractions without consideration of the national interest is bound to fail. . . . All the successful statesmen of modern times, from Richelieu to Churchill, have made the national interest the ultimate standard of their politics" (pp. 33–34). The first thing to be said for a policy of national interest, then, is that it is successful; it reflects the political wisdom of statesmen aware of the rules of the art of politics. But the success of a policy hardly guarantees its morality and, unless he is to adopt a Machi-avellian position he consistently rejects, Morgenthau cannot rest here. He therefore advances the argument by asserting: "There is a profound and neglected truth hidden in Hobbes' dictum that there is neither morality nor law outside the states" (p. 34). Here Morgenthau introduces a new set of ideas culminating, it would seem, in a Hegelian conception of the state as the ultimate source of morality.[34]

National societies, he now argues, give concrete meaning to universal moral principles; they provide "concrete standards for individual action" (p. 35). States can do this because "interests and convictions, experiences of life and institutionalized traditions have in large measure created a con-sensus" on the real meaning of moral principles. Above states "there exists no international society so integrated so as to be able to define for them the concrete meaning of justice or equality, as national societies do for their individual members. . . . The appeal to moral principles in the international sphere has no concrete universal meaning" (pp. 34–35). Regardless of

---

33. *Ibid.*, 94–95, 99–100.

34. In an interview with the author in March, 1977, Morgenthau denied that he intended such a conception in making the argument: "Hegel was the farthest thing from my mind." Nevertheless, he agreed that the interpretation was plausible.

one's interpretation of Hegel's view of the state—a subject of lively controversy—the notion of "universal concretization" is unquestionably his.

If the state is the source of concrete morality (*Sittlichkeit* in Hegel's terminology), then a policy defending its essential interests is *ipso facto* moral. Morgenthau gives the argument another twist forward when he asserts that a policy of national "egotism or selfishness," essential for national survival, is a moral duty because such a policy is the only way to achieve a "modicum of order" and "minimum of moral values" in the international sphere (p. 38). This argument parallels the notion expressed in *Scientific Man vs. Power Politics* that individuals have a paradoxical ethical obligation to be selfish.[35] More than this, the argument reflects Morgenthau's conviction that, if generally followed, policies of national interest (when rationally defined) result in international moderation, which he sees as continuous competition and threats of war but no agonistic conflict. Moral crusades and fanatical political religions provide the real danger to international peace: "What is good for the crusading country is by definition good for all mankind, and if the rest of mankind refuses to accept such claims to universal recognition, it must be converted with fire and sword" (p. 37). If states follow their national interests and eschew political moralizing, they will avoid "religious world wars" such as World War I became. Instead, he concludes, "a foreign policy derived from the national interest is in fact morally superior to a foreign policy inspired by universal moral principles" (p. 39). Thus a policy that follows the national interest is theoretically doubly moral: it protects the integrity of the very source of concrete morality and at the same time it results in relative international moderation and order.

In the specific context of the early Cold War Morgenthau believed that the danger for America posed by a policy based on "utopian principles of abstract morality" rather than on the national interest was acute. He opposed not only the internationalist rhetoric of collective security in the United Nations—an approach that led to the Korean stalemate—but also the Republican rhetoric of "liberation" for Eastern Europe. Both approaches failed to examine the "concrete circumstances of interest and power"; both failed adequately to weigh the consequences of the policy so fervently advocated: "Would the objective of the liberation of Poland justify the ruination of Western civilization, that of Poland included,

35. Morgenthau, *Scientific Man*, 92

which would be the certain result of a third world war? What resources does the United States have at its disposal for the liberation of all nations or some of them?"[36] These are the questions suggested by a sober analysis of the national interest; above all, such an analysis carefully weighs the consequences of a given policy.

Throughout his career Morgenthau continued to speak out on specific issues of American foreign policy as well as to develop his theoretical approach further. Concerning theory, perhaps his most interesting notion was to express agreement with Carr's conclusion that the nation-state is obsolete in the nuclear age. Morgenthau agreed with Carr's argument that the nation can no longer protect its citizens and thus with that reason for its obsolescence, but he did not rely on Carr's discussion of social welfare. Rather, he emphasized the fissiparous qualities of nationalism and argued that in its modern form "it has brought us disorder and war and threatens us with universal destruction." Nationalism has so intensified the struggle for power among nations that the only long-term solution is to abandon it and its apotheosis, the individual nation-state. As with Carr, Morgenthau's conclusion was frankly normative: "In the atomic age, [nationalism and the nation-state] must make way for a political principle of larger dimensions, in tune with the world-wide configuration of interest and power of the age."[37]

Until then, however, Morgenthau continued to offer advice on America's national interest on issues ranging from how to improve the foreign service to the faults of the strategic vision of Richard Nixon and Henry Kissinger. Perhaps his most consistent and prescient piece of advice was about Vietnam. As early as 1956 he warned against military involvement in Indochina, attributing the Viet Minh victory to anticolonialism.[38] He urged in 1962 that the United States seek a political solution in Vietnam, arguing against a purely military "intervention which supports to the bitter end the powers-that-be, even if their policies, by being counter-productive, jeopardize the interest of the United States."[39] As the war escalated, he continued to oppose American policies on the grounds that "they do not serve the interests of the United States, they even run counter to these

36. Morgenthau, "Problem of the National Interest," 104.
37. Morgenthau, "Nationalism," in *Decline of Democratic Politics*, 195.
38. Morgenthau, "The Immaturity of our Asian Policy," in *The Impasse of American Foreign Policy* (Chicago, 1962), 251–77.
39. Morgenthau, "Vietnam: Another Korea?" in *The Restoration of American Politics* (Chicago, 1962), 375.

interests, and the objectives we have set ourselves are not attainable, if they are attainable at all, without unreasonable moral liabilities and military risks."[40] Morgenthau opposed the war on what was for him the solid ground of the national interest. But obviously those responsible for the policy defined the American national interest very differently, thus raising the troublesome problems, first, of how to define the national interest and second, what standards to apply in judging the political and moral content of the policy purportedly based on it. In conclusion, I shall consider each of these issues in an explicitly critical way.

Moral *Realpolitik?*

In Morgenthau's hands the "national interest" could be a subtle tool of analysis, a shorthand term for a balanced foreign policy. He reminded policy makers of the inescapable importance of power but also of its limits. He distinguished Russian imperialism from genuine revolution in Asia, and he consistently favored serious negotiating over empty posturing. As his position on Vietnam demonstrates, Morgenthau could almost always be counted on to make moderate and sensible recommendations for specific policies. Yet for all his wisdom and subtlety, Morgenthau did not succeed in establishing the national interest as an objective standard, let alone one possessed of moral dignity. Moreover, even his specific policy prescriptions occasionally went awry.

The ambiguity of his view of the Soviet Union has been noted: he was inconsistent about whether it was a traditional or an ideological power and about its desire and ability to negotiate a settlement with the West. But for the sake of argument let us overlook these hesitations—after all, it is not easy to divine Soviet motives, as we have discovered throughout the postwar period—and grant Morgenthau his most frequently expressed view of the Soviet Union as a traditional great power for which communist ideology was an instrument of its aggrandizement. Given this view, does Morgenthau's urgent recommendation for a crash program of rearmament make sense? Did the United States really underestimate Soviet military power? His argument assumes that the American atomic monopoly was the only deterrent to a Soviet attack on Western Europe; his analysis of the Soviets' motives did not extend beyond an assessment of their available and theoretically employable military power. Once they had a bomb

40. Morgenthau, *A New Foreign Policy for the United States* (New York, 1969), 129.

of their own, the deterrent of the American monopoly ceased; America could not threaten atomic retaliation without risking considerable destruction to itself. As later theorists would express it, the nuclear deterrent had lost credibility. Mere numerical superiority would not suffice to make the Russians behave. In a passage from *In Defense*, Morgenthau quotes himself from *Politics Among Nations*: "Once the Soviet Union has atomic weapons, it matters little that the United States will have more atomic weapons than the Soviet Union. It requires only a limited number of atomic bombs to destroy the military potential of the United States. This destruction will deprive the United States of the ability to win a war against the Soviet Union, however much damage it might be able to do by dropping a superior number of atomic bombs on Russian territory."[41]

In expressing these views, Morgenthau anticipated a preoccupation of strategists in the late 1950s and early 1960s leading to the shift of the American nuclear strategy from massive retaliation to "flexible response"; Morgenthau urged a conventional buildup more than a decade before Robert McNamara. Morgenthau's recommendation rested on the belief that Soviet intentions followed their military capabilities closely: why else but to attack would they have all those divisions in central Europe? Freed of the fear of nuclear retaliation, they might well do so, hence the need for frantic speed in conventional rearmament in Europe. Those who had power would use it.

But in retrospect—and even at the time—it is clear that Morgenthau overestimated the Soviets' willingness to risk nuclear war even when they had the bomb themselves. He assumed too easily that they would unleash their troops in Europe once they had achieved some nuclear capability. Moreover, he failed to consider (as George Kennan did) how a massive Western rearmament would be interpreted by the Russians. Morgenthau believed that the rearmament could "bring about the conditions of a negotiated settlement"; this view is hard to understand. From Moscow's standpoint, a frantic military effort by the West could easily be seen as tightening capitalist encirclement, a prelude to a war of liberation. In the event, the establishment of NATO and the militarization of containment—a gradual rather than frantic process—did not facilitate negotiations for a balance-of-power settlement. On the contrary, it froze a bipolar status quo. Like other realists, Morgenthau hoped for a settlement involving a mutual

41. Morgenthau, *In Defense*, 173, from *Politics Among Nations* (1948), 319.

withdrawal of troops and agreed-upon spheres of influence—a latter-day Congress of Vienna approach. But neither the Russians nor the Americans defined their national interest in so apparently rational a way; they preferred—or perhaps could not escape—the certainty of ideological cold war. Although Morgenthau saw and defined the "rational core of the national interest," policy makers in Washington and Moscow did not. Morgenthau, of course, realized this; thus the persistence and urgency of his appeal to the American people "to let their voices cry out" to their leaders to "forget sentimental illusions and remember the realities of power" (p. 242).

But this very appeal suggests a wider problem with Morgenthau's analysis and its reliance on a "rational" concept of the national interest. Whenever he faced strong disagreement with his approach and recommendations, Morgenthau called his opponents prisoners of sentiment or moralistic illusion; they would have to learn to face the realities of power, to appreciate that the national interest had to take precedence. But surely even realists can disagree among themselves; not every problem with American foreign policy can be attributed to its attachment to sentimental ideals. The causes of failure and the prerequisites for success are much more complicated.

Furthermore, Morgenthau never squarely faced the problem of defining the actual content of the national interest in democratic and ideological states. Justifiably confident of his own ability to discern the rational core of the national interest, he assumed too easily that statesmen—or indeed "scientific analysis"—could do so. But Morgenthau's subtlety and wisdom were hardly universal among statesmen or academics; nor could his personal learning serve as the foundation for a "scientific" theory of international relations.

The concept of the national interest simply cannot bear the weight Morgenthau assigned to it. It is not "objective," as Morgenthau's own hesitations about its translation into policy demonstrate. Rather, it is a value, itself defined by different—albeit sometimes characteristic—hierarchies of values. Even the notion of national survival, as Arnold Wolfers argued in 1949, is ambiguous.[42] How one defines the national interest depends on the values he espouses and the way he ranks them. Should the physical survival of a state's citizens take precedence over that of a given

42. Arnold Wolfers, "Statesmanship and Moral Choice," *World Politics*, I (January, 1949); in his *Discord and Collaboration*, chap. 4.

regime? What was the objective national interest of Czechoslovakia after Munich or Poland in 1939? There is no objective answer, still less an answer guaranteed to contain moral dignity. The national interest is not automatically moral; nor does it lead necessarily to international moderation. Instead of insisting on the objective and moral quality of the national interest and on the irrelevance of overarching moral considerations in its definition, Morgenthau would have done better to explicate and defend the values that informed his own understanding of the American national interest.

Of course, in his more explicitly ethical writings Morgenthau tried to formulate such a defense. In *Scientific Man*, for example, he identifies a universal lust for power from which it follows that all action—and prototypically, political action—is in some measure evil. The problem of ethics then becomes a question of choosing the least evil alternative. But according to which standard does one choose—the "transcendent moral law" or the "political ethics of consequences"? I have noted that Morgenthau argues against the misguided "school of the dual standard" and that he insists that "there is not one kind of ethical precept applying to political action and another one to the private sphere, but one and the same ethical standard applies to both."[43] In spite of these assertions, he nevertheless distinguishes between two kinds of ethics—abstract and political—with the former being limited to impotent moralizing after the fact.[44] This ambiguity, if not contradiction, suggests difficulties both in his argument against the so-called dual standard and in his assumptions about the source and permanence of the so-called transcendent standard.

Concerning the dual standard, Morgenthau overstates his case. Presumably his chief concern is to deny on one hand perfectionist ethics of conviction that judge political action without any consideration of consequences—Weber's great bugbear; and on the other hand, to avoid a debilitating relativism that relegates politics permanently to only the most minimal (and hypocritically applied) moral standards—Carr's ultimate position. But in denying these unacceptable views one need not posit, as Morgenthau does, a single, rigidly uniform standard of morality applying equally to every situation regardless of circumstances. Morality, as the philosopher J. R. Lucas observes, "is not all of one piece. We need to

43. Morgenthau, *Scientific Man*, 195–96.
44. *Politics Among Nations* (1967), 10; see also "The Moral Dilemma of Political Action" and "The Problem of the National Interest," in *Decline of American Politics*.

distinguish different stages at which different considerations come into play."[45] To take account of the different circumstances surrounding the decision of the statesman and the individual private citizen is not necessarily to propound a dual standard of morality. Morgenthau presents a false dichotomy in his dismissal of the "school of the dual standard," and in the end he fudges it himself.

This apparent failure to recognize the importance of the circumstances in which moral decisions are made results from Morgenthau's oversimple view of politics as a mere reflection of man's universal lust for power. Man continually seeks power; politics, therefore, is a constant struggle for power. Unlike Niebuhr, Morgenthau sees no noble striving after justice for its own sake: ultimately what we want is power over our fellow men, even if we recognize and fight against such a desire. Morgenthau fails to see the extent to which the evil of power derives not from man's own nature but from the particular situation in which he finds himself. Good men can be pushed into evil action and evil men can be restrained or unleashed by the force of circumstances. Morgenthau does not distinguish between the consequences of man's inherent nature and the consequences of the position and environment in which he operates. And he has virtually nothing to say about the complicated ways individual people and the societies they live in define their ends. It is not enough to assert that power is always one's purpose. If all politics are power politics, then the distinction between international politics and domestic politics—a distinction Morgenthau occasionally (and rightly) makes—disappears: international politics, like all politics, is a struggle for power.

Morgenthau's argument against the dual standard therefore not only overstates but also reflects his overreliance on a single factor of power. His definition of political ethics—weigh consequences and follow a policy of national interest defined in terms of power—suffers from the same difficulty. Confident that the unchanging essence of international politics was the struggle for power, he was too sure that a policy based on national interest would result in moderation: power would balance power and relative peace would ensue. The implicit ideal of Morgenthau's system was the nineteenth-century balance of power, a system whose moderation was based on restraint, shared conservative values, and belief in an underlying harmony of interests. The only way to make sense of Morgenthau's expec-

45. J. R. Lucas, *The Principles of Politics* (Oxford, 1966), 317.

tation of international moderation from policies based on the national interest is to assert the continued existence of these factors—an assertion Morgenthau explicitly denies.

Finally, even Morgenthau's ultimate position on the content of the transcendent moral law has its problems. His arguments against Carr-like relativism have been mentioned: he insists that there is a rock bottom of morality common to all people and ages. How else, he asks, could we "explain that the moral ideas of Plato and Pascal, of Buddha and Thomas Aquinas are . . . acceptable to our intellectual understanding and moral sense?"[46] He upholds this position of constancy throughout *Scientific Man*. Yet as George Lichtheim has pointed out in his essay "The Tragedy of German-Jewish Liberalism," Morgenthau writes that "the philosophy and the institutions of liberalism are not the expression of eternal verities. That philosophy and those institutions arose under certain historic conditions and hence were bound to disappear under different historic conditions. It is not by accident that the rise of liberal philosophy and liberal institutions is intimately connected with the rise of the middle class." This passage could have been written by Carr or Mannheim, authors whose relativism Morgenthau criticized. But Morgenthau employs this Marxian method of debunking selectively; although liberalism is dismissed as time-bound, his own Burkean traditionalism and moral certainty have, as Lichtheim puts it, "a privileged ontological status which renders them immune to the flux of time and circumstance."[47] Thus not only does Morgenthau's definition of the political ethic reflect his preoccupation with an idealized balance of power, but his account of a supposedly universal ethic, an ultimate standard of moral judgment, rests on his own assumptions of an inescapable *animus dominandi*, and his conviction that only a profoundly conservative—indeed, morally authoritarian—society is capable of taming this lust for power and making a relatively peaceful social life possible. These assumptions are normative. Morgenthau's realism therefore stands or falls on ethical ground—on the persuasiveness of his personal moral choices.

This is perhaps an ironic conclusion to draw about a writer so insistent on empirical verisimilitude. Yet Morgenthau's values were deeply human-

---

46. Morgenthau, "Epistle to the Columbians on the Meaning of Morality," in *Decline of American Politics*, 372.

47. *Ibid.*, 248; George Lichtheim, "The Politics of Conservative Realism," in *The Concept of Ideology and Other Essays* (New York, 1967), 140–42.

istic, and as a result his views will always repay careful consideration. His own evolving definition of the American national interest never failed to embody great learning and a formidable sense of practical possibilities. Unfortunately, Morgenthau tried to generalize his own views into an "objective" concept, a rational national interest based on calculations of power. He tried to make this concept a master key to solving problems of policy, but his ambiguity on some of these problems demonstrates that even a subtle and realistic appreciation of power cannot guarantee success. Obviously, no one can be right on every issue; but neither can the national interest solve every dilemma of policy. At best, the national interest describes a starting point, an approach, to formulating policy. The content of that policy and the question of its morality depend on the values one applies to defining the interests of the national community and on the extent to which those values are translated into concrete and effective policy. In short, it is possible to disagree about what the national interest is and on how best to express it in policy.

Throughout his long career, Morgenthau was fond of quoting Edmund Burke against what he regarded as the simplistic moral arguments of his academic and political combatants. As he wrote in a reply to critics in 1952, "The issue between utopianism and realism . . . has been most succinctly put by Edmund Burke . . . : 'Nothing universal can be rationally affirmed on any moral or any political subject.'"[48] Perhaps Morgenthau should have applied Burke's dictum not only to the moral abstractions of the utopians but also to his own realistic insistence on the objectively discernible "national interest defined in terms of power."

48. Morgenthau, "Problem of the National Interest," 110.

7

George Kennan: Diplomacy and Moderation

Like E. H. Carr, George Kennan made his contribution to the idea of realism by way of active diplomacy. From his position in the United States embassy to the Soviet Union during World War II and later as head of the State Department's Policy Planning Staff, Kennan influenced the reorientation of American policy toward the Russians in 1946–1947 and played a decisive part in the formulation of the Marshall Plan. After he left the Foreign Service in 1952, Kennan became a resident fellow at the Institute of Advanced Study at Princeton, where he pursued his academic interest in the diplomatic history of early Soviet-American relations. In contrast to Carr, whose immersion in Soviet history excluded an active role in the debate on contemporary issues, Kennan continued to write and lecture on current problems in foreign policy even while producing scholarly works of history and two superb volumes of autobiography.[1]

Throughout his postwar writings on American foreign policy, Kennan stressed the virtues of sophisticated diplomacy over naive moralism and political flexibility over military rigidity. More than anything else, this emphasis on diplomacy defines Kennan's realism. Repeatedly he appealed for an approach to foreign policy that was alive to the possibilities of diplomatic maneuver while at the same time aware of the limitations imposed by history and the national interest. From his point of view, the policy of containment, which the United States adopted as a long-term strategy for dealing with the Soviet Union, fell short on both these grounds. The containment he recommended differed sharply—at least in his conception—from the policy actually followed by Truman and Acheson.

One of the tasks of this chapter is to account for this difference, to make clear the premises of Kennan's realism. To do so, I shall begin by consider-

1. George F. Kennan, *Memoirs: 1925–1950* (Boston, 1967), and *Memoirs: 1950–1963* (Boston, 1972); hereinafter cited as *Memoirs*, I and *Memoirs*, II, respectively.

ing the bases of his overall approach to politics and then discuss his specific ideas for American policy in the early postwar period. Although Niebuhr, Morgenthau, and Kennan are bracketed as founders of American realism, they disagreed significantly on several key issues. With these issues canvassed, and the questionable pedigree of containment established, I shall characterize Kennan's later—and continuing—efforts to set forth his own guidelines for a realistic American foreign policy and conclude as usual with some critical remarks. Despite his protestations of realism and his recommendations for a policy of national interest, Kennan remains a formidable adherent of a traditional morality—a learned and sensitive diplomat who by his own admission holds little sympathy for the prevailing mores of American political life.

Underlying Assumptions

Kennan nowhere offers a systematic explanation of his approach to international politics or of his political philosophy in general: he is a diplomat turned historian, not a theologian or a political theorist, and he is concerned neither to propound a doctrine of human nature nor to set forth the recurring truths of international politics in a quasi-doctrinal way. "I'm afraid," he writes in his *Memoirs*, "that when I think about foreign policy, I do not think in terms of doctrine. I think in terms of principles."[2] Yet underlying these principles one finds a conception of human nature very like Niebuhr's and a view of international politics similar to Morgenthau's in its broad outlines, but less Gothic, less insistent on the pure struggle for power, more refined. If Morgenthau's writing suggests a world of calculating Bismarcks, Kennan's implies an assemblage of Talleyrands with convictions—if that is not a contradiction in terms. One revisionist historian has perhaps too cleverly written that "in Kennan the Presbyterian elder wrestled with the Bismarckian geo-politician"; a more apt characterization suggests that "seeing Kennan's mind is like looking at the mechanism of a fine watch."[3]

Perhaps the mainspring of that mechanism is Kennan's strong conviction that man is a deeply flawed creature, but a creature nevertheless capa-

2. Kennan, *Memoirs*, I, 364.
3. Lloyd Gardner, *Architects of Illusion* (Chicago, 1970), 285; Stanley Hoffmann, "After the Creation, or the Watch and the Arrow," *International Journal*, XXVIII (Spring, 1973), 19.

ble of striving for some justice in an imperfect world. As he said in a 1947 lecture: "The fact of the matter is that there is a little bit of the totalitarian buried somewhere, way down deep, in each and every one of us. It is only the cheerful light of confidence and security which keeps this evil genius down at the usual helpless and invisible depth. If confidence and security were to disappear, don't think that he would not be waiting to take their place."[4]

Keeping evil in check requires work and faith. "It is only through effort, through doing, through action—never through passive experience," he told college students in 1967, "that man grows creatively."[5] And to the developing countries of the Third World, he recommends a measure of the self-reliance, faith, and industry shown by his Wisconsin ancestors if they wish someday to achieve comparable prosperity and development.[6] His attachment to tradition and faith may best be illustrated by the following negative portrait of "today's radical student" and the society that produced him:

> There is no strong and coherent religious faith, no firm foundation of instruction in the nature of individual man, no appreciation for the element of tragedy that unavoidably constitutes a central component of man's predicament, and no understanding for the resulting limitations on the possibilities for social and political achievement. The student is the victim of the sickly secularism of this society, of the appalling shallowness of the religious, philosophic and political concepts that pervade it.[7]

Implicit in the passage are Kennan's own values—strong, coherent religious faith, continuity between generations, a sense of the limits of human beings: "There are certain sad appreciations we have to come to about human nature on the basis of the experiences of these recent wars. One of them is that suffering does not always make men better. Another is that people are not always more reasonable than governments; that public opinion, or what passes for public opinion, is not invariably a moderating force in the jungle of politics."[8]

Kennan rejects any Kantian hopes that the increasing severity of war will drag humanity to peace via a league of democratic republics. Indeed,

---

4. Quoted in Kennan, *Memoirs*, I, 319.
5. Kennan, *Democracy and the Student Left* (New York, 1968), 10.
6. Kennan, *The Cloud of Danger: Current Realities of American Foreign Policy* (Boston, 1977), 189.
7. Kennan, *Democracy and the Student Left*, 189.
8. Kennan, *American Diplomacy: 1900–1950* (Chicago, 1951), 61.

he believes that democracies often fight the most severe wars because they hope through them to remake the world in their own democratic image. Their wars become moral crusades certified by self-righteous belief in an ethic of democratic conviction. Against this faith, Kennan argues that force, however well intentioned, "cannot in itself make a positive contribution to any democratic purpose."[9]

When Kennan applies his view of human nature to domestic political arrangements—again, not something he ever does systematically—one gets a curious mixture of Burke, Alexis de Tocqueville, and Thomas Jefferson. Kennan describes himself as "a conservative person, a natural born antiquarian, a firm believer in the need for continuity across generations in form and ceremony."[10] And, like Tocqueville, he worries about "vast, impersonal political communities," the resulting dependence upon "the bloated monstrosity and impersonality of the Federal government," and he suggests radical decentralization to "permit people to concentrate, as citizens, on the problems that are near and understandable to them, instead of burdening their consciences with what takes place in remote parts of the country, the problems of which they poorly understand. . . . Great countries, I think, are a menace to themselves and everyone else." Of course, if people in the United States cannot understand even their own regional differences, their grasp of faraway countries and alien cultures is even more simplistic—especially since the media of mass communication are dominated by the commercial interests of advertising, whose "trivial, inane forms are positively debauching in their effect on the human understanding."[11] For this reason, as well as those to be examined shortly, Kennan strongly prefers that diplomacy be left to professional diplomats.

The Jeffersonian element of Kennan's complex mix of political values enters in his appreciation of rural life and his strong concern for the quality of the environment. He deplores "the obvious deterioration in the quality both of American life itself and of the natural environment in which it had its being, under the impact of a headlong overpopulation, industrialization, commercialization and urbanization of society."[12] He condemns the imperialism of the automobile, which has already "spelled the end of our cities as real cultural and social communities." And he abominates the

9. *Ibid.*, 89.
10. Kennan, *Memoirs*, II, 264.
11. Kennan, *Democracy and the Student Left*, 204–205, 201.
12. Kennan, *Memoirs*, II, 85.

corruption of the American political structure and, even more, discourse—"the hearty bombast, the banging of the chauvinistic bell, the measureless national self-congratulation, the huffy assertions of suspicion and truculence directed to the outside world, and the ritualistic invocation of a pious anti-communism to justify anything for which a more meaningful argument might seem too subtle or difficult."[13] Clearly, Kennan is a man of strong and traditional convictions, both moral and political.

Yet in his explicit characterizations of international politics, he tries to mask these convictions behind an orthodox portrayal of the virtues of amoral hierarchy and balance of power. In *Realities of American Foreign Policy* he disdains the "utopian schemes" of "competing groups of well-meaning peace enthusiasts [who] succeeded in needling two harried Foreign Ministers, M. Briand and Mr. Kellogg, into an embarrassing . . . [sponsorship of] one of the most meaningless and futile of all international engagements."[14] So much for the "scholarly activism" of James T. Shotwell. Kennan's view of the ideal international system is hierarchical, and in contrast to his appreciation of small communities for domestic politics, he deplores "the curious liberal-American assumption that bigness on the part of a political entity is somehow bad, smallness good: that large powers are by nature wicked, small powers innocent and virtuous." As a result of this "childish daydream," the order of an international society marked by five or so great powers and a variety of hierarchically arranged political entities—which "allowed for an accommodation to real culture and physical differences"—has given way to an anarchic mélange of great powers, ineffective and overlapping international organizations, and "a horde of wholly untried and inexperienced small entities" falsely dignified with sovereign status.[15]

This anarchy, he writes, stems from the basically mistaken notion that one can apply moral ideas to international relations. He denies that the "elements of right or wrong" can be applied to "most international differences." If "conflicts are to be effectively isolated and composed, they must be handled partly as matters of *historical* equity but partly, also, with an eye to the given relations of power." Kennan softens the power determinism of Carr or Morgenthau; in a revealing simile he compares the imponderables of international conflicts with those of personal relationships:

13. Kennan, *Democracy and the Student Left*, 203, 194.
14. Kennan, *Realities of American Foreign Policy* (Princeton, 1954), 21.
15. Kennan, *Cloud of Danger*, 31, 29.

general principles do little good in promoting solutions. What will help is a good knowledge of the specifics of a problem and a skillful sense of diplomacy. Thus moderation in the international milieu is possible if diplomacy is allowed to prevail over "an abstract devotion to the principles of international legality" and "the imperious seizures of political emotionalism" to which democracies are prone.[16]

But even if Kennan criticizes the explicit pursuit of moral values in foreign policy, his own personal convictions inform his view of diplomacy. His sober view of human nature and his pessimism about the ability of either institutions or events to change it lead Kennan to regard the skillful manipulation of conflict—based on a realistic assessment of possibilities—as the best hope for avoiding war and promoting harmony. The purpose of diplomacy is to ease change, "to temper the asperities to which it often leads, to isolate and moderate the conflicts to which it gives rise, and to see that these conflicts do not assume forms too unsettling for international life in general."[17] Kennan's diplomacy is similar to Niebuhr's "instruments of rule": both are techniques essential for moderating conflict and for making even an approximation of justice possible.

Moreover, his doubts about the possibility of changing individuals extend to states as well. A unique feature of his analysis of both America and the Soviet Union is his emphasis on their historical concerns and limitations.[18] His wartime dispatches from the Moscow embassy stressed the continuity of Russian interests, her "age-old sense of insecurity," and her "traditional suspicion of the West."[19] Kennan's historical perspective led him consistently to discount the possibility of American-Soviet postwar collaboration. This conviction was firmly rooted in his diplomatic experience in the Soviet Union during the 1930s—an experience that not only convinced him that there was "little future for Russian-American relations other than a long series of misunderstandings, disappointments, and recriminations on both sides," but also inspired in him a profound disapproval of Soviet communism.[20] His desire to demonstrate the impossibility

16. Kennan, *Realities of American Foreign Policy*, 36; emphasis added.

17. Kennan, *American Diplomacy*, 98.

18. Concerning America's relations with the Orient, for example, Kennan writes, "It would seem that a nation which admits that its own capacity for assimilation is limited once you get beyond the peoples of Caucasian origin should observe a special reserve in its dealings with other peoples and in its hopes for intimacy of association with them" (*American Diplomacy*, 53).

19. Kennan, "Russia's International Position at the Close of the War with Germany," May, 1945, reprinted in *Memoirs*, I, 532–46.

20. Kennan, *Memoirs*, I, 74; the passage is a quotation from a paper written in 1938.

of collaboration to American policy makers and his intense disapproba-
tion of the Soviet regime later found expression in the so-called Long
Telegram and in the "X" article.

One of the most consistent aspects of Kennan's approach is his belief
that a thorough knowledge of historical interests and limitations is a vital
prerequisite for successful diplomacy and, through it, international moderation. Such diplomacy must be devoid of what Morgenthau called the
"crusading spirit." For Kennan, this "legalistic-moralistic" approach to
international problems and conflicts has been a perennial cause of failure
and disillusionment in the United States' foreign policy. Throughout
American Diplomacy, a series of lectures in 1950 published as his first
book, Kennan traces the effects this approach—which "runs like a red
skein through our foreign policy of the last fifty years"—has had on America's foreign relations. Where sober diplomacy tries to mute conflict, devotion to overarching principles, or slogans, leads to total war and
unconditional surrender. Where diplomacy seeks areas of negotiation and
accommodation, legalistic-moralism takes principled stands from which
no movement is possible. The indictment is by now familiar: advocates of
world government through international law underestimate the discontent felt in parts of the world and try to reduce it to a formula; they freeze
the status quo of national sovereignty and put a "legal straitjacket" on
change; they assume the continuing possibility of distinguishing international from civil conflicts; finally, they ignore the insuperable difficulties of
any system of sanctions. When these legalistic faults are grafted to that of
moralism, the result is extreme: "A war fought in the name of high moral
principle finds no early end short of some form of total domination."[21]

Kennan's answer to this recurring fault in American foreign policy is to
reassert, first, the value of professional diplomacy and second, the importance of basing policy on the national interest. But Kennan's version of the
national interest is less confident than Morgenthau's; he makes no claim
that it carries its own moral dignity. Indeed, Kennan writes that the principles of international law and morality should have "the unobtrusive, almost feminine function of the gentle civilizer of national self-interest in
which they find their true value." His statement of the national interest
carried with it a proviso: if, he writes, "we will have the modesty to admit
that our own national interest is all that we are capable of knowing and
understanding—and the courage to recognize that if our own purposes

21. Kennan, *American Diplomacy*, 95ff. The quotations are from 95 and 101.

and undertakings here at home are decent ones, unsullied by arrogance or hostility toward other people or delusions of superiority, then the pursuit of our national interest can never fail to be conducive to a better world."[22]

This statement of the national interest, urged as a corrective to American moralism, rests on the belief that a prudent calculation of interest provides the best avenue to moderation in the international sphere and therefore to a "better world"; this presumed likelihood constitutes the chief reason for following the national interest. Morgenthau, in arguing for the moral dignity of the national interest, goes well beyond this justification. In contrast, Kennan regards moderation as the main goal and highest possible achievement of diplomacy and argues that the best diplomacy bases itself on the national interest; but he does not claim that such a policy is automatically moral, just that it is far more conducive to international harmony. Nonetheless, it will be recalled from the analysis above that even this "justification by moderation" contains two problems: the actual content of the national interest and the validity of the assumption of moderation. Let us examine Kennan's attempt to solve them.

Problematic Paternity: Containment and the National Interest

Throughout his diplomatic service, Kennan consistently held the belief that America's national interest lay in a balance-of-power policy based on agreed-upon spheres of influence. Unlike Niebuhr, he never had any hope for a stable agreement among the great powers that would, as Niebuhr put it, "provide an adequate core of authority for a minimal world order."[23] For this reason Kennan remained out of sympathy with the main preoccupation of American wartime diplomacy, the pursuit of postwar collaboration with the Soviet Union. To Kennan, such collaboration was a chimera; in pursuing it the Americans were not only neglecting their own interests but also indulging in moral hypocrisy. His position on the issue of Poland illustrates this belief.

For two important reasons, Kennan maintained that there was little the Americans could do to help the Poles after the Russian army occupied Polish territory. The first, as he wrote in his diary on August 1, 1944, was that "the Russians, in the long run, would be no more inclined at present

22. *Ibid.*, 54, 103.
23. Niebuhr, *Children of Light*, 177.

than they were a hundred years ago to accept 'the contradiction of the grant to Poland of rights which were not yet given in Russia'"; the second reason lay in the Kremlin's fear that even a moderately independent government would expose Russian atrocities at Katyn and elsewhere.[24] In the face of this reality, the Americans had only two honorable alternatives. "We could," Kennan wrote, exhibit "the judgment and good taste to bow our heads in silence before the tragedy of a people who have been our allies, whom we have helped to save from our enemies, and whom we cannot save from our friends," or, in the aftermath of the Warsaw uprising, we could force a "full-fledged and realistic political showdown with the Soviet leaders," offering them the choice of "changing their policy completely and agreeing to collaborate in the establishment of truly independent countries in Eastern Europe or forfeiting Western-Allied support and sponsorship for the remaining phases of their war effort."[25] Once this moment had passed, the Americans could have no real effect on Soviet policy toward Poland; all that was left was "unreal, repetitious wrangling: I never doubted that it was all a lost cause."[26]

In the immediate postwar period Kennan tried to convince American policy makers that they should abandon their attempts at collaboration with the Russians and adopt a sensible spheres-of-influence policy. America had, as the case of Poland demonstrated, "no significant influence on events in the area under Soviet control," and by continuing to defer to the Russians for "the pipe-dream of a general European collaboration," the Americans were risking their position in "the part of Europe which really was accessible to our influence."[27] In Kennan's view the basic American problem was a legalistic-moralistic approach to the hard questions of diplomacy; this naiveté was fed by a general misconception of the nature of the Soviet regime. His desire to disabuse first, his superiors, and later, the American public of these illusions explains the content and the tone of his famous dispatch from Moscow on February 22, 1946, and his 1947

24. Quoted in Kennan, *Memoirs*, I, 208–10. Kennan's internal quotation is from Bernard Pares' *History of Russia*; the passage in question is about Russian policy in 1830.
25. *Ibid.*, 210–11. The first quotation is from his 1944 diary; the second is from the main text of *Memoirs*, I, 211. Kennan's view of the second choice is shared by Herbert Feis in his *From Trust to Terror* (New York, 1970), but this position is not widely held among historians. Adam Ulam, for example, believed the important points were conceded to the Russians at Teheran. See his *Expansion and Coexistence: The History of Soviet Foreign Policy, 1917–1967* (New York, 1968), 352–57, and *The Rivals: America and Russia Since World War II* (New York, 1971), 14–15.
26. Kennan, *Memoirs*, I, 212.
27. *Ibid.*, 256.

Foreign Affairs article, "The Sources of Soviet Conduct by X." The origin
and purpose of these essays must be kept in mind if one is fully to understand their place in Kennan's overall analysis.

Several aspects of these well-known and often-quoted essays deserve
emphasis. In the Long Telegram, written in response to an innocuous
query from the Treasury Department, Kennan stressed that the mainspring
of Soviet foreign policy was the "basic inner-Russian necessities which
existed before the recent war and exist today. At the bottom of the Kremlin's neurotic view of world affairs is the traditional and instinctive Russian
sense of insecurity." Marxist dogma—"a fig leaf of moral and intellectual
respectability"—merely adds to traditional Russian insecurity and imperialism, making it more dangerous and insidious than ever before. Since the
source of Soviet policy was internal, it followed for Kennan that only one
viable policy was open to America: to resist Soviet expansion and to wait
for "the gradual mellowing of Soviet power," as he put it in the "X"
article. Such a policy was viable because the Russians were not adventur-
ous and their expansion did not follow a fixed plan. They took no unnecessary risks. If their "adversary has sufficient force and makes clear his
readiness to use it, he rarely has to do so. If situations are properly handled
there need be no prestige-engaging showdown."[28] Thus there was still
room for diplomatic maneuver—but only if the Americans gave up their
millennial hopes of cooperation.

In 1946 Kennan reckoned that "gauged against the Western World as a
whole, the Soviets are still by far the weaker force."[29] But Kennan's definition of force was problematic, as both the favorable and unfavorable
reactions to his *Foreign Affairs* article demonstrate. In that article, Kennan
continued his earlier analysis of the "sources of Soviet conduct," concen-
trating this time exclusively on the ideological factors. He identified two
important such factors: "the innate antagonism between capitalism and
Socialism" and "the infallibility of the Kremlin."[30] Partly as a result of the
circumstances in which the article was written, Kennan excluded any
wider historical analysis of Russian policy.[31] The first of the ideological
factors meant that Americans could expect no respite from the problems

28. Telegraphic message of February 22, 1946, quoted in *ibid.*, 549, 551, 558.
29. *Ibid.*, 558.
30. Kennan, "The Sources of Soviet Conduct by X," *Foreign Affairs*, XXV (July, 1947),
566–82, reprinted in *American Diplomacy*, 114, 116.
31. See Kennan, *Memoirs*, I, 353–59; Gardner, *Architects of Illusion*, 280–92.

created by Soviet power, but the second meant that "the Kremlin has no compunction about retreating in the face of superior force," and the struggle with the West could go on indefinitely. "In these circumstances," Kennan argued, "it is clear that the main element of any United States policy toward the Soviet Union must be that of a long-term, patient but firm and vigilant containment of Russian expansive tendencies." Such containment had nothing to do with threats of "toughness" but with a "cool and collected" diplomacy that knew when to "leave the way open for a compliance not too detrimental to Russian prestige." Thus Kennan's containment was a diplomatic stance, "a political containment of a political threat," as he later wrote.[32]

This was not, of course, the version of containment recognized either by Kennan's State Department superiors or by his chief critic, Walter Lippmann. They focused on the following sentences in Kennan's article:

> The Soviet pressure against the free institutions of the Western world is something that can be contained by the adroit and vigilant application of counterforce at a series of constantly shifting geographical and political points, corresponding to the shifts and maneuvers of Soviet policy, but which cannot be charmed or talked out of existence.... [The internal weakness of Soviet society] would of itself warrant the United States entering with reasonable confidence upon a policy of firm containment, designed to confront the Russians with unalterable counter-force at every point where they show signs of encroaching upon the interests of a peaceful and stable world.[33]

To the American policy makers "counter-force" meant military force; Acheson, for example, never understood why Kennan opposed what he considered to be the inevitable consequences of containment, NATO and the division of Germany.

Lippmann criticized Kennan's neglect of the historical sources of Russian policy and feared the logical consequences of his version of containment. In *The Cold War*, published in 1947 from a series of newspaper columns he wrote in response to Kennan's article, Lippmann argued that containment would lead to universal intervention and indefinite occupation by American armed forces all over the globe. It would mean that "for ten or fifteen years Moscow, not Washington, would define the issues, would make the challenges, would select the ground where the conflict

---

32. Kennan, "Sources of Soviet Conduct," in *American Diplomacy*, 119; *Memoirs*, I, 358.

33. "Sources of Soviet Conduct," in *American Diplomacy*, 120, 126.

was to be waged, and would choose the weapons." Kennan's containment policy would send American troops scurrying all over the world and force alliances "with a heterogeneous array of satellites, clients, dependents and puppets." Such a policy ignored the historical limitations of America and of American military force: "The Americans would themselves probably be frustrated by Mr. X's policy long before the Russians were." Lippmann firmly dismissed Kennan's "dismal conclusion" that a policy of resolute containment was likely to bring about "either the break-up or gradual mellowing of Soviet power." To Lippmann it amounted to "bolstering up the wishful thinking of hoping for the best"—not exactly the soundest basis for a policy. Ironically, Lippmann accused Kennan of devaluing diplomacy: "For a diplomat to think that rival and unfriendly powers cannot be brought to a settlement is to forget what diplomacy is about."[34]

Lippman's positive recommendations were addressed to the problem of "how the continent of Europe can be evacuated by the three non-European armies which are now inside Europe"; without such withdrawal, "there is no possibility of a tolerable peace." Toward this end, Lippmann urged that the Americans "concentrate [their] effort on treaties of peace which would end the occupation of Europe." A vital part of such a treaty was a demilitarized and neutralized Germany; only this feature would have permitted a withdrawal of troops and the restoration of a healthy balance of power.[35]

Kennan writes in his *Memoirs* that he reacted to Lippmann's articles "with anguish," largely because he agreed with most of the criticisms. That containment, he insists, was not his: Lippmann "interpreted the concept of containment in just the military sense I had not meant to give it." He wrote but did not send a letter to Lippmann arguing that "the Russians don't want to invade anyone. It's not in their tradition." Kennan confesses that the article suffered from "careless and indiscriminate language" and "egregious" errors.[36] Nonetheless, Lippmann's misinterpretation, if it was such, remains instructive in a way that I shall consider below.

Kennan became the director of the State Department's Policy Planning Staff in 1947. From that position he was largely responsible for the formulation of the Marshall Plan, and he opposed what he regarded as the grow-

34. Walter Lippmann, *The Cold War: A Study in United States Foreign Policy* (Boston, 1947), 7, 13, 50.
35. *Ibid.*, 50.
36. Kennan, *Memoirs*, I, 357, 358.

ing militarization of containment in Europe during 1948 and 1949. In November of 1948 he wrote for Secretary of State Marshall a paper that decried the "general preoccupation with military affairs, to the detriment of economic recovery and of the necessity for seeking a peaceful solution to Europe's difficulties."[37] Kennan considered that it was a mistake to begin talking about a North Atlantic alliance at all. He regarded the security anxieties of the Europeans as "a little silly," and, unlike most of his State Department colleagues—and certainly unlike Hans Morgenthau—the failure of the Russians to demobilize did not worry him: "The Russians had no idea of using regular military strength against us. Why then direct attention to an area where we were weak and they were strong?"[38] Kennan was at pains to distinguish the military capability of the Soviet Union from what he regarded as its intention, which, according to Kennan, was not military aggression.

Kennan's opposition to NATO and his position on Germany—he urged a Lippmann-like formula of demilitarization and neutralization—reflected his basic unwillingness to accept a permanent division of Europe. He writes that he "clung desparately to the hope of getting the Russians to retire some day from the heart of the continent, and fought to prevent our adopting a stance which threatened to destroy every possibility of such a retirement for an indefinite number of years to come."[39]

Kennan regarded the division of Europe into two hostile blocs as fundamentally unstable, as a "great geopolitical disbalance to which the outcome of World War II had led." His preoccupation with the instability of rigid alliances has led one scholar to suggest that he was "haunted by the ghost of 1914."[40] For him a prerequisite to international moderation and a restoration of normal diplomacy was superpower withdrawal from Europe and the pursuit of a balance-of-power policy. This was his goal; its prudent pursuit was his version of America's national interest. From his point of view the obstacle to a wider appreciation of the national interest was America's legalistic-moralistic attitude toward foreign relations. Initially, this attitude led Americans to romanticize the Soviet regime and to pursue the chimera of collaboration. Kennan's 1946 and 1947 essays were attempts to shake Americans out of this attitude, to get them to realize that

37. Quoted in *ibid.*, 410.
38. *Ibid.*, 408.
39. *Ibid.*, 447.
40. *Ibid.*, 463, Hoffmann, "After the Creation," 34.

Soviet power would not dissolve into universalist cooperation. Yet Kennan was dismayed when he saw his principle of containment, a principle he regarded as a working precept of diplomatic intercourse with the Russians, turned into a doctrine to be applied universally. Kennan saw evidence of this transformation in American policy concerning Germany, NATO, and later, Korea, where he opposed attacking beyond the Thirty-eighth Parallel and argued for the admission of communist China to the United Nations. The cause of this universalization he regarded, once again, as the red skein of legalistic-moralism; his remedy was to preach the gospel of the national interest.

Kennan's last important paper as a member of Truman's State Department was written in 1952 during his brief and unhappy tenure as the American ambassador to the Soviet Union. Kennan writes that the document was "utterly without effect," but he regards it as the definitive summation of his views on American-Soviet relations.[41] There is no question that this remarkable analysis—it stands, perhaps, as the first "revisionist" interpretation of the origins of the Cold War—provides invaluable insight into Kennan's realist critique of American foreign policy.

In the paper, Kennan tried to show that the hardening of the postwar world into two rigid, militarized blocs resulted from a "cosmic misunderstanding between the Kremlin and the Western powers." Kennan rests most of his case on a subtle analysis of the position and motives of the Soviet leaders. At the end of World War II, they had "no desire to face another foreign war for a long, long time to come"; at the same time they wished to extend their influence by all means short of general war. For this reason, and not—*pace* Morgenthau—because they intended to fight, they maintained a large standing army; a large army was a traditional Russian policy anyway. After the Western powers shed their illusions of collaboration in 1947 and 1948, they opposed Soviet interests in Germany and Austria, launched the Marshall Plan, and the Americans gave aid to Greece. All these policies came to the Soviets as an unpleasant surprise: "The imposition of the Berlin blockade and the Soviet crackdown in Czechoslovakia were reactions to these reverses in the cold war."[42]

But Western statesmen misunderstood Russian intentions. With their

41. Kennan, *Memoirs*, II, 142.
42. Kennan, "The Soviet Union and the Atlantic Pact," Foreign Service Dispatch 116 of September 8, 1952, quoted in *ibid.*, 336.

eyes fixed firmly on the size of the Red Army, they interpreted these moves as evidence of new Soviet aggression. (Once again, contrary to Morgenthau, Kennan believed that the West overestimated Soviet power.) The 1948 war scare followed. These statesmen failed to see the true nature of the Soviet threat: "They were capable of thinking about international developments only in the old-fashioned terms of full-fledged war or full-fledged peace." They responded by rearming and by concluding the North Atlantic Alliance. The Soviets could not help but see this act as aggressive: "It was no wonder that the Soviet leaders found it easy to conclude that the Atlantic Pact project concealed intentions not revealed to the public, and that these intentions must add up to a determination on the part of the Western powers to bring to a head a military conflict with the Soviet Union as soon as the requisite strength had been created on the Western side." The Western "inability to put the need for rearmament and military alliance to their peoples in less primitive and more accurate terms," the course of the Korean conflict, and the traditional Soviet distrust of the West all fed the logic of misunderstanding.[43]

Even in 1952 Kennan seemed to think that the force of this logic could be broken, or at least weakened, if Western leaders played down the military aspects of their policy, if they took care to show that with NATO they were not undertaking "feverish preparations" for war but were merely building a fence "rather in the normal and prudent desire to have clarity on all sides and to prevent any and all misunderstandings." If the Americans in particular failed to do this and did not reach a "reasonable and sensible compromise" between political and military requirements, they would only increase the risk of war: "It is not for us to assume that there are no limits to Soviet patience in the face of encirclement by American bases." His prescription, then, was for the Americans to engage the Soviets "on their curious level of 'partial war'" and as far as possible to keep the conflict political and not military—in short, to pursue diplomatic containment.[44]

Implicit in this prescription—and explicit in another *Foreign Affairs* article in 1951—is Kennan's notion that a prudent policy of diplomatic resistance to the Soviet Union could not fail to bring about the "gradual mellowing" of the Soviet regime: he was convinced that "there can be no

43. *Ibid.*, 333.
44. *Ibid.*, 349–50.

genuine stability in any system which is based on the evil and weakness in man's nature."[45] The policy of containment actually adopted by the United States after 1947 had failed to bring about this "mellowing." Kennan's conviction notwithstanding, the Soviet regime has remained obdurate and stable; the containment policy adopted by the United States since 1947 has failed to induce any discernible "mellowing." Kennan, the reluctant "father of containment," would probably answer that his policy was misunderstood and misapplied. Thus from the point of view of its "father," the policy of containment was stillborn.

A Civilized Voice in the Wilderness: Realism or Nostalgia?

After he left the Foreign Service on terms that were less than amicable— John Foster Dulles was not a secretary Kennan admired—Kennan went to the Institute for Advanced Study in Princeton, where he pursued his scholarly research into diplomatic history. But he continued to press his views on American foreign policy in a number of different forums, becoming identified in the process with Niebuhr and Morgenthau as a spokesman for realism. In general his prescriptive writings have developed the two themes already discussed—first, the danger of naive moralism and the need for prudent diplomacy, and second, the real character of Soviet intentions and the right way for the West to deal with them: in short, the sources of Soviet conduct and the political containment of their ambitions. Recently, Kennan has added a third theme: the urgent need for serious nuclear disarmament if a war to end all wars—and life—is to be avoided.[46] In all these lectures and essays of persuasion—even his *Memoirs* try to convince one that the Cold War need not have been so bitter and intense—Kennan insists quietly and elegantly on the dangers of self-righteousness and the need for a detached sense of proportion. Only in his very worried warnings about nuclear war does a note of stridency creep in—and it reflects the depth of his horrified concern. Indeed, in one of these essays of warning

45. Kennan, "America and the Russian Future," *Foreign Affairs*, XXIX (April, 1951), reprinted in *American Diplomacy*, 148.
46. Kennan, "How to Break the Nuclear Impasse: A Modest Proposal," *New York Review of Books*, XXVIII (July 16, 1981), 14–17; "On Nuclear War," *New York Review of Books*, XXVIII (January 21, 1982), 8–12; "Two Views of the Soviet Problem," *New Yorker*, LVI (November 2, 1981), 54–65; see also *The Nuclear Delusion: Soviet-American Relations in the Atomic Age* (New York, 1983).

Kennan, the consummate professional diplomat, refers warmly and approvingly to the mass peace movement.[47] What are we to make of Kennan's overall views? Let us consider, in turn, his view of the Soviet Union, his assessment of American policy in dealing with its rival, and his larger vision of international moderation.

Kennan's portrayal of the Soviet Union has been criticized as inconsistent over the Cold War period, and there is no doubt that a comparison of his most recent writing with his 1947 "X" article is startling.[48] But simply to call Kennan inconsistent misses the point: one discovers the real keys to his approach in his underlying convictions and the polemical context in which he was writing. His basic view, I think, does not change, but his sense of the fallacious prevailing orthodoxy does. In short, Kennan tailors his argument to meet his latest opponent. And since those opponents have changed over the past thirty-five years, so too have the emphases of his argument. But the basic line—with one exception—remains consistent.

Beneath Kennan's realism, as we have seen, lies a strong and traditional sense of morality, which deeply disapproves of Soviet communism. This fundamental abhorrence for the Soviet regime—yet attraction to the Russian people—recurs throughout Kennan's writings. It comes through in his diary accounts of his rare excursions into the countryside, where he could meet ordinary Russians as "one of them"; in his horror at the continued suffering of the population at large; in his conviction that "communism is like a malignant parasite which feeds only on diseased tissue"; and in his belief, which has perhaps retreated to a mere hope, that, if resolutely opposed, the regime would necessarily disintegrate because it was based only on the evil in men.

In fact, "America and the Russian Future," the 1951 article in which Kennan considered the possibility of Russia's liberalization, argues from moral principle. As Martin Wight has shown, Kennan's elaboration of the "attributes we, as responsible members of the world community [are] entitled to look for" in the Soviet Union constitutes an application of Robert Phillimore's principle of international society: "No State has a right to establish a form of government which is built upon professed hostility to the government of other nations."[49] Indeed, Hans Morgenthau, demon-

47. Kennan, "On Nuclear War," 8.

48. Christopher Lasch, *A World of Nations: Reflections on American History, Politics and Culture* (New York, 1974), 205–16.

49. Martin Wight, "Western Values in International Relations", in Herbert Butterfield and Martin Wight (eds.), *Diplomatic Investigations* (London, 1966), both quotes on 99.

strating the greater purity of his realism, wrote of this same essay that "even if the Russian government were to meet the requirements stipulated [by Kennan], would not the task of American foreign policy, though made easier in detail, remain precisely what it is today?"[50] Morgenthau viewed the Soviet Union strictly as a power; the plight of its people was not relevant to his calculations in the way that it was to Kennan's.

Kennan's opposition to the wartime policy of collaboration flowed in some measure from his disapproval of the Soviet regime; more important, as his attitude to the Polish question demonstrated, was the antipathy he felt for the hypocrisy and self-delusion that the policy necessarily involved. His determination to disabuse the American policy makers of their universalist illusions stems at least partly from this antipathy; and this determination helps to explain the form of the "X" article, which especially in its omission of any historical analysis, was not typical of Kennan's writing.

Of course, it was just this omission, in addition to the ambiguity of much of Kennan's language ("unalterable counter-force") that moved Walter Lippmann to criticize the essay so severely. Kennan's moral censure of the Soviet regime, his unhappiness at being the agent of a futile policy of collaboration, and his long-standing impatience with the naiveté of his Washington superiors all found expression in the Long Telegram and the "X" article. When Lippmann reacted as he did, criticizing the very aspects of American policy Kennan had himself opposed, Kennan could not have failed to be upset—Lippmann had drawn from his essay all the wrong conclusions.

Lippmann's criticisms as well as the prevailing rhetoric of liberation and rollback in the early Eisenhower administration led Kennan in *Realities of American Foreign Policy* (1954) to emphasize the difference between "the congenital and deep-seated hostility of the Soviet regime" and the intentions of its leaders. "Hostility is one thing; intentions another." Concerned about the belief that war with the Soviets was inevitable, Kennan repeated the arguments of his 1952 ambassadorial dispatch about the absence of any Soviet desire for general war: "The Soviet leaders are not like many of us; they do not suppose that military victory solves all problems; they know that it is only a beginning and not an end." Liberation of Eastern Europe was a dangerous chimera, an example of the naive, oversimple

50. Hans Morgenthau, "American Diplomacy: The Dangers of Righteousness," *New Republic*, CXXV (October 22, 1951), 17.

thinking America would have to replace with "deliberateness of states-manship" and a "high degree of national self-discipline" if political containment were to succeed. "An approach directed strictly to countering the Soviet threat as a straight military problem," Kennan concluded, was fundamentally mistaken, not least because the world was moving quickly away from the bipolarity of the early postwar years.[51]

Kennan's impatience with the persistence of that bipolarity resulted in his controversial proposals in the 1957 Reith Lectures for a neutral, disarmed, but reunified Germany attended by the withdrawal of American troops.[52] These lectures reveal much about Kennan's vision of international moderation as well as his evolving argument about the nature of the Soviet threat. His ideas for Germany and for halting the growing dependence on nuclear weapons were essentially pleas to return to a more "normal" state of international affairs—one with a truly independent Europe as free as possible from superpower domination and from the constant threat that a continent stuffed with tactical nuclear weapons would represent.

Perhaps because he believed so strongly in the need for these measures as a way to break the enduring impasse of the Cold War, his portrayal of the Soviet regime was unusually benign. He urged Western leaders to avoid indulging in summit meetings, which raise millennial expectations, and he advised people in the West to cultivate "detachment and reservation of judgment" concerning "internal happenings in Russia. Their world is not our world; their fortunes need not always be the diametrical opposite of our own." Once again he cautioned against an exclusively military conception of containment, scoring the continuing "obsession that the Russians are yearning to attack and occupy Western Europe, and that this is the principal danger."[53] These lectures, in short, sought ways to moderate the Cold War by making room for genuine nineteenth-century-style diplomacy. Kennan could never accept the political rigidity that followed the war and was reinforced by the cold, calculating logic of deterrence.

In a later set of lectures, delivered after his brief stint as ambassador to Yugoslavia and published in 1964 as *On Dealing with the Communist World*, Kennan reiterated his commitment to a foreign policy whose goal was coexistence with the Soviets instead of "victory" over them. Quite

51. Kennan, *Realities of American Foreign Policy*, 68–70, 99, 101.
52. Kennan, *Russia, the Atom and the West: The B.B.C. Reith Lectures, 1957* (London, 1958) chap. 3.
53. *Ibid.*, 15, 64.

presciently, he warned against dismissing too easily the views of those who "would willingly see us sacrifice all the positive values of life to the struggle against communism." Such views were gaining wide currency, he thought, and deserved to be taken seriously enough to refute. Hence he confronted the issue of coexistence versus victory by asking what "victory" would mean. In the atomic age the search for a final showdown can lead only to unparalleled catastrophe; the challenge therefore was to pursue a policy of coexistence that did not result in a "spineless pacifism."[54]

Probably the most interesting aspect of this discussion of coexistence is his treatment of the issue of East-West trade. In what now seems like an advance critique of Henry Kissinger's policy of detente, Kennan deplored the notion that "trade with a Communist country, even on normal commercial terms, represents an act of graciousness on our part for which we should demand political concessions in return." He doubted that economic transactions concluded on the basis of mutual interest could easily be controlled and directed by Western political authorities; he pointed to the basic differences in interest between Americans and the European allies and questioned the likelihood of coordinating policies; and he concluded that "to demand political concessions as a *quid pro quo* for normal commercial transactions is, after all, only another way of renouncing trade altogether; for Communist countries will never yield to overt demands of this nature."[55]

His overall recommendation was to "relax" and avoid making "such heavy sledding" over the issue one way or the other. European countries that wished to pursue trade with Eastern bloc countries should not be inhibited from "experimenting," but Kennan foresaw neither great dangers nor world-shattering breakthroughs. He has remained consistent in this view: from his 1947 recommendation that the Truman administration "play it straight" with the Soviet Union and invite it to participate in the Marshall Plan to a 1982 speech, Kennan has opposed the use of trade to wrest political concessions. As in the 1964 lectures, his reasons have been mainly practical—such attempts simply would not work. But in his most recent writing, he has been increasingly willing to make virtually a moral case against such uses of trade. Indeed, one can almost detect an echo of Richard Cobden: "If we really want to seek peace, we will have to abandon every form of economic warfare. There should be no place in the

54. Kennan, *On Dealing with the Communist World* (New York, 1964), 6, 18.
55. *Ibid.*, 31, 32.

policies of a democratic government for efforts to set back the economic development of another great people. Those are devices with which one prepares a war, not devices with which one avoids a war."[56]

Throughout his years as a private citizen, Kennan remained active in contemporary debates on policy, and his brief tenure as ambassador to Yugoslavia reinvigorated his public persona. Of course, his views had always earned a respectful hearing among the foreign policy elites, but to the wider public he was perhaps less familiar. His position on the Vietnam War, and later, on student unrest after 1968, thrust him into greater prominence. Like Hans Morgenthau, Kennan opposed the war on what he considered the firm ground of the American national interest; and though perhaps less trenchant than Morgenthau in that opposition, he was nevertheless willing to argue for his position in highly public forums.

In early 1966 Kennan appeared before the Senate Foreign Relations Committee as part of a series of televised hearings chaired by Senator J. William Fulbright on the direction of the war. Those testifying besides Kennan were Secretary of State Dean Rusk, Lieutenant General James M. Gavin, and General Maxwell D. Taylor. The hearings marked an important phase in the developing opposition to escalating the war. At the time of the hearings there were about 200,000 troops in South Vietnam; the immediate occasion for the hearings was a request for supplemental funding of $275 million to the Agency for International Development for use in Vietnam.

In his testimony, Kennan argued that the war was a mistake for essentially three reasons. First, Vietnam did not constitute a vital interest for the United States: "It is difficult to believe that any decisive developments of the world situation would be determined in normal circumstances by what happens on that territory." While recognizing that the United States had—ill-advisedly—committed its prestige to South Vietnam by its very presence, Kennan insisted that the American "military involvement has to be recognized as unfortunate, as something we would not choose deliberately if the choice were ours to make all over again today." He concluded that "it should be our government's aim to liquidate this involvement just as soon as this can be done without inordinate damage to our own prestige." As for how this could be done, Kennan endorsed General Gavin's idea of pursuing a defensive military strategy—placing our troops in defen-

---

56. Kennan, *Nuclear Delusion*, 249; "play it straight" from *Memoirs*, I, 342.

sible enclaves—and pursuing negotiations to withdraw in the least costly way possible.[57]

Thus for Kennan, the first error was the failure to consider the importance of Vietnam in the overall direction of American foreign policy. During close questioning about the costs to American prestige if we should withdraw, he answered, in effect, that the costs of staying were greater. He discounted the domino effect, and when Senator Bourke Hickenlooper asked whether American withdrawal could be used as a "propaganda tool and weapon," Kennan replied, "Senator, it would be a six months' sensation, but I daresay that we would survive it in the end, and there would be another day." Kennan worried more that the war increasingly dominated our foreign policy and badly distorted our relationship with the Soviets. This second basic reason for his opposition to continued involvement was perhaps most important: "This involvement seems to me to represent a grievous misplacement of emphasis on our foreign policies as a whole." Against those who saw in the successful pursuit of far-flung "limited wars" the great power battleground of the future, and therefore virtually by definition a vital American priority, Kennan argued:

> There are a great many new nations, small nations, nations with inexperienced governments, nations with shallow traditions of national life, dotted all around this world. Believe me, they are going to fight with each other, and it seems to me that our role here as a great power must be to try to isolate, to moderate these conflicts, to settle them as quickly and as easily as we can, not to worry too much about the issues because there will be right and wrong on both sides, but to try to keep these local conflicts from doing great damage to world peace.
>
> Now the problem we face with relation to Vietnam today is how do we best serve world peace at this moment? Do we serve it best by increasing the measure of our involvement in Vietnam? By trying to root out the Viet Cong by fire and sword? By increasing the intensity of this conflict in a single area to the neglect, I must say, of our world responsibilities, our responsibilities in other areas? Or do we serve it better by trying as best we can to bring about some sort of a resolution of the fighting in Vietnam and applying ourselves then again imaginatively and courageously and enthusiastically to the solution of the great, really great, and fateful problems that we still have outstanding with the Soviet Union?[58]

Kennan's extemporaneous eloquence in this passage on the dangers of an excessively bipolar and military view of the world reflects his long-

57. J. William Fulbright (ed.), *The Vietnam Hearings* (New York, 1966), 108–109.
58. *Ibid.*, 124, 150–51.

standing belief that subtle diplomacy, not force, should be the tool of great statecraft. If Max Weber looked at the world of states rather as Hieronymus Bosch portrayed hell, Kennan was more an impressionist: the hard edges of endemic conflict could be blurred by the deft and prudent application of diplomatic imagination. What horrified him about Vietnam was the seemingly inexorable logic of military escalation that governed American policy.

For Kennan, this logic was bound to fail—the third main reason for his opposition. "Any total rooting-out of the Viet Cong from the territory of South Vietnam could be achieved, if it could be achieved at all, only at the cost of a degree of damage to civilian life and of civilian suffering, for which I would not like to see this country responsible." He argued that increased pressure on the North would only bring in China, and he offered a poignant reminder that strategic bombing, whatever its purported local military advantages, carried heavy political costs:

> Our motives are widely misinterpreted, and the spectacle—the spectacle emphasized and reproduced in thousands of press photographs . . . the spectacle of Americans inflicting grievous injury on the lives of a poor and helpless people, and particularly a people of different race and color, no matter how warranted by military necessity or by the excesses of the adversary our operations may seem to us to be or may genuinely be—this spectacle produces reactions among millions of people throughout the world profoundly detrimental to the image we would like them to hold of this country. I am not saying that this is just or right. I am saying that this is so, and that it is bound in the circumstances to be so, and a victory purchased at the price of further such damage would be a hollow one in terms of our world interests, no matter what advantages it might hold from the standpoint of developments on the local scene.[59]

One could hardly imagine a more incisive critique of the American policy of bombing the North and of establishing "free-fire zones" in the South. Indeed, the passage seems an especially apt comment on the bombings of North Vietnam ordered by Richard Nixon and Henry Kissinger in December, 1972, after the latter had already announced that "peace is at hand."

Thus the Kennan who began his testimony by saying, "I have not been anxious to press my views on the public," presented a realist's dissent from the Vietnam War. Vietnam was not a vital American interest, the war distorted the priorities of our foreign policy, and it was in any case prob-

59. *Ibid.*, 110, 112.

ably not winnable at a cost we would regard as acceptable. There is one other aspect of Kennan's position on the Vietnam War that deserves to be highlighted—his claim that his opposition was merely practical and not moral.

At least until his most recent writings—and this is the exception to his consistent line mentioned above—Kennan always insisted that his policy recommendations reflected not his moral values but his realistic assessment of American interests. This insistence has been a hallmark of postwar American realism, and in his testimony on Vietnam Kennan repeated it: "I am trying to look at this whole problem not from the moral standpoint, but from the practical one." He thoroughly abominated the Viet Cong and professed the "deepest sympathy" for a country that "fell under [their] exclusive power." But the issue, Kennan averred, was not moral: the United States simply could not "shoulder the main burden of determining the political realities in any other country, and particularly not in one remote from our shores, from our culture, and from the experience of our people." (Kennan would later take a roughly similar position regarding the Soviet invasion of Afghanistan and the events in Poland.) Regardless of our moral preferences we must bow to international reality. Kennan ended his testimony by quoting John Quincy Adams on the dangers of American crusades abroad.[60]

But Kennan's opposition inevitably reflected his values, his moral vision. Indeed one pro-administration critic of the realist dissenters from the war accused Kennan of being a "very exasperating" and "incurable moralist [who] moralizes without a license." Kennan and Morgenthau doubtless were very exasperating to administration officials—the Johnson White House even launched a "Project Morgenthau" to rebut the professor—and it is hard to imagine how, and to whom, one would apply for a license to moralize. But there is a real point here: Kennan and, as I have already argued, Morgenthau reached their conclusions not by some amoral calculation of interest and power but by applying their values to judge political consequences and possibilities. Kennan believed military victory to be possible "only at the cost of a degree of damage to civilian life and of civilian suffering, generally, for which I would not like to see this country responsible." For him, maintaining tolerable relations with the Soviet Union for the sake of peace took precedence over "winning" in Vietnam.

60. *Ibid.*, 114; on Poland and Afghanistan see Kennan, *Nuclear Delusion*, chap. 11 and 227–28.

These are at least in part moral judgments. And even when they are strictly "political" they reflect a personal, transcendent hierarchy of values. In short, Kennan's values relate almost dialectically to his "realistic" assessments. There is nothing wrong in this—indeed, it is hard to see how it could be otherwise—but one might hope that Kennan would more openly acknowledge the considerable extent to which his policy recommendations flow not merely from Bismarckian *Realpolitik* but from his own deeply held moral convictions. One of the attractions of his latest essays, in my view, is precisely this acknowledgment.[61]

In his most recent writing on the Soviet Union Kennan has returned to his old theme of political containment but with a sharper attack on the opposing "militarists," on the new prevailing view of the Soviet Union. If the wartime seekers of collaborative world government ignored all that was evil and calculating in the Soviets, the new militarists offer an "endless series of distortions and oversimplifications," which paint the Russian leaders as reckless and aggressive expansionists on a par with the Nazis.[62] Kennan condemns this "naiveté of cynicism and suspicion" and its dangerous—and ultimately self-fulfilling—"demonizing" of the leaders of a "great and long-suffering people." He stresses once again the limited aims and persistent problems of the Soviet leadership, reminding his opponents that every great power seeks to expand its influence and that pursuit of influence does not entail a disposition for military invasion and formal takeover.

A tone of exasperation creeps into these essays by a distinguished author who would rather, one feels, be enjoying his retirement in rural serenity. But even in his eighties Kennan retains a formidable sense of duty, and his admirably deep concern at the recent turn in American foreign policy moves him to keep lecturing and writing. Throughout his long career Kennan has never shrunk from intellectual controversy—indeed, one suspects that at some level he thrives on it. The American political process, however, has always repelled him, and his sense of distaste can only have grown. More than any of his fellow American realists, Kennan remains a figure fundamentally out of sympathy with the existing structure of American democracy and indeed with the whole direction of American foreign

61. David Little, *American Foreign Policy and Moral Rhetoric: The Example of Vietnam* (New York, 1969), 17; for Kennan's recent approach see *Nuclear Delusion*, esp. 201–11.
62. Kennan, "On Nuclear War," 10; "Two Views of the Soviet Problem," 55.

policy after the election of Harry Truman in 1948—when "the vultures of domestic politics swarmed back onto the scene, insisting that the external relations of the country were no longer important enough to be permitted to interfere with the struggle for internal political power." On many different occasions Kennan has asked whether a country with so "primitive" a political process "should not recognize certain limitations on its ability to play a major active role in international affairs."[63]

This passage provides invaluable insight not only into Kennan's character as a diplomat without relish for the struggle for power but also into his idiosyncratic contribution to the idea of realism. Kennan's vision of international relations consists of moderate conflict with limited states, change eased by professional diplomacy, frank recognition of spheres of influence but without a rigid division into blocs, a sobering and universal awareness of the limitations of force—in short, an idealized picture of the prerevolutionary, preideological international system of the early eighteenth century. Kennan's realism, therefore, is tempered with a body of strongly held moral convictions that find expression in his preference for the simpler, more orderly world of the past. His differences with his State Department superiors, and later with the whole cast of American foreign policy, reflected more than conflict between a putative realism and a naive legalistic-moralism: these differences reflected a fundamental clash of visions. Kennan's moral universe simply did not coincide with the one that dictated the logic of the Cold War. Underlying his realism is a wish for a different world. Consider the following striking passage: "The sources of tragedy in international life lie in the differences of outlook that divide the human race; and it seems to me that our purposes prosper only when something happens in the mind of another person, and perhaps in our own mind as well, which makes it easier for all of us to see each other's problems and prejudices with detachment and to live peaceably side by side."[64]

As his own anguished appeals to end the nuclear arms race demonstrate all too well, that "something" has failed to happen, and prejudices and suspicions continue to swell the arsenals of the world. "Realism" has not proven the equal of Cold War and nuclear deterrence; instead its arguments have been employed by many perhaps less sensitive than Kennan to justify their continued pursuit.

In the end, Kennan's version of realism has failed significantly to influ-

63. Kennan, *Memoirs*, II, 321, 315.
64. Kennan, *Dealing with the Communist World*, 18.

ence American policy at least partly because it rests on so personal a foundation. His self-professed antiquarianism, his nostalgia for a hierarchical ordering of states, his horror at the requirements of mass democracy—all these important aspects of his approach reflect his individualist values. The point is not to judge these values—though there is much in them to admire—but to recognize both their existence and their considerable distance from the austere world of constant struggles for power usually associated with realism.

Finally, could Kennan's prescriptions for a moderate postwar world have worked? Certainly they possessed consistency and even elegance. Applied with skill and tact, Kennan's flexible, essentially nonmilitary containment might have succeeded. The inevitable conflict between America and the Soviet Union might have taken a more civilized form. Europe might have regained a measure of political independence. The race in nuclear armaments might have been less all-consuming, and our societies less militarized. Costly intervention in Vietnam (and perhaps Afghanistan) would have been avoided. Given the current state of Soviet-American relations, the counterfactual possibilities of Kennan's version of containment obviously seem attractive, even tantalizing. Of course, there is no way to prove or disprove a scenario, rather as one cannot prove or disprove Kant's vision in *Perpetual Peace*. Yet I suspect that ultimately, the success of Kennan's ideas would have depended on the extent to which men on both sides—diplomats and their superiors, military men and civilian planners, congressmen and *apparatchiki*—shared his civilized values. Unfortunately for all of us, too few of them did.

8

Henry Kissinger: Realism in Power

When Richard Nixon asked Henry Kissinger to leave the Harvard faculty to become his national security adviser, the triumph of the realist analysis of American foreign policy seemed at hand. Kissinger had studied the ideas of the realists and as an academic had contributed to the growing body of realist criticisms of the American approach to international affairs. Like Hans Morgenthau, he had great appreciation for the success of the nineteenth-century balance of power and for the basic principle that states should follow their national interests. Like George Kennan, he valued skilled, professional diplomacy and the careful assessment of realistic possibilities. And like Weber, he had a profound faith in the creative possibilities of personal statecraft together with a thorough distrust of entrenched bureaucracy.

His appointment therefore seemed to confirm the argument of many (including Morgenthau) during the 1968 election campaign that Nixon would be more likely than Hubert Humphrey to end the Vietnam War and that American foreign policy would move away from misguided crusades toward the prudent calculation of interest urged by all realists. Many hoped or expected that Kissinger would bring to American foreign policy the historical perspective and conceptual sophistication it lacked for much of the postwar period. Journalists hurried to read Kissinger's academic writings, and academics endeavored to explain them to a larger public. Indeed, after Kissinger's remarkable rise to public prominence, it became fashionable to compare his brilliance to Metternich's or, later, to condemn his apparently amoral "Machiavellianism." Certainly Kissinger's books and essays presented an almost unique opportunity to compare his theory with his practice, and doubtless this has contributed to the fascination and controversy he has inspired.

My goal in this chapter is not to join these continuing controversies, but rather to demonstrate the remarkable extent to which Kissinger draws from, develops, and writes variations on the realist themes that have been identified so far. In the basic assumptions underlying his thought, in his conception of leadership and the limits of ethics, and in his critique of American foreign policy, Kissinger shows a deep sympathy for the ideas of all the realists we have considered with the single exception of Carr in his socialism and sociology of knowledge. Kissinger's highly personal synthesis of these ideas not only reflects his particular world-view but also demonstrates—if such a demonstration is needed—the continuing importance of realism among a new generation of scholars and statesmen. For the debates about Kissinger's ideas and tenure have taken at least two forms: some, like Morgenthau and Kennan, have argued that Kissinger misapplied realist ideas in his policies, while others have asserted that those ideas were misguided in the first place.

Thus the chapter will also present a brief characterization of Kissinger's attempt to make his version of realism the foundation of a new era in American foreign policy, one that would ensure a "stable structure of peace." Led by Kissinger's two enormous volumes of memoirs (2,807 pages covering less than six years) the literature on the Nixon-Kissinger foreign policy has already grown to a mountain, and obviously anything like a complete treatment cannot be undertaken here. Instead I shall try to suggest in summary fashion the ways Kissinger's policies in office reflected his ideas in the academy and begin to assess the extent to which flaws in the ideas led to failures in policy. Kissinger's reliance on great power diplomacy, his assumption of unquestioned priority of international over domestic politics, his Weberian conception of the statesman's personal responsibility for the ethical dilemmas of foreign policy—all these tenets of realism informed Kissinger's approach. Arguably, they resulted in policies that can only cast doubt on the wisdom and practicality of realism, at least as interpreted by Kissinger.

The chapter begins with an account of Kissinger's basic philosophy as expressed in his remarkable undergraduate thesis, "The Meaning of History," and of his doctoral dissertation, later published as *A World Restored*; it then moves to characterize his overall analysis of American foreign policy before he came to office. With these tasks accomplished, I shall conclude with some brief consideration and criticism of his tenure in office along the lines just described.

Foundations

A working philosophy of history provides for Henry Kissinger the foundation to his later thought that the doctrine of human nature provides for such other realists as Niebuhr. Kissinger's undergraduate thesis, "The Meaning of History: Reflections on Spengler, Toynbee and Kant," tries to define such a philosophy by considering the hoary philosophical issue of freedom versus necessity. "The philosophy of history," he writes at the outset, "is inseparable from metaphysics and involves a deep awareness of the mysteries and possibilities not only of nature, but of human nature." Kissinger's concern with philosophy of history, therefore, goes well beyond the usual questions associated with it: whether there is a recurring pattern to the past, whether history represents progress, whether writers in the present can ever understand and evoke the past. These problems are dismissed by Kissinger as "merely empirical." His interest in history is as a "key to action": "Necessity describes the past, but freedom rules the future."[1]

In an essay that includes the sentence "Birth is the beginning of death, life, the process of mortality" it is not surprising to find as its daunting central question the metaphysical problem of whether freedom remains possible and of what it consists. A measure of its ambition and achievement—or perhaps of the inordinate interest Kissinger arouses—is the publication by the Cambridge University Press of a book on the unpublished undergraduate thesis.[2] In any case, Kissinger attacks the problem of defining freedom through an ethical conception of history by considering the historical theories of Oswald Spengler and Arnold Toynbee. Ultimately he rejects these theories in favor of an idiosyncratic reading of Kant, whose morality, according to Kissinger, "derives from a mystic relation to the Infinite, a personal experience which elevates man above the realm of necessity."[3]

Spengler's attractiveness to Kissinger lay in his notion of *erfühlen*, or intuitive perception. This concept has authoritatively been explained as a way to understand history by leaps of creative imagination rather than by careful empirical treatment of facts—disclaimed by Spengler as plodding.[4]

1. Henry A. Kissinger, "The Meaning of History: Reflections on Spengler, Toynbee and Kant" (A.B. thesis, Harvard University, 1951), 9–10, 24–25.
2. *Ibid.*, 10; Peter Dickson, *Kissinger and the Meaning of History* (New York, 1978).
3. "Meaning of History," 25.
4. H. Stuart Hughes, *Oswald Spengler: A Critical Estimate* (New York, 1952), 67.

Kissinger recognizes and applauds this aspect of Spengler's project, writing that his "vision transcended the mere causal analysis of data and the shallow dogmatism of many progress theories." But for Kissinger the real value of the notion of *erfühlen* consists in its ability to "point the way toward insights of compelling beauty," to understand through creative intuition the real meaning of events even while in the midst of them: "Spengler grasped the essential mystery of life that Kant found in the experience of freedom. He realized that every event represents not only an effect, but also an inward experience, the key to results incommensurable with our intentions."[5] This idea of intuiting the meaning of events played an important part in Max Weber's conception of the inner bearing of the true leader. Kissinger draws on both thinkers in his own definitions of freedom and leadership.

Although Kissinger adopts Spengler's *erfühlen*, he rejects his deterministic view of history—"a mere repetition of power phenomena"—and the specific use to which Spengler puts *erfühlen*. Kissinger criticizes Spengler's preoccupation with decline: "A disintegrating society offers no obvious field of activity for leadership." Moreover, he treats states as all-powerful in their demands, a position that could only inhibit the development of a truly normative philosophy of history and thus of the possibility of freedom. In his conclusion on Spengler Kissinger foreshadows his later argument about freedom: "The recognition of limits, that one is man and not God, may in nations, as in individuals, serve as the basis for ethical criteria and *the* concept of the moral personality of man."[6] Thus Kissinger adopts Spengler's notion of intuition even as he dismisses the cyclical and deterministic view of history which *erfühlen* is meant to yield. By recasting this idea into a strictly personal revelation, Kissinger lays the groundwork for his later argument for the notion of freedom as intuition once the limits of knowledge are accepted.

But before he can develop this argument, Kissinger has first to dispose of Arnold Toynbee's attempt to discern the meaning of history through a combination of empirical analysis and faith in a universal Christian church. Given his attraction to Spenglerian intuition, one would not expect Kissinger to applaud Toynbee's empirical method. And in fact, in his introduction, Kissinger writes of Toynbee that "a philosophy of history without a profound metaphysics will forever juxtapose surface data and can never

5. Kissinger, "Meaning of History," 115, 131, 214.
6. *Ibid.*, 117, 215, 119.

satisfy the totality of man's desire for meaning." Later, in considering
Toynbee's famous notion of challenge-and-response, Kissinger asserts
that "Toynbee's empiricism allows him to distinguish challenges only by
their origin and magnitude, not by their inner meaning." The notion of
inner meaning is crucial to Kissinger's view of history and freedom; he
accuses Toynbee of mixing a theological and biological approach without
recognizing that it is "impossible to unite general laws with the unique
merit of Christianity." Concerning Christian views, Kissinger notes that "a
philosophy of history based on theology is feasible, as Bossuet and Niebuhr demonstrate. Yet their formulation derives in the first instance, from
a frank recognition of a normative pattern and a profound metaphysics."[7]
Thus Kissinger prefers even a Christian philosophy of history based on a
"normative pattern" to Toynbee's because it contains a "profound metaphysics"—something that Toynbee's definitely lacks.

Kissinger's ultimate criticism of Toynbee is that he attempted to define
freedom as an artifact, an aspect of objective reality; but, Kissinger argues,
"freedom cannot be proved syllogistically . . . an inner experience, again,
remains inaccessible to an empiricist." His conclusion of the chapter on
Toynbee bears quotation: "If freedom is not an attribute of external, objective reality, it must result from an inward state that imposes its patterns
on phenomena. If morality is not denoted by successful activity, we must
find better criteria for ethical conduct. The two realms of freedom and
necessity are perhaps reconcilable through our experience of freedom in a
however determined world. The meaning of history may appear as the
emanation of man's moral personality."[8]

With this conclusion on Toynbee, Kissinger comes finally to consider
the way man might achieve the inner state of freedom. He finds the key to
this problem in Kantian metaphysics, in Kant's division of reality into
phenomenal (that which can be apprehended by pure reason) and noumenal (things-in-themselves: the objects of speculative reason). Noumena
reveal themselves to man through inward experience; and man may
achieve freedom only insofar as he is noumenal: "The meaning of life
becomes the emanation of a personality, not an attribute of the empirical
world. Purposiveness is not revealed by phenomenal reality but constitutes
the resolve of the soul. Freedom does have a place in a determined universe."[9]

7. *Ibid.*, 23, 244, 243, 238. *Faith and History* is the only work by Niebuhr that Kissinger
cites.
8. *Ibid.*, 259.
9. *Ibid.*, 274.

Kissinger goes on to write that "the experience of freedom in a determined world implies that we can transcend necessity only by imparting our
individuality to the inexorable unfolding of events." This romantic, not to
say Nietzschean, conception of freedom later finds expression in his treatment of Metternich and Castlereagh and serves, I think, as a credo for his
own statecraft. Kissinger does, however, use the structure of Kant's argument to produce conclusions quite different from those of Kant himself,
both in the matter of inner transcendence and in the moral conclusions
that transcendence is said to yield.[10] Moreover, Kissinger explicitly rejects
Kant's teleology as undermining the will to act: if nature "guarantees" that
perpetual peace through a league of democratic republics is the end of
history, why should individual men and women struggle to bring about
this outcome?[11]

Thus for Kissinger man imparts his own meaning to history. His motive
for doing so "issues from an inward experience which teaches man his
limits and his intrinsic worth. This is the ultimate basis of human freedom,
the condition of mankind's self-transcendence." As a result of this transcendent inward experience (which Kissinger describes in language that is
positively Hegelian: "a mystic attitude, an inward state that feels the cosmic in the universe, an occasion when time stands still and man partakes of
eternity"), man knows freedom; thus equipped he attempts to give meaning to history.[12]

What defines this knowledge of freedom? Kissinger's answer amounts
to a remarkable (though no doubt unconscious) synthesis of Reinhold
Niebuhr and Max Weber: freedom involves "the inward necessity of a
recognition of limits," the "recognition of necessity which enables [man]
to transcend the determined inevitability of his environment." The notion
of an inner experience of limits leads, for Kissinger, to a Weberian formulation of the problem of ethics: "Freedom invariably involves the recognition of limits and the acceptance of one's humanity. But the moral content
of ethical freedom resides in the sanction ascribed to that necessity, in the
inner content of the reconciliation. . . . Ethics must always reside in an
inward state, in a personal recognition of limits . . . the ultimate liberation
derives from within us, from an experience both personal and essentially

10. *Ibid.*, 235. On Kissinger's misreading of Kant, see Dickson, *Kissinger and the Meaning of History*, 51–83.
11. Kissinger, "Meaning of History," 295–301; *cf.* Kant, "Idea for a Universal History
from a Cosmopolitan Point of View," in Hans Reiss (ed.), *Kant's Political Writings* (Cambridge, 1970).
12. Kissinger, "The Meaning of History," 286, 324.

incommunicable." In sum, then, Kissinger argues that freedom grows out of an intense inner experience which accepts the inevitability of human limits. Only through such an experience can man create and apprehend the meaning of history and transcend its external limitations. And only through such an experience can one recognize the ethical content of one's actions. "The meaning of history," he concludes, "results from an inward apprehension that determines the will by its very conception without any regard to its immediate empirical attainability." Kissinger expresses this same idea more vividly in *A World Restored*: "For men become myths not by what they know, nor even by what they achieve, but by the tasks they set themselves."[13]

The affinity of Kissinger's position with that of Niebuhr and Weber stands out clearly. Niebuhr's ultimate limitation—original sin and pride—in Kissinger's scheme becomes necessity: to achieve anything truly noble man must recognize his own limits. For Niebuhr man can (at least try to) transcend himself—and thus come closer to God—only by recognizing his ultimate lack of freedom. He is most free, paradoxically, in the profound realization of his unfreedom. For Kissinger only the recognition of the limits imposed by necessity allows one to transcend those limits and experience true freedom. Both men regard a deep realization of one's limits to be the prerequisite of freedom.

Of course, as a theologian, Niebuhr argues that an inescapable original sin accompanies every attempt at self-transcendence. Sinful human pride taints all of our achievements; even our best approximations of justice are morally ambiguous. Nations are apt to forget this; hence the need to remind them of their unjustified self-righteousness, and hence Niebuhr's moral distinction between nations according to their openness to such reminders. Kissinger demonstrates no such concerns: he wishes to find a way for individual freedom and creativity in an apparently determined universe. He implies that once transcended inwardly, the bonds of necessity need not hinder the genuinely creative statesman eager to impart meaning to history. Kissinger indicates no moral qualification to this attempt: ethics, too, derive from the same inward experience. Niebuhr would have regarded this view, if not as blasphemous, then as another example of sinful human pride.

Certainly in its account of the source and content of moral judgment, it

---

13. *Ibid.*, 325, 335, 345, 291; Kissinger, *A World Restored: Metternich, Castlereagh, and the Problems of Peace, 1812–1822* (Boston, 1957), 322.

suffers from the same difficulty as Weber's ethic of responsibility—the problem of providing concrete content to standards that emanate from "inner strength." Though he shares Weber's hopes for leadership—indeed, exceeds them—Kissinger, too, fails to define the precise character of the morality followed by the free and responsible actor. All we are told is that "it resides in an inward state." Still, Kissinger's insistence on the importance of recognizing limits explains his clear preference, expressed in *A World Restored*, for the conservative statesman who accepts the limits of his time and humanity but tries nevertheless to leave his mark on history within and despite those limits. The radical, though less profound, at least recognizes the existence of external limits in his attempt to overturn and replace them. Only the liberal leader, governed by a shallow doctrine of progress and illusions of rational reform, fails to appreciate the meaning of the limits of necessity; his efforts are bound to end in defeat.[14]

Like Niebuhr, Kissinger views history as normative but in a different way. Niebuhr sees in history divine self-revelation, the apprehension of which leads man to a fuller appreciation of his limits and possibilities: rightly understood, history confirms personal revelation and leads man closer to God—the only object of the revelation.[15] In contrast, Kissinger regards history as an opportunity and a testing ground: an opportunity for freedom and a test of creativity, of the ability to impose one's personality on history—especially against that powerfully impersonal enemy of creativity, bureaucracy. Kissinger's abhorrence of the plodding spirit of bureaucracy rivals Weber's; and like Weber, Kissinger seeks an antidote for it in the personal creativity of a strong leader. In his philosophy of history Kissinger tries to discover the key to this creativity, to learn from a deep understanding of the past how to act in the present—not in the simplistic sense of reasoning by analogy but in the sense of applying one's inward experience of freedom to his actions in an uncertain present. In short, he builds a paradigm for the liberated—and thus creative—statesman. Kissinger's undergraduate thesis provides the theoretical underpinning for his later study of Castlereagh and Metternich at the Congress of Vienna—of makers of history in action. Both statesmen confronted the problem of freedom and necessity, and Kissinger's study of them supplied empirical verification for his uniquely personal, normative view of history.

14. Kissinger, *World Restored*, chap. 17. See also the discussion in Stanley Hoffmann, *Primacy or World Order: American Foreign Policy Since the Cold War* (New York, 1978), 35–42.
15. Niebuhr, *Nature and Destiny of Man*, II; see the discussion above in Chapter 5.

Creativity Versus Bureaucracy and the Search
for a Legitimate Order

So much has been written about Kissinger's analysis of the nineteenth-century balance of power and his supposed preoccupation with Metternich or Bismarck that I shall confine myself to a few general remarks about the relation of *A World Restored* to other realist writings.[16]

Because the book is a mixture of history, theoretical analysis of international relations, and personal reflections on the nature of leadership, it lacks the rigor of any one form. For example, Kissinger places great stock in his concept of international legitimacy, defining the success of the Vienna settlement as the result of its ability to fashion an order "in which change could be brought about through a sense of obligation instead of through an assertion of power"; it constituted, in short, "an order based on 'legitimacy.'"[17] The quotation marks around "legitimacy" are not accidental: Kissinger uses the term so loosely and idiosyncratically that even he draws attention to his peculiar usage. As Stanley Hoffmann has demonstrated, Kissinger's conception of legitimacy is extraordinarily elusive.[18] The issue is the extent to which a common normative vision, a shared sense of justice, defines the principle.

Sometimes Kissinger treats a legitimate order simply as a series of "workable arrangements" about the "permissible aims and methods of foreign policy" without reference to justice, whereas at other times (and more frequently) "the legitimizing principle establishes the relative 'justice' of competing claims." If the latter formulation were consistent, Kissinger would be a dissenter from the traditional realist view that power relationships are the real keys to the stability of a given order; but it is not. The book betrays a debilitating ambiguity on the precise content of a "legitimizing principle," on what legitimacy consists in. On the key issue of the self-restraint of would-be revisionist powers, for example, one never learns if it results from common belief in the principle, which itself might be no more than "no one is to help himself without consultation." If this were the principle, then Kissinger would stake out a position just this side

---

16. Among the many such works see Stephen R. Graubard, *Kissinger: Portrait of a Mind* (New York, 1973); John D. Montgomery, "The Education of Henry Kissinger," *Journal of International Affairs*, IX (Spring, 1975), 49–62; S. G. Walker, "Beliefs and Behavior in Henry Kissinger," *Journal of Conflict Resolution*, XXI (March, 1977), 129–68.
17. Kissinger, *World Restored*, 172–73.
18. Hoffmann, *Primacy or World Order*, 38–40.

of tautological—even Hitler "consulted" before acquiring the Sudeten-land. Alternatively, self-restraint might simply be the product of external constraints, of the balance of power, which Kissinger defines as "the classic expression of the lesson of history that no order is safe without physical safeguards against aggression."[19]

Overall Kissinger fudges the issue, content to invoke the "great tradition of the eighteenth century," a time when cosmopolitan statesmen "were products of essentially the same culture, professing the same ideals, sharing similar tastes." In these passages Kissinger echoes the diplomatic realism of George Kennan, praising the archetypal diplomat, who was "coolly and unemotionally arranging his combinations in an age increasingly conducting policy by 'causes.'"[20] He notes the passing of this age of cosmopolitan culture, yet his conception of the international order depends on it. Kissinger's attempt in office to recreate the order of an earlier time in a century infinitely less amenable to the separation of ideological from "power" factors may have demonstrated his heroic qualities of freedom and leadership, indeed his personal creativity, but the difficulties of the policy reflect the inapplicability of the concept. In the late twentieth century, to deny the relevance of ideology is to proclaim another competing ideology.

The Weberian and romantic aspects of *A World Restored* come through in its reflections on leadership, in particular on the contrasting fates of Metternich and Castlereagh. Kissinger admires Metternich for his imagination, his skill at negotiation, and his ability "to dominate Europe morally and then to construct a group of powers which made a major conflict impossible physically." But he criticizes Metternich's contribution to Austria's domestic sterility and petrifaction and concludes that his agile diplomacy, remarkable though it was, "left the fundamental problems unsolved"; his final legacy was "manipulation and not creation." He explains the cause for Metternich's failure in phrases straight from "The Meaning of History": "Lacking in Metternich is the attribute which has enabled the spirit to transcend an impasse at so many crises of history: the ability to contemplate an abyss, not with the detachment of a scientist, but as a challenge to overcome—or to perish in the process."[21]

Castlereagh, of course, did just that, but his chief failure was his inabil-

19. Kissinger, *World Restored*, 3, 145, 318.
20. *Ibid.*, 319–20.
21. *Ibid.*, 318, 322.

ity to carry his country with him. One is not sure whether Kissinger believes this failure stems more from Castlereagh's own shortcomings or
from the bureaucratic and mediocre nature of all domestic politics; when
he later discusses the failures of his own policy he expresses no such ambiguity. For whatever reason, Metternich and Castlereagh were "both defeated in the end by their domestic structure: Castlereagh by ignoring it,
Metternich by being too conscious of its vulnerability."[22] Kissinger treats
these failures as regrettable—as unfortunate examples of the restraints the
pettiness of domestic politics place upon statesmen of vision.

Like Weber, Kissinger regards the creativity of such statesmen as perhaps the only chance to slow the advance of bureaucracy. If the essence of
the true statesman is creativity, the essence of bureaucracy is instrumental
rationality. All politics is a "conflict between inspiration and organization": "Inspiration implies the identification of the self with the meaning
of events. Organization requires discipline, the submission to the will of
the group. Inspiration is timeless, its validity inherent in its conception.
Organization is historical, depending on the material available at a given
period. Inspiration is a call for greatness; organization a recognition that
mediocrity is the usual pattern of leadership."[23] In a revealing elaboration
of this contrast between the inspiration of leadership and the organization
of bureaucracy, Kissinger applies the same dichotomy to international and
domestic politics, asserting that "many nations exhibit a powerful if subconscious rebellion against foreign policy." This rebellion makes the task
of the creative statesman far more lonely and difficult: "The statesman
must therefore be an educator; he must bridge the gap between a people's
experience and his vision, between a nation's tradition and its future."[24]
The leader's intuition must serve as the guide for the nation in a hostile
world. Kissinger's view here echoes that of Weber in "Politics as a Vocation," but in the case of Kissinger one senses an element of personal ambition absent in Weber.

A World Restored was an addition to the growing corpus of realist
literature. Kissinger's analysis of the Congress of Vienna was very much in
tune with the Hans Morgenthau of *Politics Among Nations*, and his appreciation of diplomacy recalled George Kennan. The conservative bias of
the book, its assumption that a study of the attempt to hold back ideology

22. *Ibid.*, 323.
23. *Ibid.*, 317.
24. *Ibid.*, 329.

by shrewd balance-of-power manipulations had continued relevance, and its treatment of domestic politics as a mundane inhibition on international creativity all struck familiar realist chords. In addition, his evocation of the Weberian notion of leadership and sole ethical responsibility, plus his secular romanticization of Niebuhr's conception of human limits, mark Kissinger as a thinker deeply in sympathy with the realist tradition as I have defined it. Yet in these foundations to his thought, Kissinger fails to solve some of the characteristic problems of that tradition: his notion of power and legitimacy is ambiguous; his conception of human nature and the meaning of history is personal and "incommunicable," as is his view of ethics; and his depreciation of the role of domestic politics as well as the technical aspects of international relations fails to advance from Kennan's visceral distaste for the same factors.

The Critique of American Foreign Policy

In this area as well, Kissinger reveals himself to be an almost ideal-type realist. In *Nuclear Weapons and Foreign Policy* (1957), *The Necessity for Choice* (1961), and *The Troubled Partnership* (1965) he developed familiar themes: the costs of American inexperience in the world; the danger of its naive attitude to power; America's continuing illusions about a reformed international system; its failure to integrate force and diplomacy; its childish hopes for the achievements of summits; its reluctance to assume the responsibilities of world leadership. Was it, for example, Kissinger, Kennan, or Niebuhr who pointed to "our lack of tragic experience" as a cause of our frequent insensitivity to the concerns of our European allies?[25] At the same time, Kissinger shows none of the caution expressed by Morgenthau or Kennan in the mid-1950s about the ability of the United States to play an active global role. In a passage critical of Kennan's 1957 Reith Lectures he writes: "We must be willing to face the paradox that we must be dedicated both to military strength and to arms control, to security as well as to negotiation, to assisting the new nations towards freedom and self-respect without accepting their interpretation of all issues. If we cannot do *all* of these things we will not be able to do *any* of them."[26]

Kissinger's first book on policy, *Nuclear Weapons and Foreign Policy*,

25. Of course, it was all three. The phrase quoted is from Kissinger, *Nuclear Weapons and Foreign Policy* (Garden City, N.Y., 1957), 242.
26. Kissinger, *The Necessity for Choice: Prospects of American Foreign Policy* (New York, 1960), 9.

is especially interesting because it represents an attempt to bring the traditional realist maxim about integrating force and diplomacy into the nuclear age: in urging America to prepare to fight limited nuclear wars Kissinger tried to define a "strategic doctrine which gives our diplomacy the greatest freedom of action and which addresses itself to the question of whether the nuclear age presents only risks or whether it also offers opportunities."[27] Couching his argument in terms borrowed from *A World Restored* ("The quest for absolute security inevitably produces a revolutionary situation") Kissinger in 1957 clearly felt that there were such opportunities. In many ways, as in its discussion of deployment and its proposal to divide the military into a "strategic force and a tactical force," the book is a relic of an earlier age; but in others, it is quite revealing.

For example, Kissinger criticizes Achesonian containment and "situations of strength" not because the policy is basically wrongheaded but because of its inflexibility, its failure to "translate power into policy," and its failure to signal to the Russians how the situations of strength would be demonstrated. Kissinger's preoccupation in the book is to argue against the notion that nuclear weapons have rendered the application of power and force irrelevant; nothing could be more dangerous. "Foreign policy cannot be conducted without an awareness of power relationships"; Americans, he writes, must overcome their "reluctance to think in terms of power." Even in the nuclear age Kissinger's universe is the classical one of diplomacy and traditional military power: he has little interest in the exigencies of domestic politics. In this, as in his treatment of national interest, or his emphasis on "the capacity to think conceptually," Kissinger sounds much like Morgenthau or Kennan.[28]

He is more original in his curious mixture of the different ideological and power emphases of Niebuhr, Kennan, and Morgenthau. Like Niebuhr, he viewed the Soviet Union as a revolutionary, ideological power that could not be treated as just another great power, as Morgenthau tended to do. But unlike Niebuhr, he issued no ideological challenges or moral strictures: except for the standard recital of American responsibilities, his rhetoric was strictly that of a *Realpolitiker*, similar to Morgenthau's. Like Kennan and Morgenthau, he criticized inflexible, Dullesian diplomacy; but unlike them, he accepted the division of Europe and

27. *Nuclear Weapons and Foreign Policy*, 15.
28. *Ibid.*, 243, 248; on the national interest, see Kissinger, *American Foreign Policy: Three Essays* (New York, 1969), 91–97.

wanted no part of their schemes to neutralize Germany and supposedly restore Europe to flexible alignments. Later, when American policy toward Europe became more active under John F. Kennedy (with flexible response and the multilateral force) Kissinger adjusted his critique accordingly: we were too paternalistic and failed adequately to appreciate the security anxieties of the Europeans—anxieties Kennan always regarded as silly.[29] Kissinger may have been as fascinated with traditional diplomacy as Morgenthau and Kennan were, but in his prescriptive writings he explicitly avoided expressing the nostalgia for cabinet diplomacy that flavors their (and his earlier) work—even if his personal preference for such diplomacy remained.

Thus as a writer in opposition, Kissinger placed himself on the hard side of the containment consensus, closer to the Kennan of the "X" article than the Kennan of the Reith Lectures or *Memoirs*. He reiterated the realist theme of appreciating power and applying it when necessary, but he judged that necessity far more liberally than Niebuhr, Morgenthau, or Kennan, all of whom regarded the strategy of a limited nuclear war—a position Kissinger later abandoned—as beyond the pale.[30] As the founding fathers grew to chafe at America's unreflective application of global containment, Kissinger sought to give containment a new life, to convert it into a "stable structure of peace." Let us turn now to his attempt to match his theory with his practice, focusing on three issues: Kissinger's notion of a central balance among the great powers, that is, the frequently invoked "stable structure of peace"; his classically Weberian attitude that domestic politics should be subordinated to the higher needs of foreign policy; and his personal approach to the moral problems of statecraft.

Realism à la Kissinger in Power:
A Characterization and Critique

In his two massive volumes of memoirs Kissinger explains the premises underlying his policy, providing an authoritative account of his ideas, which attempts not only to persuade but also to lay down the terms of

29. Kissinger, *The Troubled Partnership: A Reappraisal of the Atlantic Alliance* (New York, 1965), chap. 1.

30. In office Kissinger did not pursue the strategy of limited war recommended by his earlier book. See *American Foreign Policy* (3d ed.; New York, 1977), chap. 14. For Niebuhr's opposition see *Structure of Nations and Empires*, 279–82; Morgenthau's, *New Foreign Policy for the United States*, chap. 8; Kennan's, *Russia, the Atom and the West*, chap. 4.

future debate. The concern here is not to offer a global evaluation of his policy—a task well beyond the scope of this essay—but rather to trace its relation to realism, or in Kissinger's preferred term, the "geopolitical approach."

Kissinger argues that his policy, based on a geopolitical conception of our fundamental national interests, was designed to correct the defects of containment (primarily, as we have seen, a "sentimental moralism" and diplomatic inflexibility) and, moreover, "to lay the foundation for a long-range American foreign policy even while liquidating our Indochina involvement." He recognizes that at the time he and Nixon took office the Vietnam War had destroyed the domestic consensus around containment; but, significantly, he blames the evaporation of this consensus not on the flaws of the policy but on the "collapse" of the "internationalist Establishment before the onslaught of its children who questioned all its values." Thus the task of the new administration was to prevent a return to "sulking isolation" by means of an ambitious scheme whose goal was to assure a lasting equilibrium.[31] Four years later, when direct American involvement in Vietnam had finally ended, Kissinger explained that he hoped "the nation's foreign policy could combine the exuberant idealism of the Kennedy Administration . . . with the unsentimental emphasis on national interest of the Nixon Administration."[32]

What were the precise components of Kissinger's realistic scheme? And how did he and President Nixon try to implement it? The key goal was "global equilibrium." "Such an equilibrium," Kissinger claims in terms that recall *A World Restored*, "could assure stability among the major powers, and even eventual cooperation, in the Seventies and Eighties." Kissinger is never explicit on the precise character of this equilibrium, but it is clear that what he has in mind is stability, the maintenance of America's privileged position in the world. "Like it or not, we were assuming the historical responsibility for preserving the balance of power," and we would need to learn that the "management of the balance of power is a permanent undertaking, not an exertion that has a foreseeable end. . . . Management of the balance requires perseverance, subtlety, not a little courage and above all understanding of its requirements."[33]

This understanding, which serves as Kissinger's definition of geopoli-

31. Kissinger, *White House Years* (Boston, 1979), 65.
32. Kissinger, *Years of Upheaval* (Boston, 1982), 72.
33. Kissinger, *White House Years*, 192, 115.

tics, is possessed only by creative statesmen such as Kissinger himself, Nixon (most of the time), Chou En-lai, and De Gaulle. A bureaucracy—governed by rigid procedures, jealous of its prerogatives, which moves "by almost imperceptible steps toward a goal it may itself only dimly perceive"—is by definition incapable of this understanding, this "sense of nuance and proportion." Kissinger devotes long passages to recounting his skirmishes with the "bureaucratic steamroller," with area experts who objected to geopolitical considerations as "gratuitous," and, especially, with Nixon's hapless secretary of state, William P. Rogers.[34] Kissinger's onslaught against bureaucrats continues even in his second volume, after he was appointed secretary of state and hence became head of, and responsible for, an enormous foreign policy bureaucracy. He blames the delay of the airlift of arms to Israel during the 1973 war on "bureaucratic foot-dragging and logistical problems"; he ascribes leaks during preparations for the strategic arms negotiations in January, 1974, to "the bureaucracy's revenge for my freewheeling diplomacy during Nixon's first term"; and he laments the degeneration of his Year of Europe initiative to a "bureaucratic exercise that stifled . . . instead of reviving consultation."[35] Kissinger's geopolitical equilibrium clearly had very little room for civilized, orderly diplomacy in the style of Kennan.

One of the main tactics Kissinger developed to promote this equilibrium was "linkage." (Resolute use of force, as we shall see, was another.) He writes that it is "synonymous with an overall strategic and geopolitical view. To ignore the interconnection of events was to undermine the coherence of *all* policy." Sometimes the linkage is made direct and specific, as in the 1971 India-Pakistan War, during which Kissinger threatened the Soviets to get them to restrain the Indians, or in the Four Power Berlin Agreements and *Ostpolitik*. At other times the linkage exists "by virtue of reality" when events inevitably have consequences "beyond the issue or region immediately concerned."[36] Examples here are the "opening" to China or, less happily, the election in Chile of Salvador Allende, which was supposed to have dire consequences all over the globe.

The chief object of linkage, of course, was the Soviet Union, and Kissinger's ambivalent attitude toward America's chief antagonist reveals many of the hesitations common to all the realists. On one hand, there is an

---

34. *Ibid.*, 914, 39, 350.
35. Kissinger, *Years of Upheaval*, 501, 1017, 70.
36. Kissinger, *White House Years*, 129.

almost wistful appreciation of the Soviets' domestic advantages: "The Soviet leadership is burdened by no self-doubt or liberal guilt. It has no effective domestic opposition questioning the morality of its actions. The result is a foreign policy free to fill every vacuum, to exploit every opportunity, to act out the implications of its doctrine. Policy is constrained principally by calculations of objective conditions."[37] The passage seems to exude envy: no Congress, no liberals, no bother about morality. On the other hand, Kissinger stresses the importance of the "durable impulses of nationalism and ideology that lie behind Soviet policy." He regards the continuing debate about Soviet intentions as beside the point: their policy is "essentially one of ruthless opportunism." "To foreclose Soviet opportunities," Kissinger concludes, "is thus the essence of the West's responsibilities. It is up to us to define the limits of Soviet aims."[38]

To fulfill our responsibilities, "we would pursue a carrot and stick approach, ready to impose penalties for adventurism, willing to expand relations in the context of responsible behavior." This would be a continuing task—remember the "fallacy that there is some terminal point to international tension"—but the Soviets "can adjust to steady firmness." Over time, the "latent weaknesses" of the Soviet system—political instability, an inefficient economic system, suppressed nationalities—will make themselves felt. "Coexistence on the basis of a balance of forces should therefore be within our grasp—provided the nature of the challenge is understood," that is, that we understand that even a tamer Soviet Union will still need careful watching.[39]

Despite his claim to originality, Kissinger's description sounds uncannily similar to Kennan's original statement of containment: "the adroit and vigilant application of counter-force at a series of constantly shifting geographical and political points, corresponding to the shifts and maneuvers of Soviet policy." Kissinger's plan to moderate Soviet behavior ultimately seems indistinguishable from Kennan's hope for the "break-up or gradual mellowing of Soviet power" except in its operational details: geopolitical equilibrium turns out to be an attempt at containment *redux*. In practice, the notion of a new concert based on detente with the Soviet Union and a triangular geopolitical equilibrium managed by linkage and creative diplomacy proved extraordinarily difficult.

37. *Ibid.*, 117.
38. *Ibid.*, 118–19.
39. *Ibid.*, 120.

Kissinger himself provides some of the evidence of the problems with linkage. First, the Soviets proved harder to train than he had imagined. Their negotiating style, Kissinger writes concerning Andrei Gromyko, was to begin "*tabula rasa*; it started as if it had no history, and it established no claim or obligation for the future." This is a long way from the shared values of the eighteenth-century "scientists of power" Kissinger admired in the statesmen of the Congress of Vienna. A more significant failure of linkage is Kissinger's tacit admission that the Soviets, for most of his first term, were either unable or unwilling to help him negotiate an end to the Vietnam War. He exults at the failure of the Soviets to cancel the May, 1972, summit in the wake of our mining of Haiphong harbor but is curiously silent about its implications for linkage. For the fact is that the summit could succeed precisely because we did *not* insist on linking progress in Vietnam to the SALT treaty and to a general detente—as Kissinger had said we would. The Soviets merely ignored—at no cost to themselves—our new moves against Hanoi.[40]

Kissinger later acknowledges specific failures of linkage with the Soviets, but he blames them on Watergate and on the obtuseness of his domestic critics, who turned "our policy toward the Soviets . . . into a caricature of itself."[41] But apart from these domestic considerations (to be discussed presently), Kissinger's scheme was unsuited to a complex world of economic interdependency, ideological conflict, and revolutionary instability throughout the Third World. As several scholars and critics have pointed out, his neoclassical vision of achieving a working agreement, a "principle of legitimacy," among the great powers vastly overestimated the ability of these powers to impose their vision of order on the world—even assuming that they could reach such an agreement, which they clearly failed to do, Kissinger's virtuoso diplomacy notwithstanding.[42]

Moreover, as Hans Morgenthau pointed out in one of his last essays, policy under Kissinger was directed toward maintaining a fundamentally "unviable status quo" in the "outlying political areas throughout the world." Morgenthau argued that the roots of instability in the developing

40. *Ibid.*, 701, 1188–97.
41. Kissinger, *Years of Upheaval*, 241, 300–301.
42. See especially Hoffmann, *Primacy or World Order*, and his reviews of Kissinger's memoirs: *New York Review of Books*, XXVI (December 6, 1979) and XXIX (April 29, 1982); Roger Morris, *Uncertain Greatness: Henry Kissinger and American Foreign Policy* (New York, 1977); Seyom Brown, *The Crises of Power: An Interpretation of U.S. Foreign Policy During the Kissinger Years* (New York, 1978); and George Ball, *Diplomacy for a Crowded World* (Boston, 1976).

world lay not in "Communist subversion" but in "profound popular dissatisfaction with the social, economic and political status quo": "Since the causes and effects of instability persist, a policy committed to stability and identifying instability with communism is compelled by the logic of its interpretation of reality to suppress in the name of anti-communism all manifestations of popular discontent and stifle the aspirations of reform. Thus in an essentially unstable world, tyranny becomes the last resort of a policy committed to stability in the last resort." Kissinger's support of the Shah of Iran, his reaction to the election of Allende, and his wish to send troops to Angola would all seem to confirm Morgenthau's judgment. Kissinger, he concluded, "put his extraordinary gifts at the service of lost causes. His failures . . . derived from [his] overall perception of the world as it exists and his conception of the world to be created by foreign policy."[43] Given the extent to which that conception encapsulated the tenets of realism, Morgenthau's verdict is especially ironic: a realist condemns a self-conscious attempt to apply the ideas of realism.

If Kissinger's vision of geopolitical equilibrium was unsuitable internationally it had even greater difficulties gaining understanding and acceptance within the United States. We have seen that virtually all the American realists have denigrated the American capacity to define and execute a subtle foreign policy; indeed, this incapacity provided the impetus for their continuing efforts to educate the American public. We have seen too that from Weber on, realists have treated domestic politics as either an enabling or, more often, an inhibiting factor in the pursuit of international advantage. Sharing these views, yet theoretically aware of the consequences of inadequate domestic support, Kissinger nevertheless designed a foreign policy that made extraordinary demands on the domestic polity. Manipulating rewards and punishments in Bismarckian fashion against an inscrutable foe when one is not operating in Bismarck's autocratic political system may exceed the ability of even the most creative statesman. Grain sales cannot be promoted and canceled at the stroke of a diplomat's pen, as Kissinger learned to his chagrin in his dealings with Secretary of Agriculture Earl Butz, "who had no intention of facing the wrath of the farmers."[44] Trade develops its own momentum, fueled by "the passionate view of many businessmen that profits should not be sacrificed to

43. Hans J. Morgenthau, "Three Paradoxes," *New Republic*, CLXVIII (October 11, 1975), 17.
44. Kissinger, *Years of Upheaval*, 248.

politics."[45] In addition to the "nightmarish" interest-group politics that dogged Kissinger's fine tuning of detente—"each issue seemed to produce its own constituency with no obvious logical relationship to any other"—he and Nixon never managed to establish a relationship even approaching trust with Congress or with the foreign policy elites.[46] As Stanley Hoffmann has concluded, Kissinger's "strategy requires total control by the Executive; when idealists or suspicious cold warriors insist on having their say, the delicate mix of policy instruments risks being destroyed."[47]

Thus if "the acid test of policy is its ability to gain domestic support"[48]—Kissinger's own maxim—his policy manifestly failed. Yet throughout his memoirs he shows no understanding of why this might be so or of the difficulties his design presented. One could hardly expect him to admit abject failure in building a domestic base for the "stable structure of peace," but some thoughtful reflection on what went wrong would clearly have been helpful. Instead Kissinger tries in retrospect to win all the arguments he failed to carry while in office. Critics are assailed for "overweening self-righteousness" and their "headlong retreat from responsibility"; liberal dissenters in particular have their arguments summarized virtually in caricature.[49] Like other realists fighting other foes, Kissinger blames American illusions, and by the end of his tenure in office he was reduced to repeating the lectures of the original realists in a gaggle of speeches across the nation. He preached new sermons on old realist texts, but without much success.[50] The reason Kissinger offered for the unraveling of his design was "the domestic passion play" of Watergate—the *diabolus ex machina* that ultimately seems to account for every failure. "A normal Nixon Presidency," he writes in *Years of Upheaval*, "would have managed to attain symmetry between the twin pillars of containment and coexistence."[51]

Kissinger's attitude to the Watergate scandals and to the Vietnam War

45. Kissinger, *White House Years*, 901.
46. Kissinger, *Years of Upheaval*, 1006.
47. Stanley Hoffmann, "The Return of Henry Kissinger," *New York Review of Books*, XXIX (April 29, 1982), 20.
48. Kissinger, *World Restored*, 326.
49. Kissinger, *White House Years*, 515, 153; for examples of Kissinger's distorted summaries of "liberal arguments" (he never cites anyone specific) see *Years of Upheaval*, 240–42, and his treatment of William Shawcross, 346.
50. For a representative sampling of these speeches, see Kissinger, *American Foreign Policy*, 3d ed., chaps. 8, 9, 11, 12, and 14.
51. Kissinger, *Years of Upheaval*, 245 ("passion play"); 300.

seems to me to demonstrate the deep flaws of his personal version of Weber's ethic of responsibility. Throughout his long account of Nixon's second term and "the gathering impact of Watergate" Kissinger shows no real understanding of the depth of its assault on the American constitutional system. Instead he suggests that "somebody had implemented Presidential musings that could only be regarded as juvenile" and thus had childishly "set at risk both our social cohesion and our ability to fulfill our international responsibilities." For himself, he "could not imagine a President as politically experienced as Nixon would permit the White House to be involved in so pointless an exercise." By his own account, Kissinger did little over the eighteen months of the developing crisis to supplement this original surmise; domestic politics were strictly insulated from foreign policy in the Nixon White House, and he did not go out of his way to inform himself. In short, on the issue of the morality of Nixon's behavior—and of his own complicity in it—Kissinger is strikingly and uncharacteristically reticent. His remarks at Nixon's final cabinet meeting (spoken, he now writes, to "preserve Nixon's dignity") reveal his real concern: "We must demonstrate that the country can go through its constitutional processes [impeachment and trial]. For the sake of foreign policy we must act with assurance and total dignity. If we can do that, we can vindicate the structure of peace."[52]

What worried Kissinger about Watergate was its effect on the foreign policy he was trying to pursue. He was so certain of the creativity of that policy, of its definition of the American national interest, and of its incomparably greater importance to the future of the country than any silly break-in and cover-up that he treated Watergate as an ever-escalating impediment to his vision of stability, not as an issue in its own right calling for a stand. The real locus of political ethics for Kissinger, as for Weber, was in international relations; the ethic of responsibility applied in that milieu, and the vital issues there overrode domestic concerns and excused excesses. (See his weak account of wiretapping his aides.[53]) "My predominant concern during Watergate," he writes, "was to sustain the credibility of the United States as a great power."[54] One cannot help questioning whether a fundamental conception of morality less dependent on an "inward recognition of limits" and less confident of one's own ability to

52. *Ibid.*, 76, 1204.
53. *Ibid.*, 115–22.
54. Kissinger, *White House Years*, 1386.

transcend those limits by an exercise of personal creativity would have yielded conclusions so concerned to retain power. Kissinger's interpretation of Weber's description of the statesman's duty to draw a line and say, "here I stand, I can do no other," was always to stay and pursue the "stable structure of peace." My point is not to condemn Kissinger's decision but to ask whether he recognized it as an ethical choice at all: if foreign policy always subsumes domestic politics in its higher aims, many hard dilemmas are decided in advance.

Finally, there is Kissinger's handling of the Vietnam War. It was a war he inherited, and a war Nixon had pledged to end. Kissinger and Nixon might have drawn a lesson from the domestic turmoil of the Johnson years, which shattered the containment consensus, to concoct a face-saving scheme for early American withdrawal. In healing divisions at home, the new and complex goals connected with detente and "geopolitical equilibrium" would have had far better prospects of acceptance. (Kissinger himself later recognized the cost of Vietnam to his other aims. In his final showdown with South Vietnamese President Nguyen Van Thieu, he told him that "for four years we have mortgaged our entire foreign policy to the defense of one country.") It would have been entirely consistent with a realistic, geopolitical view of the world to conclude that American interests were not being served by fighting, and losing, a prolonged war in a peripheral area for limited ends against an enemy whose stake was unlimited. As described above, this was Morgenthau's position from the beginning, and Kennan and Niebuhr joined him in this view. The costs of the intervention—in lives, in national unity, indeed in achieving "victory," assuming we could even define it—far outweighed in their view any possible gains. And given the level of domestic dissent, a continuation of the war seemed to them pointless and, as Niebuhr put it in 1969, "immoral."[55]

Instead, Kissinger embraced the primary and most misleading rationale for the war—that we were fighting to demonstrate the credibility of our resolve and commitments throughout the world—and made it his own. From this basic conviction that "humiliation" in Vietnam would have been "profoundly immoral and destructive of our efforts to build a new and ultimately more peaceful pattern of international relations" all else followed.[56] Although he recognizes that "the process of honorable withdrawal was inevitably confusing to a public that was still being asked to

---

55. *Ibid.*; Niebuhr, "Toward New Intra-Christian Endeavors," 1663.
56. Kissinger, *White House Years*, 228.

sacrifice in the name of an abstract, unprovable goal of America's global credibility," Kissinger never confronts the fundamental issue of how prolonging a bitter war served even that goal.[57] Again, he is so inwardly confident in the morality of his approach that he is blind to the arguments of his critics, even when those critics shared—indeed, taught him—his basic approach.

Kissinger reveals in *White House Years* that he opposed Vietnamization because it undermined our ability to "retain flexibility" with Hanoi. Throughout his long account of the decisions surrounding the policy toward and the negotiations with the North Vietnamese, he repeatedly complains that the inexorable troop withdrawals were depriving him of the leverage he needed to make Hanoi "sue for a respite, if not for peace."[58] For all its purported subtlety and nuance, Kissinger's policy was essentially identical to the unsubtle strategy of "pressure-attrition-ouch." If the United States kept up the pressure in a variety of (mainly military) ways, Hanoi would finally give in and negotiate an "honorable" peace with us.

The trouble with this strategy, as Kissinger uncomfortably recognized, is that if it did not work when America had more than 500,000 men in South Vietnam, it was unlikely to work when, for domestic reasons, it was pulling out troops 50,000 at a time. Thus were born the bombings of Cambodia and the later invasions of Cambodia and Laos: they were designed to demonstrate to Hanoi that the United States could and would keep up the pressure, that it could still respond to the communists' military moves. And thus was born the paradox of widening the war ostensibly to end it.

One does not have to enter the controversy over William Shawcross' account in *Sideshow* to recognize the moral and political insensitivity of this policy. Kissinger's own description of the decision to undertake the secret bombing of Cambodia in 1969 is damning enough. The administration, still "savoring the honeymoon that follows the Inauguration of any president," as early as January 25 was seeking means to retaliate against the North in the event of an anticipated offensive. Renewed bombing of the North was ruled out: "None of us had any stomach for the domestic outbursts we knew renewed bombing would provoke."[59] Military moves

57. Kissinger, *Years of Upheaval*, 84.
58. Kissinger, *White House Years*, 284–88, 311.
59. *Ibid.*, 239; William Shawcross, *Sideshow: Kissinger, Nixon and the Destruction of Cambodia* (New York, 1979).

in the South were also impossible. Military leaders suggested bombing North Vietnamese and Viet Cong "sanctuaries" within Cambodia. The secret raids were ordered in March. Even granting the military usefulness of such air strikes, it is important to remember that the impetus behind them was to "signal" Hanoi that we could still keep up the military pressure. The bombing was kept secret in a process Kissinger calls "double-bookkeeping," ostensibly to obviate the need for the Cambodian leader Norodom Sihanouk to protest, but really, as Nixon straightforwardly admits, "to provoke as little public outcry as possible."[60] The story of the 1970 invasions is essentially the same. Negotiations were going nowhere, and Hanoi launched an offensive; to drive the communists to negotiate on our terms we needed to respond with unambiguous force.

Arguments about the military value of these assaults are beside the point. Their purpose was to send Hanoi a message: "Come to reasonable terms or else." Kissinger is emphatic on this point: the escalations were necessary if we were to obtain what he called an honorable peace. At every impasse he was cold-bloodedly prepared to use greater force to extract concessions from Hanoi. The December, 1972, bombings were the most extreme and gratuitous example of this willingness. Yet at the same time Kissinger rises in indignation because the North Vietnamese considered themselves in a life-and-death struggle; they "did not treat negotiations as an enterprise separate from the struggle; they were a form of it." Hanoi was "interested in victory, not a cease-fire, and in political control, not a role in free elections."[61] Obviously, from the American point of view Hanoi's attitude was unfortunate; what is astonishing is that a self-proclaimed realist like Kissinger should find it unexpected and reprehensible. For in trying to win, Hanoi was simply applying Kissinger's own maxims—but against him.

The most striking aspect of Kissinger's treatment of the Vietnam War in all its facets is the apparent depth of his conviction that he was right and all of the critics from every direction were wrong—wrong in their tactical

60. Richard Nixon, *RN: Memoirs* (New York, 1978), 242. "Double-bookkeeping" in Kissinger's letter to *The Economist*, September 6, 1973, p. 7.

On Cambodia, see also Shawcross, "Through History with Henry Kissinger," *Harper's*, CCLXI (November, 1980), 35–44, 89–97; William Beecher, "A Scrutiny of Kissinger on Bombing of Cambodia," Boston *Globe*, October 22, 1979, p. 2; Wolfgang Saxon, "Kissinger Revised His Book More Than He Reported," New York *Times*, October 31, 1979, p. 14; Neal Ascherson, "Deaths That Haunt Dr Kissinger," London *Observer*, November 18, 1979, pp. 11–12; Bruce Page, "The Pornography of Power," *New Statesman*, November 23, 1979, pp. 808–11. Also see the Appendix to *Years of Upheaval*, 1215–30.

61. Kissinger, *White House Years*, 260–67.

sense ("Cambodia was not a moral issue . . . what we faced was an essentially tactical choice"[62]), wrong in their reading of his motives, wrong in their calculations of the consequences of American withdrawal. Kissinger's certainty raises an important problem for the Weberian distinction between an ethic of conviction or intention and an ethic of responsibility or consequence. All of the realists, Kissinger included, accept this dichotomy and urge the virtues of an ethic of responsibility. Yet beyond providing a well-taken critique of moral crusades and a series of synonyms for "responsibility" ("prudence," "modesty," a "rational concept of national interest"), none of them have succeeded in giving concrete content to this ethic. Rather, they repeat that the quality of the statesman's sense of responsibility is the relevant criterion; his judgment of consequences and his willingness to accept responsibility are regarded as the crucial issues. In Kissinger's account of Vietnam, and indeed of all his foreign policy, his confidence in his ability to judge consequences is so great that the ethic of consequences in effect merges with the ethic of intentions. To say, "trust my calculation of consequences—my sense of responsibility is beyond question" differs very little from saying, "trust me—my intentions are good." Kissinger's conception of personal leadership and his attempt to vindicate that leadership with a historical account of extraordinary breadth and ambition in my view amount to precisely this equation of intention and consequence. And his untiring efforts to place the blame for the failures of his policy anywhere but on himself do not speak well of his adherence to the Weberian notion of personal acceptance of responsibility.

Thus in the "paradoxical brilliance" of Henry Kissinger, the idea of realism finds ironic fulfillment.[63] His reliance on great power diplomacy and a conservative concept of international legitimacy proved too simple for a complex world yet too complicated and elitist for the domestic polity on whose behalf it was advanced. His assumption of the primacy of foreign relations ran aground when domestic politics asserted an overwhelming predominance over even the most pressing international issues. And the realist insistence on an ethic of responsibility ended in Kissinger as an ethic of personal vision essentially unknowable to anyone but the statesman himself.

The final and perhaps most ironic aspect of Kissinger's tenure has been

62. *Ibid.*, 515.
63. Hans Morgenthau's phrase, in "Three Paradoxes," 17.

the course of American foreign policy since he left office. Far from building a "new world equilibrium" and setting American foreign policy on a more stable, realistic course, the policy hardly endured to the end of his tenure. Gerald Ford banned the mere mention of the word "detente" during the 1976 presidential campaign, and Jimmy Carter was elected president on a platform of replacing Kissingerian geopolitics with the promotion of human rights. Four years of well-meaning pursuit of "world order" have in turn given way to a nostalgic reassertion of American nationalism which has indicted not only Carter but also Kissinger as too "soft" on the Soviets, too easily deceived by the pursuit of detente, too reluctant to assert and use American military power. E. H. Carr's conclusion that "the constant interaction of irreconcilable forces is the stuff of politics" may be right after all.[64] The search for the "rational core of the national interest" remains as elusive as ever.

64. Carr, *Twenty Years' Crisis*, 94.

9

Theory, Policy, and Ethics: The Realist Contribution Assessed

In contrast to what they considered the utopian illusions of liberal internationalists and naive moralists, the realists considered here sought to define an alternative approach to international relations that reflected a truer understanding of people and states. If Leopold von Ranke wanted to write history "as it really was," the realists wanted to explain the behavior of nations "as they really act." They reached back to Thucydides, Augustine, or Hobbes to uncover what Hans Morgenthau called the "perennial forces" governing the relations of states, and as we have seen, their explanation had three distinct aspects. Realists tried to develop a general theory of the essence of politics among nations; they applied the insights of their general approach to advocate or oppose specific policies in contemporary international politics; finally, by urging an ethic of responsibility and prudence, the realists sought to provide a general answer to the recurrent and perhaps ultimately insoluble moral dilemmas of statecraft. With the detailed examination of the views of individual realists on all these issues now complete, my goal in this concluding chapter is to assess their entire approach. In the interest of brevity, I shall not attempt to recapitulate all the arguments of the figures treated in the preceding chapters. Rather, I shall highlight those facets of their thought most relevant to a general evaluation of their overall analysis, proceeding in turn through the aspects of theory, advocacy, and morality.

Theory: Dogma or Framework?

Academic preoccupations being what they are, perhaps no aspect of realism has attracted more attention than its claim to provide a general theory of international relations. Part of the difficulty, of course, is that scholars fundamentally disagree about what would define an "adequate" theory of international relations; perhaps, as Robert Gilpin has recently suggested, the discipline, no less than its object of study, is in a state of anarchy. Must an adequate theory generate testable hypotheses, with its propositions rigorously, even deductively, related, so that prediction, at least under controlled circumstances, becomes possible? Or is it enough for a theory to define key questions and concepts, to seek to identify patterns in the behavior of states in history, to try to understand how and why states act as they do, with an awareness that "the more we understand the clearer we should be about the limits and uncertainties of prediction?"[1] These are fundamental issues at the heart of the discipline which obviously cannot be treated in any depth; what must occupy us here is an assessment of the realist contribution to this debate. There are four key components to the realist approach, which are worth considering in turn.

First are the assumptions about the character of human nature. Realists assume an ineradicable tendency to evil, a universal *animus dominandi* among all men and women. The specific views of each of the realists have been developed sufficiently to obviate repetition here; but it should be mentioned that even E. H. Carr, who seemed not to share a Niebuhrian concept of original sin, nevertheless posited a search for power and security as a fundamental human motivation. And Morgenthau, the most self-consciously theoretical of all the early realists, in an essay called "International Relations as an Academic Discipline," asserted that "the element of universality, transcending any particular area and common to all, may be called human nature. However different in its specific manifestations at different times and places, it is the same everywhere and at all times."[2] This treatment of human nature, reaching back to Thucydides, informs every facet of realist analysis.

Second, realists assume that the important unit of social life is the collectivity and that in international politics the only really important collective actor is the state, which recognizes no authority above it. States exist in an "anarchical society" (to adopt Hedley Bull's felicitous term) and generally succeed in placing their interest as states above all other claims, whether individual, collective, or cosmopolitan. In the literature this is usually called the "state-centric assumption" and is taken to be a hallmark of realism. Together with the first, this second assumption has important

---

1. Robert Gilpin, "The Richness of the Tradition of Political Realism," *International Organization*, XXXVIII (Spring, 1984), 287; Hoffmann, *State of War*, 16n.
2. Morgenthau, *Decline of Democratic Politics*, 121.

consequences for the realists' treatment of change. If there is to be a fundamental change in the character of world politics—something both Morgenthau and Kennan in their later writings felt to be imperative for survival—"this transformation," as Morgenthau put it in *Politics Among Nations*, "can only be achieved through the workmanlike manipulation of the perennial forces that have shaped the past as they will shape the future. The realist cannot be persuaded that we can bring about that transformation by confronting a political reality that has its own laws with an abstract ideal that refuses to take those laws into account." Or as Kennan has put it more recently in *The Nuclear Delusion*:

> No one could be more aware than I am of the difficulty of ruling out war among the great states. It is not possible to write any sure prescription as to how this might be achieved, particularly because the course of international life is not, and cannot be, determined over the long term by specific treaties or charters agreed upon at a single moment in history and reflecting only the outlooks and circumstances of that particular moment. It is the ingrained habits and assumptions of men, and above all of men in government, which alone can guarantee any enduring state of peaceful relations among nations.

Thus change, though necessary to ensure peace, can occur only through the inspired manipulation of "the ingrained habits and assumptions of men."[3]

For their third assumption, realists hold power and its pursuit by individuals and states to be ubiquitous and inescapable. From Weber to Kissinger, conflicts of power constitute the essence of international politics. Hobbes's conception of the state of nature as a state of war is adopted without his distinction between individuals and nations. In an anarchic milieu, states are engaged in an unending quest for power. Sometimes, as I shall argue shortly, realists go further and write as if power were fungible, treating it as the currency of international politics, convertible for a great variety of uses. The conflicts among states vary in intensity according to the scope of national ambitions, the stability of a central balance of power, and the skill of great power diplomats; but from these conflicts there can be no escape. This theoretical assumption becomes almost imperceptibly normative when realists argue that a skilled and sophisticated diplomacy on behalf of states that calculate their interests rationally and without moral sentimentality can do much to promote and preserve such a stable central balance.

It follows from this third assumption that the important subjects for

3. Morgenthau, *Politics Among Nations*, 6th ed., 12; Kennan, *Nuclear Delusion*, xxix.

theoretical consideration are the permanent components of power, the historically proven methods for its control, and the evolving instruments of its manipulation. International institutions, networks, or norms are considered significant theoretically only to the extent that they structure or affect the competition for power, for the prevailing relations of power between sovereign nation-states ultimately determine the character of these institutions and norms. And realists from Max Weber on treat domestic politics as another factor among many that combine to equip a nation more or less stoutly for the struggle with other states.

Fourth, realists assume that the real issues of international politics can be understood by the rational analysis of competing interests defined in terms of power. As we saw in Chapter 6, Morgenthau reduces all foreign policies essentially to two ideal types—to maintain or to increase power; for him, one of the major tasks of theoretical analysis is to unmask the outward forms that this quest for power takes. As Keohane and others have pointed out, states are assumed to be unitary rational actors who are more or less skilled at calculating the risks and advantages of different policies aimed at amassing power in a milieu of uncertainty. This theoretical assumption once again tends to bleed into normative exhortation, when states are urged to follow a policy of "national interest defined in terms of power" not only because such a policy will be more successful— if this were all, realists could justly be accused of being Machiavellian amoralists—but also because universalized policies of national interest, as long as they are rationally defined, lead to international moderation.[4]

The qualification "rationally defined" is key to the realist enterprise: realists believe that a "rational core" to the national interest can be uncovered by objective analysis. Obviously there is some ambiguity about whether this objective analysis is purely theoretical or normative; I have tried to show that the realists fail to resolve this ambiguity. Indeed, Morgenthau clearly had some hesitation about the possibility of "objective" theory: "There is a rational element in political action which makes politics susceptible to theoretical analysis, but there is also a contingent element in politics which obviates the possibility of theoretical understanding."[5] Nevertheless, each of the realists was confident in his ability to recommend (and obviously, in Kissinger's case, to pursue) particular poli-

---

4. For similar accounts of realist assumptions (I differ slightly from both) see Keohane, "Theory of World Politics," 508; and Gilpin, "Richness of Political Realism," 290, 299.

5. Morgenthau, "The Functions of a Theory of International Relations," in *Decline of Democratic Politics*, 69.

cies; much of that confidence came from their assurance that they understood the rational requirements of successful policy.

If these four main assumptions characterize the realists' approach to theory, how can one evaluate their contribution? Let me repeat that one's evaluation obviously depends on what one expects theory to accomplish. Many recent authors have adopted the notion of philosopher of science Imre Lakatos that a successful theory must generate "progressive research programs"; this idea has replaced an earlier vogue for an idea taken from another philosopher of science, Thomas Kuhn, and his concept of a governing "paradigm." My own view is that these borrowings from philosophers attempting to understand the history of natural science, especially physics, are highly problematic when applied to the social sciences in general and to international relations in particular. Keohane himself admits that "if we took literally the requirements that [Lakatos] laid down for 'progressive' research programs, all actual theories—and perhaps all conceivable theories—would fail the test." And Lakatos himself, in terms reminiscent of Morgenthau at his sharpest, was scathing about "scientifically" oriented social science: "One wonders whether the function of statistical techniques in the social sciences is not primarily to provide a machinery for producing phoney corroborations of 'scientific progress' where, in fact, there is nothing but an increase in pseudo-intellectual garbage." Keohane ends his discussion of standards by adopting a sensible criterion, whose definition hardly required invoking Lakatos: "How much insight does realism provide into contemporary world politics?"[6] It is this standard I propose to adopt.

Apart from the inconsistencies among the individual realists in fleshing out their assumptions, as a general theory of international relations whose point is simply to aid our understanding of contemporary events, realism has some widely recognized deficiencies. First, as I have argued particularly in relation to Carr and Morgenthau, the conception of power on which it relies is far too broad and undifferentiated. Power is treated as an end—both ultimate and intermediate—and as a means. If as an end, power is intermediate, realism contributes little to our understanding of how a nation defines its *ultimate* ends—particularly since nations are said in the final analysis to pursue a policy of national interest defined in terms of

6. Keohane, "Theory of World Politics," 505; Imre Lakatos, *The Methodology of Scientific Research Programmes*, ed. John Worrall and Gregory Currie (Cambridge, 1978), 88–89n.

power, even if they think they are doing something else. In Carr's case, this is because material interests basically determine even our moral ideas; for Morgenthau the national interest is akin to a physical conception of equilibrium to which even the most moralistic nation must eventually return. In neither version does one get any account of the political process of determining the goals of policy. Whether the international system structurally imposes goals on states, or states as actors define their goals, which in turn affect the system, is unclear; and scholarly successors to the original realists (for example, Kenneth Waltz or Raymond Aron) can be found on both sides of this question. Simply asserting that states inevitably seek power, either immediately or ultimately, provides no real solution.

When realists treat power as a means, they leave unanswered important questions about how and under what circumstances which kind of power can be used. Too often power is simply asserted to decide the outcome of a given struggle—at least when one reads the theoretical writings of Weber, Kissinger, Carr, or Morgenthau. In their more specific policy essays, they recognize, often with great subtlety, limitations on power. Morgenthau criticized the application of military power to Vietnam; Kennan wanted a political, not a military, containment; Carr saw that economic power and power over opinion were important factors that went beyond an assessment of the military balance. Thus, when they applied their general ideas to specific events, the realists employed a conception of power far more nuanced and differentiated than their theory taken at face value would suggest. Morgenthau's conception of the American national interest, for example, invariably reflected a keen and discriminating sense of when active intervention, political or military, would work and when it would not. Kennan's notion was perhaps even more subtle, if also seemingly more averse to any use of force. And as a diplomat, Henry Kissinger proved far more flexible and inventive than he was as a theoretician or ghostwriter of Nixon's bloated annual addresses on the "state of the world."

Thus in their rather too loose theoretical application of the concept of power, the realists have invited a series of correctives, some of which they in effect wrote themselves by paring down their broader assertions about power in their essays on specific policy. Their assumption about the basic structure of the international milieu, however, has "remained at the center of contemporary international relations theory in the United States." Though their conception of structure has been criticized as empty, static, or dogmatic, as Waltz points out, "structures appear to be static because they often endure for long periods. Even when structures do not change, they are dynamic, not static, in that they alter the behavior of actors and affect the outcome of their interactions."[7] Realists have long recognized the importance of structural factors—a central strength of their approach.

At the same time, the overwhelming emphasis on the importance of the anarchic international milieu has led realists to underplay or ignore, at least in their theoretical writings, the crucial interactions between domestic and international politics. Following Weber, realists tend to regard domestic politics and institutions merely as (somewhat irritating) variables that affect a state's ability to compete effectively in the international milieu. This view has resulted in sliding from putatively empirical assertion (for example, states must necessarily follow certain policies dictated by structure regardless of their regime or ideology) to normative exhortation, as in Weber's Inaugural Lecture or in Morgenthau's plea for the national interest, or in Kissinger's attitude toward Watergate. Much of the stuff of international relations lies in the complex mutual interaction between the international structure and the social, ideological, and political factors in a given state. Realists have perhaps unwittingly contributed to an unfortunate compartmentalization of domestic and international history and theory, leading to fruitless methodological arguments about which factors have "primacy," when we should be studying how they affect one another.

The obverse of the realist emphasis on the importance of the international state of nature is an insistence on the durability of the nation-state. To be sure, there is E. H. Carr's embarrassing 1945 prediction of its imminent demise and the perhaps less familiar delineation by Morgenthau of "the contrast between the technological unification of the world and the parochial moral commitments and political institutions of the age." The latter, he wrote in 1961, date from "an age which modern technology has left behind, have not kept pace with technological developments and, hence, are incapable of controlling their destructive potentialities."[8] But even if realists in their later writing regarded the nation-state as an obstacle to peace more and more to be deplored, empirically and theoretically they opposed a trend of thinking that has tried to remove a unitary concept of the nation-state from its traditional pride of place in the analysis of international relations.

7. Keohane, "Theory of World Politics," 511; Kenneth Waltz, *Theory of International Politics* (Reading, Mass., 1979), 69–70.
8. Morgenthau, "International Relations," in *Restoration of American Politics*, 174.

As a sympathetic interpreter of Niebuhr and Morgenthau has put it, "Transnationalism is a premature form of universalism because the prevailing forces of international politics are still moving along other pathways and patterns." Those pathways and patterns continue to be the power and prestige interests of nation-states. "The academicians' illusion," he continues, "rests in part on the belief that a few limited and segmental relations between specialized national groups across national boundaries is representative of political and social relations as a whole." This conclusion by Kenneth Thompson can, I think, be taken as a definitive statement of the realist attitude to "transnationalism" though its characterization of the phenomenon it criticizes may be open to question.[9]

The realists themselves could be accused of harboring the same "academicians' illusion" in their theoretically based confidence in the contribution a professional and cosmopolitan corps of diplomats makes to easing international tension. As shown above, George Kennan frankly stated his belief in the efficacy of professional diplomacy, and Hans Morgenthau devoted the closing chapters of *Politics Among Nations* to discussing how the ancient art of diplomacy could be continued. Kissinger's estimate of Metternich emphasized that "with his cosmopolitan education and rationalist philosophy, Austrian only by the accident of feudal relationships, [he] could be imagined equally easily as the minister of any other state."[10] Thus despite their general insistence on the primacy of issues of military security pursued by unitary nation-states, the realists depend on a transnational society of accomplished diplomats to produce the moderation they expect from a balance-of-power system.

Moreover, it cannot be denied that some basic changes in the agenda of international relations have occurred. "A new and unprecedented kind of issue has emerged. The problems of energy, resources, environment, population, the uses of space and the seas now rank with questions of military security, ideology and territorial rivalry which have traditionally made up the diplomatic agenda."[11] The author of this statement was no starry-eyed internationalist but Henry Kissinger, as secretary of state in 1975. To conclude that new factors have emerged is not to deny the con-

9. Kenneth W. Thompson, "Science, Morality, and Transnationalism," *Interpretation*, IX (September, 1981), 424, 422. The essay seems to conflate the approach to transnationalism of Robert O. Keohane and Joseph S. Nye in *Power and Interdependence: World Politics in Transition* (Boston, 1977) with the radically normative work of Richard Falk in *The Study of Future Worlds* (New York, 1975).

10. Kissinger, *World Restored*, 321.

11. Quoted in Keohane and Nye, *Power and Interdependence*, 26.

tinued salience of old ones; but it does question a theory which denies that anything important has changed.

Despite these faults, has realism in its theoretical guise nevertheless contributed to our understanding of world politics? Unquestionably; scholars operating more or less under the realist assumptions just outlined continue to produce work of interest to specialists and nonspecialists alike. Stanley Hoffmann has written that "if our discipline has any founding father, it is Hans Morgenthau"; he has even suggested that Morgenthau's shortcomings were fruitful: "He was both a goad and a foil. Indeed, the more one agreed with his approach, the more one was irritated by his flaws and eager to differentiate one's own product. A less arrogantly dogmatic scholar, a writer more modest both in his empirical scope and in his normative assertions, would never have had such an impact on scholarship." The judgment seems apt as long as one remembers that Morgenthau himself, especially in his policy writings, was capable of reining in his tendency to overgeneralize or to invoke the timeless "laws of political reality." It may be that realism is better conceived as a *Weltanschauung* than as a conventional theory or explanation: the very breadth of its vision helps to explain both its oversimplifications and its profound insights. Those insights have proven sufficiently fruitful and enduring to conclude that realism is neither a passing academic fad nor a fusty dogma of power; as Keohane concludes in his recent review of the field, realism "continues to provide the basis for valuable research in international relations."[12]

Advice to the Prince: Speaking Truth to Power

In its second manifestation, realism has persistently demonstrated a willingness to engage the controversial issues of contemporary foreign policy. Here, too, an assessment of the realist contribution is mixed but on balance positive, especially if one weighs in the admirable willingness of the senior figures of American realism to admit their past mistakes and reshade the emphases of their central arguments to account for changes both anticipated and unexpected. Looking at the record of Niebuhr, Morgenthau, and Kennan (and excluding for the moment Weber, Carr, and Kissinger) one cannot fail to be impressed by its consistency after their surprising

12. Hoffmann, "American Social Science," 45; Keohane, "Theory of World Politics," 520.

initial disagreements about early Cold War policy had been worked out.

But if one considers the six realists together—and as I have tried to establish, they share enough common assumptions to be so taken—one concludes unmistakably that realist arguments can be driven in very different directions. In Chapter 2 I noted the extent to which Max Weber's commitment to the advance of German culture and civilization colored his approach. His realism grew very largely out of his nationalism, and thus his advice to the prince (recall his encounter with Ludendorff) inevitably reflected his cultural values; realism, as such, was almost incidental to his view. Realism would not have dictated the sacrifice of Ludendorff to the Allies for the sake of German honor.

In the case of E. H. Carr, the combination of a Marxian sociology of knowledge and a preoccupation with power led him to justify the appeasement of Hitler's Germany on grounds of realism. By yielding to the new reality of power in central Europe in the context of a peaceful negotiation, Britain and France would implicate Germany in the new status quo and turn it into a satisfied power; power and morality, in the sense of recognizing inevitable change and accommodating it peacefully, would both be served. Obviously, Carr's realism failed to account for the "unrealistic" scope of Hitler's demonic ambitions. And in his treatment of postwar international relations, Carr allowed his distinctly personal, socialist values to affect his analysis of the new bipolar system in a way that, paradoxically, treated factors of ideology and social welfare as more important than power.

With Niebuhr, Morgenthau, and Kennan, both the strengths and weaknesses of realism as a guide to policy are cast in sharp relief. Despite their general agreement on the essence of international politics and on the need for the United States to place its foreign policy on a realistic foundation, they disagreed significantly in their precise definition of the American national interest in the early Cold War. From the mid-1950s on, their prescriptions might differ in detail but on such important issues as the Vietnam War they came down squarely together.

For Niebuhr, the best hope for relative international harmony after World War II lay in a solution based on the "instruments of rule," that is, a central principle of organization and a balance of power among the constituent units. The individual's dual nature as sinful creature and transcendent spirit makes it impossible to move beyond these instruments; but by using them, citizens can seek approximations of justice in their national groups. Niebuhr hoped that a genuine agreement among the great powers of America, Britain, and the Soviet Union would provide the central organizing principle, working in the context of an international body that could place "moral and constitutional checks" on their national pride. The balance of power among all the nations could be satisfied by maintaining comparably tolerable standards of political and economic health. A careful manipulation of these instruments would encourage the process of building a world community. Nations would begin to look beyond their own immediate interests and learn to temper their pride and will-to-power. Possessing a sober awareness of the corruption within them, men and women would reach for a higher approximation of justice on the international level.

Niebuhr's vision was spoiled by the excessive pride manifested in the imperialism of the Soviet Union and by the stubborn insistence of American liberals on the illusion of human perfectibility. For Niebuhr, these two factors were closely linked. American liberals, the potential "prophetic minority" within the United States, failed to appreciate the force of individual and especially national pride; hence they ignored the danger presented to any approximation of justice by the spread of Soviet communism. Niebuhr, who had come to abhor the "monstrous evil" of communism, set about both to restore their awareness of sin and to promote firm resistance to communist expansion. Since Russian will-to-power meant that the instruments of rule could not be applied internationally, Niebuhr urged their application in the noncommunist West. In this way, at least some justice could still be attained. Niebuhr therefore supported both halves of the containment walnut: he believed the policy was durable enough to stop the Russians and at the same time permit the pursuit of relative justice in the West. If Niebuhr's message in these early postwar years now seems unduly strident, it is because he was sharper and far more memorable in denouncing liberal illusions than he was in showing the way to justice.

Morgenthau and Kennan shared a vision of a moderate balance-of-power international system, but they looked at it through different eyes. An emigré from Nazi Germany, Morgenthau viewed international relations in stark, Weberian terms: "In the life of nations peace is only respite from trouble—or the permanent peace of extinction." Kennan, however, was a cosmopolitan (at times seemingly expatriate) diplomat: he believed that nasty conflicts could be finessed into tolerable political and ideological incompatibilities. This difference in perspective accounts for the considerable discrepancy in the policies prescribed by Morgenthau and Kennan up to 1952.

Morgenthau identified Russian imperialism as the real threat from the Soviet Union; communist ideology was merely an instrument of that imperialism. Since conventional military strength was the prime Russian advantage in Europe and the Soviets' acquisition of the atomic bomb erased Western invulnerability, Morgenthau urged that the United States and Western Europe (including West Germany) rearm "with frantic speed, determination and circumspection."[13] This rearmament was imperative not because war was necessarily likely or imminent—he argued that nuclear weapons made modern war irrational—but because equal military power was a prerequisite for a negotiated settlement. Only Western military strength could, in the context of negotiated spheres of influence, induce the Red Army to withdraw from central Europe and thus create the conditions for the genuine balance of power that Morgenthau sought. Morgenthau's goal of a healthy European balance required careful control over Germany, whether or not divided—he feared German revisionism—and constant attention to the balance of forces between America and the Soviet Union. If America faced these realities and learned at the same time to fight the "ideological battle for the minds of men" in Asia, a stable balance-of-power system could be restored and maintained; moderation would result from the manipulation of power. Such was Morgenthau's vision.

Kennan held a different view. He, too, sought a return to a balance-of-power system, but in his ideal world, power would be tamed by civilized diplomacy. For him the possession of power matters far less than the intent to use it. The task of diplomacy is to deflect any such intentions, and rigid military alliances make that task nearly impossible. Kennan therefore opposed massive rearmament, the division of Germany, and the conclusion of the North Atlantic Alliance because he thought it would harden the Russians' position and make withdrawal from central Europe impossible. Resolute political resistance, backed up by military strength, would have sufficed to contain the Soviet threat. Kennan based his prescription on an analysis of the motives of the Soviet leaders. They would press every political advantage, trading on the presence of their huge army, but they

13. Morgenthau, *In Defense of the National Interest*, 179.

would not attack. If America fully understood this, it would pursue policies that would both mute the conflict of inimical ideologies and allow the large armies to be withdrawn and reduced. Hence all of Kennan's prescriptions were designed to give diplomacy a chance; Morgenthau's, despite their apparent emphasis on negotiation, would have made it virtually *pro forma*—the comparative balance of power would have effectively decided the real questions already.

These differences among Niebuhr, Morgenthau, and Kennan demonstrate once again that realism by no means leads to the same conclusions about policy. Niebuhr supported the general direction of American policy following the Truman Doctrine; Morgenthau and Kennan opposed it for different reasons. Yet if the founding fathers of American realism could themselves reach such different conclusions from basically the same assumptions, then others—who did not necessarily share Niebuhr's concern for justice, or Kennan's distaste for power, or Morgenthau's sense of moderation—could invoke realism to justify a wide range of policies. Walter Lippmann's interpretation of Kennan's "X" article is instructive here: as employed by Kennan, containment did have an elastic meaning. So did Morgenthau's "national interest" and Niebuhr's admonition to "defend our far-flung lines." One need not blame the realists for the later, global application of containment—indeed, they opposed it—to recognize how easy it was to turn realism and the national interest into a shorthand justification for any policy, including wholesale military intervention.

Perhaps in their eagerness to expose the moralistic illusions of American policy and to awaken America to the danger of the Soviet threat, the realists taught their lessons too well: they ended up propounding a competing doctrine of their own, based on a somber view of human nature, the inescapability of power politics, and the objective standard of the national interest. They became, in Raymond Aron's phrase, "crusaders of realism."[14] Preoccupied with America's "sentimental illusions," they presented what amounted to a single-cause explanation of every American failure. The "red skein" of legalistic-moralism accounted for everything. It explained the hesitation over Poland, the concern for the United Nations, the refusal—and the decision—to rearm. Where Morgenthau saw a sentimental underestimation of Russian power, Kennan identified a universalist tendency to see everything in simple, military terms. Nearly every policy

14. Aron, *Peace and War*, 599.

Niebuhr opposed seemed in his account to rest on optimistic illusions about human nature or a general failure to understand the tragic dilemmas of existence. If a policy were bad, almost inevitably it stemmed from American innocence about the factors of power which corrupt all political life.

Tracing the essays that flowed from these remarkable figures throughout the postwar period, one senses some regret at their early fierceness. As noted in Chapter 5, Niebuhr tried to reclaim retrospectively many of the thunderbolts he had hurled against his intellectual opponents, and both Morgenthau and Kennan in their later essays write somewhat plaintively of their failure, in Morgenthau's words, "to influence political action." Kennan at one point even mentions experiencing a state of "intellectual brokenheartedness."[15] But, of course, influencing political action is hardly the only way to judge success, as intellectuals with the integrity of these three men surely knew. Their consistent position on two of the greatest issues of postwar American foreign policy—Vietnam and the nuclear arms race—went far toward demonstrating the virtues of realism as a foundation for criticism and dissent.

Morgenthau and Kennan were among the earliest opponents of the American intervention in Vietnam, and because of their identification with realism and power politics, they were among the most effective and irritating to the Johnson and Nixon administrations. Niebuhr, too, came to oppose the war by 1967, regarding it as another example of the "illusion of American omnipotence." Their opposition was telling precisely because they applied their customary standard of national interest to refute the arguments of those favoring the war, exposing the inconsistencies of administration spokesmen such as Dean Rusk with relentless logic. It was hard for proponents of the war to accuse Morgenthau or Kennan of innocence or naiveté. At the same time, the depth of the national division over our "national interest" in Vietnam illustrates vividly that this concept cannot provide a master key to the dilemmas of policy. The virtually unison critique of American policy in Vietnam advanced by Morgenthau, Kennan, and Niebuhr more than anything else reflected the consistency of their values and mode of analysis. For each of them, Vietnam was at best a peripheral interest for the United States, whose pursuit was grotesquely out of proportion to what should have been America's larger goals and

15. Morgenthau, *Truth and Power: Essays of a Decade, 1960-1970* (New York, 1970), 433; Kennan, *Memoirs*, II, 261.

whose cost domestically and internationally was enormous. As argued in the specific chapters, they reached this conclusion by integrating their moral vision with their political judgment—indeed, it is hard to see how they could be entirely separate.

Fundamentally the same argument can be made about their position on nuclear weapons. Analytically, both Kennan and Morgenthau discerned from the very beginning of the atomic age that nuclear weapons constituted a revolution in the relationship between war and politics. In effect, the overwhelming destructive capability of these weapons, and the difficulty of controlling violence once they were used, severed the link between war and politics summarized in the famous phrase by Karl von Clausewitz. No longer could war simply be the "continuation of policy by other means." While still in government Kennan argued that "we take care not to build up a reliance upon [atomic weapons] in our military planning." For Kennan, the bomb was a "sterile and hopeless weapon," or as he put it more recently, "the most useless weapon ever invented. It is not even an effective defense against itself. It is only something with which, in a moment of petulance or panic, you commit such fearful acts of destruction as no sane person would ever wish to have upon his conscience." Morgenthau has written in similar terms, deploring a "constant . . . urge to reconcile the irreconcilable and to find a way of waging nuclear war without incurring one's destruction." For him, nuclear weapons and the threat of destruction they entail demonstrated the obsolescence of the nation-state as a guarantor of security and gave new life to Kantian universalism.[16]

The consistency and conviction of these positions taken by Kennan and Morgenthau (here obviously only mentioned) reflect their similar moral vision as much as their pure "realism," for avowed realists (such as Paul Nitze or Ernest Lefever) have been found among those urging unstinting attention to the precise nuclear balance. Here again my point is simple: the consistency of the advice given by Morgenthau, Niebuhr, or Kennan results more from the compatibility of their values than from the tenets of an abstracted realism. Thus particular realists can, and with impressive frequency have, come to the same conclusions about specific questions of policy; but whether realism as an explanation of world politics necessarily yields such agreement is altogether more questionable. In my view, the enduring merit of the senior American realists on questions of policy lies in

16. Kennan, *Nuclear Delusion*, 4, 176–77; Morgenthau, *New Foreign Policy*, 215.

their rigorous application of external standards, political and moral, to the hardest dilemmas of policy. For reasons connected with the intellectual climate of their early careers, they chose to obscure the ethical component of their approach; but that component is both vital and unmistakable.

Henry Kissinger, too, brought both realism and personal values with him into office, but as I argued in Chapter 8, neither his particular version of realist ideas nor his Weberian conception of statecraft proved to be especially compelling. In addition to the problems of his idealized picture of a world dominated by great powers orchestrated by virtuoso American policy, and the terminal failure to build a domestic consensus behind the "stable structure of peace" already discussed, another point bears mentioning here. As his remark on the new agenda of world politics quoted just above suggests, in the last three years of his tenure in office Kissinger spent most of his energy not on pursuing his classically realist conception of a great power balance but on the issues of the new agenda. The economic challenges from the OPEC cartel and from our traditional European allies; the rising voices of Third World countries demanding a "new international economic order"; the new urgency of liberation movements in southern Africa; the problems of defining a new law of the sea; the fundamental danger to any international order represented by seemingly inexpiable conflict in the Middle East—of all these issues only the last bore any relation to the idealized picture of world politics which Kissinger brought to office. Realist assumptions were of little help in dealing constructively, say, with the Group of 77.

On issues like Vietnam, Chile, or military intervention in Angola, on which Kissinger could claim to act on realist premises, he found himself opposed not only by "moralists" but by the very realists who had helped to define the tradition. Both Morgenthau and Kennan criticized his handling of Vietnam, and in a concise sentence characteristic of his sharp insight, Kennan demurred from Kissinger's predictions of doom following the congressional ban on aid to "our" faction in Angola: "It is not everyone who can be made successful, even with the greatest effort of outside aid." Thus, although Kissinger was steeped in the tradition of American realism, and a significant contributor to its development, the task of applying its general tenets to specific dilemmas of policy proved in the end to be overwhelming. And to the extent that he did succeed, it was because he could change course, improvise, and adapt to new challenges with unusual facility. Even so, by the end of his term as secretary of state he was urging friends and associates to read *The Decline of the West* and warning his allied audiences that "we must not paralyze ourselves with illusions of impotence."[17] The stable structure of peace resting on the sound foundation of realistic geopolitics seemed in 1976 to be a very distant mirage.

Thus the truth realism spoke to power varied by spokesman, and the ultimately consistent message of Niebuhr, Morgenthau, and Kennan depended on the values integrated in their realist world-view. This conclusion hardly counts as an indictment; indeed, their prescience and integrity make it easy to commend their approach. But it cannot be said that realism itself leads necessarily to wise and moderate foreign policy, or even that those calling themselves realists will agree on the content and means of such policy.

Statecraft and Ethics, Responsibility and Power

How well has realism illuminated the ethical dilemmas of statecraft? The accomplishments are important: realists have cleared away the easy optimism of the interwar idealists and exposed the illusions of facile liberalism. They have reminded us that we live in a world of states that claim our highest loyalties and provide a context of order for our moral lives. From Weber on, realists have insisted on the inescapable responsibility of power and have urged statesmen and citizens to apply an ethic of responsibility to the moral judgment of state behavior. Yet despite these accomplishments, the general answers of the realists to the thorny problems of ethics and foreign policy have proven to be disappointing and inadequate. As promised, I shall not reproduce in summary all the arguments treated in the essay so far but will instead confine myself to a few general points.

First, although realists have consistently asserted that in determining foreign policy, considerations of morality should always give way to an "unsentimental" application of the national interest defined in terms of power, their own conception of morality pervades every aspect of their argument. In their assumptions about human nature and about the essence of domestic and international politics and in their estimate of how best to control the universal lust for power, the realists express a set of values which the rest of us may or may not share. As George Lichtheim has written, "To Mr. Morgenthau's rhetorical question 'Why is it that all men

17. George Kennan, "Containment of the Kremlin," Washington *Post*, February 16, 1976, p. 15; Kissinger, *American Foreign Policy* (3d ed.; New York, 1977), 387.

lust for power?' the answer is 'some don't.'"[18] Intent on reminding us of
the limits of morality, the realists have proven unhelpfully obscure in explaining what values inform their own judgments. They have instead argued unconvincingly that values do not enter in, that "good" policy is
simply a matter of following the national interest. But the national interest
is not an objective datum, an amoral law of interstate existence. Rather, it
is defined according to a particular hierarchy of values. Even the Athenians
had to *choose* to kill the Melians; and their choice, their definition of the
national interest, reflected a hard and murderous morality.

Thus although the realists have adopted Weber's ethic of responsibility,
they have failed to present any coherent and convincing criteria for judging
what is responsible. The issue, after all, is *how* to weigh consequences—
inescapably a matter of values. As I have argued throughout this book, the
realists themselves had personal criteria which they applied in making their
own judgments—or for Kissinger, in justifying his own actions. But their
insistence on the irrelevance of ethics to interstate relations (or in Morgenthau's case on the moral dignity of the national interest, a false solution
that begs the question of its definition) seemed to prevent them from
frankly acknowledging that their judgment of morality and their definition
of the national interest rested on their own hierarchy of values. The chapters above have tried to uncover these hierarchies and to demonstrate how
they informed the approach and recommendations of each writer. My
point here is to emphasize that this is a process of argument they deliberately avoided, in an effort to distinguish themselves sharply from the cheer-
fully optimistic moralists whom they criticized.

Kennan, for example, made his appeal to the national interest seemingly
unaware of the extent to which his conception of it rested on his own
admirably traditional values. Had he more explicitly articulated those
principles (which he does only reticently and retrospectively in his memoirs), had he explained how they could moderate the international conflict, had he outlined clearly his standards of prudential morality—had he
done any of these things instead of simply repeating a message of modesty
and national interest, his contribution to the discussions of ethics would
have proven far more permanent and valuable. As it was, he did not go
much beyond prescribing an idealized balance-of-power system. And because he never seemed to recognize the extent to which such a system

18. Lichtheim, "Politics of Conservative Realism," in *Concept of Ideology*, 261.

required at least a minimal code of internationally shared values, Kennan never considered whether, or how, the necessary consensus around those values could be built.

Similarly, as a theologian Niebuhr was aware that consistent realism leads to the cynicism that exempts political acts from all moral scrutiny. He did not share the confidence of Morgenthau and Kennan that a policy of national interest was a foolproof recipe for moderation. He was convinced that without an overarching conception implicating justice, a balance-of-power system would break down into war or international anarchy. Consequently, Niebuhr tried to build for the policy of containment a sound moral foundation, to define what an ethically responsible foreign policy would mean. But his foundation rested on a shaky moral distinction between nations, an oversimplified portrayal of the motives of the Soviet Union, and a premature celebration of America's achievement of relative justice. Niebuhr was right to insist that a lasting settlement had in some way to implicate justice, but his notion of justice and responsibility remained sermonic and obscure: it was not easy to know how America could, or should, avoid the "peril of moral and spiritual complacency." The result of Niebuhr's efforts was a questionable moral justification of American policy that made it easy for others to invoke his name on behalf of policies he himself came to deplore.

In urging states to pursue their national interests, realists assumed that international moderation would result. Morgenthau even claimed that for this reason, there is moral dignity in the national interest. Thus behind the Gothic facade of the universal struggle for power lurks a masked version of the harmony of interests. Apart from Weber—who rejected such "feeble eudaemonism" even in disguise—each of the realists came to this assumption in different ways: Carr by the notion that satisfied powers adopt "satisfied" ideologies; Morgenthau by a balance-of-power conception emphasizing external restraints; Kennan and Kissinger, in their very different ways, through an appreciation of eighteenth-century cosmopolitan diplomacy. The realist position on the moral issue in statecraft concludes therefore with a paradoxical assumption of moderation. And concerning moral judgment, it leads to an unhelpful dead end. Because realists do not explain the considerations involved in defining responsibility, either they doom us to the perpetual contemplation of the tragic antinomies of international conflict, or they offer an unconvincing sleight of hand by claiming moral dignity for the national interest.

Beyond this, ethical conduct in statecraft involves more than a lonely statesman, who, burdened by the responsibility of power, reluctantly orders actions in the name of the state he would reject as an individual. Issues of global distributive justice, treatment of refugees, human rights, support for oppressed peoples and minorities, how to act in cases of civil war or struggle for liberation—all these have an important ethical dimension. On all these issues, realists have little beyond their individual intuitions to offer; and their influential definition of the moral problem in statecraft may even have inhibited the informed consideration of these wider problems. By dismissing most moral arguments as irrelevant to students of international relations, the realists have unfairly relegated discussions of ethics to philosophers and moralists—of whom many have indeed proven to be naive—and the literature on the subject remains underdeveloped.

What would defining criteria for an ethic of responsibility entail? The question deserves a book of its own. But at the very least the problem demands an explicit recognition that dilemmas of ethical choice cannot be solved by relying on the inner qualities of statesmen; that just as there is no escape from power in international relations, there is no escape from moral decision; and that an appeal to national interest is no guarantee of moderation. A genuine ethic of responsibility would take account of the common interests of the society of states not simply by exhorting such interests into being à la Shotwell, but by nurturing and building on those norms that demonstrably do exist. Moreover, this ethic would emphasize that in their own long-term national interest states would have to pursue collective as well as national goals. States would need to encourage and participate constructively in schemes of joint management, regional cooperation, and functional organization. In short, a substantive ethic of responsibility would confront the whole range of normative issues facing the modern nation-state, and it would do so not by wishing the state out of existence but by nudging it toward the structural changes that would enlarge the scope for ethical behavior.

Those seeking to develop such an ethic should not shrink from the inevitable charges of utopianism and naiveté: as Friedrich Meinecke once wrote, "It is seldom that great ethical ideas in life arise which do not carry with them some admixture of illusion." As we live with the unprecedented possibility of global destruction, the "admixture of illusion" contained in Immanuel Kant's vision of perpetual peace may yet prove realistic. Or as Hans Morgenthau once put it: "In the long run, the voice of truth, so vulnerable to power, has proved more resilient than power. It has built empires of the mind and the spirit that have outlasted, and put their mark upon, the empires of power. . . . [Recent] experience has dispelled the illusion that truth can show power the way in direct confrontation. But historical experience reassures us that truth can indeed make people 'see a lot of things in a new light.' And when people see things in a new light, they might act in a new way."[19] Perhaps, then, we can hope that the conflicts of power analyzed in such depth by realists from Weber to Kissinger will yield eventually to the voice of a higher truth.

19. Meinecke, *Machiavellism*, 209; Morgenthau, *Truth and Power*, 9.

Bibliography

This list is organized by chapter with works by the individual realists arranged chronologically: books first, articles and collections second. Critical works on the specific authors follow this listing. More general works of theory and history are set out in turn after the sections on the individual chapters.

I. Works by Max Weber
(arranged alphabetically by editor)

Eldridge, J. E. T., ed. *Max Weber: The Interpretation of Social Reality.* New York: Scribner's, 1972.

Gerth, H. H., and C. Wright Mills, eds. *From Max Weber: Essays in Sociology.* London: Routledge & Kegan Paul, 1948.

Parsons, Talcott, ed. *The Protestant Ethic and the Spirit of Capitalism.* New York: Scribner's, 1958.

Roth, Guenther, and Claus Wittich, eds. *Economy and Society.* 2 vols. Berkeley and Los Angeles: University of California Press, 1978. Includes *Parliament and Democracy in a Reconstructed Germany.*

Runciman, W. G., ed. *Weber: Selections in Translation.* Cambridge: Cambridge University Press, 1978.

Shils, Edward A., and Henry A. Finch, eds. and trans. *The Methodology of the Social Sciences.* New York: Macmillan–Free Press, 1949.

Winckelmann, Johannes, ed. *Gesammelte Politische Schriften.* 2d ed. Tübingen: J. C. B. Mohr, 1958; 3d ed., 1971.

CRITICAL WORKS ON WEBER

Aron, Raymond. *German Sociology.* Translated by M. and T. Bottomore. New York: Free Press, 1964.

———. *Main Currents in Sociological Thought,* 2 vols. Harmondsworth: Penguin, 1967.

———. "Max Weber and Power Politics." In *Max Weber and Sociology Today,* edited by Otto Stammer. New York: Harper Torchbooks, 1971.

Beetham, David. *Max Weber and the Theory of Modern Politics.* London: George Allen & Unwin, 1974.

Bendix, Reinhard. *Max Weber: An Intellectual Portrait.* Garden City, N.Y.: Doubleday, 1960.

239

————, and Guenther Roth. *Scholarship and Partisanship: Essays on Max Weber.* Berkeley and Los Angeles: University of California Press, 1970.

Giddens, Anthony. *Politics and Sociology in the Thought of Max Weber.* London: Macmillan, 1972.

Hughes, H. Stuart. *Consciousness and Society: The Reorientation of European Thought 1890–1930.* Garden City, N.Y.: Doubleday, 1959.

Jaspers, Karl. *Three Essays: Leonardo, Descartes, Weber.* Translated by Ralph Manheim. New York: Harcourt, Brace and World, 1964.

Loewenstein, Karl. *Max Weber's Political Ideas in the Perspective of Our Time.* Translated by R. and C. Winsten. Boston: University of Massachusetts Press, 1966.

Mayer, J. P. *Max Weber and German Politics: A Study in Political Sociology.* 2d ed. London: Faber & Faber, 1946.

Mommsen, Wolfgang. *Max Weber und die Deutsche Politik, 1890–1920.* Tübingen: J. C. B. Mohr, 1959.

————. *The Age of Bureaucracy: Perspectives on the Political Sociology of Max Weber.* New York: Harper Torchbooks, 1974.

Roth, Guenther, and Wolfgang Schluchter. *Max Weber's Vision of History: Ethics and Methods.* Berkeley and Los Angeles: University of California Press, 1970.

Runciman, W. G. *Social Science and Political Theory.* Cambridge: Cambridge University Press, 1965.

————. *A Critique of Max Weber's Philosophy of Social Science.* Cambridge: Cambridge University Press, 1972.

Weber, Marianne. *Max Weber: A Biography.* Translated by Harry Zohn. New York: John Wiley, 1975. Original ed.: *Max Weber: Ein Lebensbild.* Tübingen, 1926.

Wrong, Dennis H., ed. *Makers of Modern Social Science: Max Weber.* Englewood Cliffs, N.J.: Prentice-Hall, 1970.

II. Works by the Idealists

Adler, Mortimer J. *How to Think About War and Peace.* Chicago: University of Chicago Press, 1944.

Becker, Carl L. *How New Will the Better World Be?* New York: Knopf, 1944.

Butler, Nicholas Murray. *The International Mind: An Argument for the Settlement of International Disputes.* New York: Scribner's, 1913.

————. *The Path to Peace: Essays and Addresses on Peace and Its Making.* New York: Scribner's, 1930.

————. *Between Two Worlds: Interpretations of the Age in Which We Live.* New York: Scribner's, 1934.

Davies, David. *The Problem of the Twentieth Century.* London: Benn, 1930.

Dickinson, G. Lowes. *The European Anarchy, 1904–1914.* London: Swarthmore Press, 1916.

————. *Causes of International War.* London: Swarthmore Press, 1920.

Duguit, Leon. *Law in the Modern State.* New York: B. W. Huebsch, 1919.

Murray, Gilbert. *The Ordeal of This Generation*. New York: Harper and Brothers, 1929.

Reves, Emery. *A Democratic Manifesto*. New York: Random House, 1944.

Shotwell, James T. *Intelligence and Politics*. New York: Harcourt Brace, 1921.

———. *War as an Instrument of National Policy*. New York: Harcourt Brace, 1929.

———. *On the Rim of the Abyss*. New York: Macmillan, 1936.

———. *The Great Decision*. New York: Macmillan, 1944.

Streit, Clarence. *Union Now*. New York: Harper, 1939.

Toynbee, Arnold J. *Survey of International Affairs*. Annual from 1920 to 1937. London: Oxford University Press for the Royal Institute of International Affairs.

Zimmern, Alfred E. *America and Europe and Other Essays*. New York: Oxford University Press, 1929.

———. *Neutrality and Collective Security*. Chicago: University of Chicago Press, 1936.

———. *The League of Nations and the Rule of Law, 1918-1935*. London: Macmillan, 1936.

(Critical works pertinent to this chapter are listed below in Section VIII.)

III. Works by E. H. Carr

Karl Marx: A Study of Fanaticism. London: Dent, 1934.

International Relations Since the Peace Treaties. London: Macmillan, 1937. Revised and enlarged edition: *International Relations Between the Two World Wars*. London: Macmillan, 1947.

Britain: A Study of Foreign Policy from the Versailles Treaty to the Outbreak of War. London: Longmans, Green, 1939.

The Twenty Years' Crisis, 1919-1939: An Introduction to the Study of International Relations. London: Macmillan, 1939; 2d ed., 1946.

Conditions of Peace. London: Macmillan, 1942.

Nationalism and After. London: Macmillan, 1945.

The Soviet Impact on the Western World. London: Macmillan, 1947.

What Is History? London: Macmillan, 1961.

ARTICLES AND COLLECTIONS

"British Foreign Policy." *Listener*, XXXVI (October 10, 17, 24, 31, 1946).

"The Moral Foundations for World Order." In Ernest Llewellyn Woodward *et al.*, *Foundations for World Order*. Denver: University of Denver Press, 1949.

Studies in Revolution. London: Macmillan, 1950.

From Napoleon to Stalin and Other Essays. London: Macmillan, 1981.

CRITICAL WORKS ON E. H. CARR

Abramsky, C. S., ed. *Essays in Honour of E. H. Carr*. London: Macmillan, 1970.

Bull, Hedley. *"The Twenty Years' Crisis* Thirty Years On." *International Journal* (Toronto), XXIV (Fall, 1969), 625-38.

Reviews of *Twenty Years' Crisis:*

Times Literary Supplement, No. 1971 (November 11, 1939), unsigned.
Spectator, CLXIII (November 24, 1939), by Alfred E. Zimmern.
New Statesman, XVIII (November 25, 1939), by Richard Coventry.
Saturday Review, XXVI (February 17, 1940), by Crane Brinton.

IV. Works by Reinhold Niebuhr

Unless otherwise specified, Reinhold Niebuhr's publisher is New York: Charles Scribner's Sons; date of publication follows the titles.

Leaves from the Notebook of a Tamed Cynic. Chicago: Willett, Clark and Colby, 1929.
Moral Man and Immoral Society: A Study in Ethics and Politics. 1932.
Reflections on the End of an Era. 1934.
An Interpretation of Christian Ethics. 1935.
Beyond Tragedy: Essays on the Christian Interpretation of History. 1937.
Christianity and Power Politics. 1940.
The Nature and Destiny of Man: A Christian Interpretation. Volume I: *Human Nature.* 1941; Volume II: *Human Destiny.* 1943. Reprint with new preface, 1964.
The Children of Light and the Children of Darkness: A Vindication of Democracy and a Critique of Its Traditional Defense. 1944. Reprint with new foreword, 1960.
Discerning the Signs of the Times: Sermons for Today and Tomorrow. 1946.
Faith and History: A Comparison of Christian and Modern Views of History. 1940.
The Irony of American History. 1952.
Christian Realism and Political Problems. 1953.
The Self and the Dramas of History. 1955.
The Structure of Nations and Empires: A Study of the Recurring Patterns and Problems of the Political Order in the Nuclear Age. 1958.
Reinhold Niebuhr on Politics. Edited under Niebuhr's guidance by Harry R. Davis and Robert C. Good. 1960.
A Nation So Conceived: Reflections on the History of America from Its Early Visions to Its Present Power. With Alan Heimert. 1963.
Man's Nature and His Communities. 1965.
The Democratic Experience: Past and Prospects. With Paul E. Sigmund. New York: Praeger, 1969.

SELECTED ARTICLES

"Will America Back Out? Our Stake in Europe's Future." *Nation,* CLX (January 13, 1945), 42–45.
"Russia and the Peace." *Social Progress,* XXXV (January, 1945), 8–9, 22–23.
"Is This 'Peace in Our Time'?" *Nation,* CLX (April 7, 1945), 382–84.
"A Lecture to Liberals." *Nation,* CLXI (November 10, 1945), 491–93.
"The Russian Adventure." *Nation,* CLXII (February 23, 1946), 232.

"The Myth of World Government." *Nation,* CLXII (March 16, 1946), 312–14.

"Europe, Russia and America." *Nation,* CLXIII (September 14, 1946), 288–89.

"Will Germany Go Communist?" *Nation,* CLXIII (October 5, 1946), 371–73.

"The Fight for Germany." *Life,* XXI (October 21, 1946), 65–72.

"American Scene." *Spectator,* CLXXVIII (February 14, 1947), 198.

"The Sickness of American Culture." *Nation,* CLXVI (March 6, 1948), 267–70.

"For Peace We Must Risk War." *Life,* XXV (September 20, 1948), 38–39.

"The Illusion of World Government." *Foreign Affairs,* XXVII (April, 1949), 379–88.

"Streaks of Dawn in the Night." *Christianity and Crisis,* IX (December 12, 1949), 162–64.

"The Theory and Practice of U.N.E.S.C.O." *International Organization,* IV (February, 1950), 3–11.

"The Conditions of Our Survival." *Virginia Quarterly Review,* XXVI (Autumn, 1950), 481–92.

"A Protest Against a Dilemma's Two Horns." *World Politics,* II (April, 1950), 338–44.

"American Conservatism and the World Crisis: A Study in Vacillation." *Yale Review,* XL (March, 1951), 385–99.

"Can We Organize the World?" *Christianity and Crisis,* XIII (February 2, 1953), 1–2.

"The Peril of Complacency in Our World." *Christianity and Crisis,* XIV (February 8, 1954), 1–2.

"British Experience and American Power." *Christianity and Crisis,* XVI (May 14, 1956), 55–57.

"Is This the Collapse of Tyranny?" *Christianity and Society,* XXI (Summer, 1956), 4–6.

"The Moral World of John Foster Dulles." *New Republic,* CXXXIX (December 1, 1958), 8–10.

"Toward New Intra-Christian Endeavors." *Christian Century,* LXXXVI (December 31, 1969), 1662–67.

CRITICAL WORKS ON REINHOLD NIEBUHR

Bennett, John C. "Niebuhr's Ethic: The Later Years." *Christianity and Crisis,* XLII (April 12, 1982), 91–95.

Bingham, June C. *Courage to Change: An Introduction to the Life and Thought of Reinhold Niebuhr.* New York: Scribner's, 1961.

Fox, Richard Wightman. *Reinhold Niebuhr: A Biography.* New York: Pantheon, 1985.

Harland, Gordon. *The Thought of Reinhold Niebuhr: An Introduction.* New York: Oxford University Press, 1960.

Kegley, Charles W., and Robert W. Bretall, eds. *Reinhold Niebuhr: His Religious, Social and Political Thought.* Vol. II of the Library of Living Theology. New York: Macmillan, 1956. 2d ed., edited by Charles W. Kegley. New York: Pilgrim Press, 1984.

Landon, Harold R., ed. *Reinhold Niebuhr: A Prophetic Voice in Our Time.*

Greenwich, Conn.: Seabury Press, 1962. Essays by Paul Tillich, John C. Bennett, and Hans J. Morgenthau.

Lefever, Ernest, ed. *The World Crisis and American Responsibility: Analyses by Reinhold Niebuhr.* New York: Association Press, 1958.

Merkley, Paul. *Reinhold Niebuhr: A Political Account.* Montreal: McGill-Queens University Press, 1975.

Schlesinger, Arthur, Jr. "Policy and National Interest." *Partisan Review,* XVIII (November–December 1951), 706–11.

Stone, Ronald H. *Reinhold Niebuhr: Prophet to Politicians.* Nashville: Abingdon Press, 1972. Reprint. Washington, D.C.: University Press of America, 1981.

Thompson, Kenneth W. "Beyond National Interest: A Critical Evaluation of Reinhold Niebuhr's Theory of International Politics." *Review of Politics,* XVII (April, 1955), 167–89.

V. Works by Hans J. Morgenthau

Scientific Man vs. Power Politics. Chicago: University of Chicago Press, 1946.

Politics Among Nations: The Struggle for Power and Peace. New York: Alfred A. Knopf, 1948. 2d ed., 1954; 3d ed., 1960; 4th ed., 1967; 5th ed., 1973; 6th ed., edited and revised by Kenneth W. Thompson, 1985.

In Defense of the National Interest: A Critical Examination of American Foreign Policy. New York: Knopf, 1951.

The Purpose of American Politics. New York: Knopf, 1960.

A New Foreign Policy for the United States. New York: Praeger, 1969.

COLLECTIONS AND SELECTED ARTICLES

"American Diplomacy: The Dangers of Righteousness." *New Republic,* CXXV (October 11, 1951), 17–20.

Dilemmas of Politics. Chicago: University of Chicago Press, 1958.

Politics in the Twentieth Century. 3 vols. Chicago: University of Chicago Press, 1962. Vol. I: *The Decline of Democratic Politics;* Vol. II: *The Impasse of American Foreign Policy;* Vol. III: *The Restoration of American Politics.*

Truth and Power: Essays of a Decade, 1960–1970. New York: Praeger, 1970.

"Three Paradoxes." *New Republic,* CLXXVIII (October 11, 1975), 16–21.

CRITICAL WORKS ON MORGENTHAU

(See also Section VIII below.)

Lichtheim, George. "The Politics of Conservative Realism." In *The Concept of Ideology and Other Essays.* New York: Vintage, 1967.

Newman, J. R. "The Balance of Power and the Voice of God." *New Republic,* CXXV (October 22, 1951), 18.

Taylor, A. J. P. "No Illusions: And No Ideas." *Nation,* CLXXIII (September 8, 1951), 196.

Thompson, Kenneth W., and Robert J. Myers. *Truth and Tragedy: A Tribute to Hans Morgenthau.* Washington, D.C.: New Republic Books, 1977.

Tucker, Robert W. "Professor Morgenthau's Theory of 'Realism.'" *American Political Science Review,* XLVI (March, 1952), 214–24.

VI. Works by George F. Kennan

American Diplomacy: 1900-1950. Chicago: University of Chicago Press, 1950. Expanded ed., 1984.

Realities of American Foreign Policy. Princeton: Princeton University Press, 1954.

Russia, the Atom and the West: The B.B.C. Reith Lectures, 1957. London: Oxford University Press, 1958.

Soviet Foreign Policy, 1917-1941. Princeton: D. Van Nostrand, 1960.

Russia and the West Under Lenin and Stalin. Boston: Atlantic-Little, Brown, 1961.

On Dealing with the Communist World. New York: Harper & Row for the Council on Foreign Relations, 1964.

Memoirs: 1925-1950. Boston: Atlantic-Little, Brown, 1967.

From Prague After Munich: Diplomatic Papers, 1938-1940. Princeton: Princeton University Press, 1968.

Democracy and the Student Left. Boston: Atlantic-Little, Brown, 1968. [New York: Bantam.]

Memoirs: 1950-1963. Boston: Atlantic-Little, Brown, 1972.

The Cloud of Danger: Current Realities of American Foreign Policy. Boston: Atlantic-Little, Brown, 1977.

The Nuclear Delusion: Soviet-American Relations in the Atomic Age. New York, 1982. Expanded ed., 1983.

SELECTED ARTICLES

"The Sources of Soviet Conduct by X." *Foreign Affairs,* XXV (July, 1947), 566-82.

"American and the Russian Future." *Foreign Affairs,* XXIX (April, 1951), 351-70. Both essays are reprinted in *American Diplomacy.*

"How to Break the Nuclear Impasse: A Modest Proposal." *New York Review of Books,* XXVIII (July 16, 1981), 14-17.

"Two Views of the Soviet Problem." *New Yorker,* LVII (November 2, 1981), 54-65.

"On Nuclear War." *New York Review of Books,* XXVIII (January 21, 1982), 8-12.

"Nuclear Weapons and the Atlantic Alliance." With McGeorge Bundy, Robert S. McNamara, and Gerard Smith. *Foreign Affairs,* LX (Spring, 1982), 753-69.

"The President's Choice: Star Wars or Arms Control." With McGeorge Bundy, Robert S. McNamara, and Gerard Smith. *Foreign Affairs,* LXIII (Winter, 1984), 264-79.

"Morality and Foreign Policy." *Foreign Affairs,* LXIV (Winter, 1985-86), 205-19.

CRITICAL WORKS ON KENNAN

(See also Section VIII below.)

Gaddis, John Lewis. "Containment: A Reassessment." *Foreign Affairs,* LV (July, 1977), 873-88.

Gardner, Lloyd C. *Architects of Illusion.* Chicago: Quadrangle, 1970.

Gellman, Barton. *Contending with Kennan: Toward a Philosophy of American Power.* New York: Praeger, 1984.

Hoffmann, Stanley. "After the Creation, or the Watch and the Arrow." *International Journal,* XXVIII (Spring, 1973), 18–39.

Lasch, Christopher. " 'Realism' as a Critique of American Diplomacy." In *The World of Nations.* New York: Vintage, 1974.

Taylor, A. J. P. "Democracy and Diplomacy." In *Europe: Grandeur and Decline.* Harmondsworth: Penguin, 1967.

VII. Works by Henry Kissinger

"The Meaning of History: Reflections on Spengler, Toynbee and Kant." A.B. thesis, Harvard University, 1951.

A World Restored: Metternich, Castlereagh and the Problems of Peace, 1812-1822. Boston: Houghton Mifflin, 1957.

Nuclear Weapons and Foreign Policy. Garden City, N.Y.: Doubleday, 1957.

The Troubled Partnership: A Reappraisal of the Atlantic Alliance. New York: McGraw-Hill for the Council on Foreign Relations, 1965.

White House Years. Boston: Little, Brown, 1979.

Years of Upheaval. Boston: Little, Brown, 1982.

ARTICLES AND COLLECTIONS

The Necessity for Choice: Prospects of American Foreign Policy. New York: Harper Brothers, 1960.

"The White Revolutionary: Reflections on Bismarck." *Daedalus,* XCVII (Summer, 1968), 888–924.

American Foreign Policy: Three Essays. New York: Norton, 1969. 2d ed., 1974; 3d ed., 1977.

"Henry Kissinger: An Interview with David Frost." *NBC News Special Report,* October 11, 1979, interview transcript.

For the Record: Selected Statements, 1977-1980. Boston: Little, Brown, 1981.

Observations: Selected Speeches and Essays, 1982-84. Boston: Little, Brown, 1985.

CRITICAL WORKS ON KISSINGER

Ascherson, Neal. "Deaths That Haunt Dr. Kissinger," London *Observer,* November 18, 1979, pp. 11–12.

Beecher, William. "A Scrutiny of Kissinger on Bombing of Cambodia." Boston *Globe,* October 22, 1979, p. 2

Brown, Seyom. *The Crises of Power: An Interpretation of U.S. Foreign Policy During the Kissinger Years.* New York: Columbia University Press, 1978.

Buchan, Alastair. "A World Restored?" *Foreign Affairs,* L (July, 1972), 644–59.

———. "The Irony of Henry Kissinger." *International Affairs,* L (July, 1974), 367–79.

Chomsky, Noam. "Deception as a Way of Life." *Inquiry,* April 7, 1980, pp. 21–28.

Dickson, Peter. *Kissinger and the Meaning of History.* New York: Cambridge University Press, 1978.

Draper, Theodore. "Appeasement and Detente." *Commentary,* LXI (February, 1976), 27–38.

Graubard, Stephen R. *Kissinger: Portrait of a Mind.* New York: Norton, 1973.

Hersh, Seymour. *The Price of Power: Kissinger in the Nixon White House.* New York: Summit Books, 1983.

Hoffmann, Stanley. "Weighing the Balance of Power." *Foreign Affairs,* L (July, 1972), 618–43.

———. "Will the Balance Balance at Home?" *Foreign Policy,* No. 7 (Summer, 1972), 60–83.

———. "How to Read Henry Kissinger." *New York Review of Books,* XXVII (December 6, 1979), 14–31.

———. "The Return of Henry Kissinger." *New York Review of Books,* XXIX (April 29, 1982), 14–26.

Montgomery, John D. "The Education of Henry Kissinger." *Journal of International Affairs,* IX (Spring, 1975), 49–62.

Morris, Roger. *Uncertain Greatness: Henry Kissinger and American Foreign Policy.* New York: Harper & Row, 1977.

Page, Bruce. "The Pornography of Power." *New Statesman,* November 23, 1979, pp. 808–11.

Saxon, Wolfgang. "Kissinger Revised His Book More Than He Reported." New York *Times,* October 31, 1979, p. 14.

Shawcross, William. *Sideshow: Kissinger, Nixon and the Destruction of Cambodia.* New York: Simon and Schuster, 1979.

———. "Through History with Henry A. Kissinger." *Harper's,* CCLXI (November, 1980), 35–44, 89–97.

Stoessinger, John G. *Henry Kissinger: The Anguish of Power.* New York: Norton, 1976.

VIII. Critical Works on Realism and Morality

Aron, Raymond. *Peace and War: A Theory of International Relations.* Translated by R. and A. B. Fox. Garden City, N.Y.: Doubleday, 1966.

———. *Politics and History.* Edited by Miriam Conant. New York: Free Press, 1978.

Ashley, Richard K. "Political Realism and Human Interests." *International Studies Quarterly,* XXV (June, 1981), 204–36.

———. "The Poverty of Neo-Realism." *International Organization,* XXXVIII (Spring, 1984), 225–86.

Bainton, Roland H. *Christian Attitudes Toward War and Peace.* Nashville: Abingdon Press, 1960.

Beard, Charles. *The Idea of National Interest: An Analytical Study in American Foreign Policy.* New York: Macmillan, 1934.

Beitz, Charles. *Political Theory and International Relations.* Princeton: Princeton University Press, 1979.

Berki, R. N. *On Political Realism.* London: Dent, 1981.

Berlin, Isaiah. "Realism in Politics." *Spectator,* CXCIII (December 17, 1954), 774–76.

Bull, Hedley. *The Anarchical Society: A Study of Order in World Politics.* New York: Columbia University Press, 1977.

Butterfield, Herbert. *The Statecraft of Machiavelli.* London: Bell, 1944.

———. *Christianity and History.* New York: Scribner's, 1950.

———. "The Scientific vs. the Moralistic Approach in International Affairs." *International Affairs,* XXVII (October, 1951), 411–22.

———. *Christianity, Diplomacy and War.* London: Epworth, 1953.

———. *International Conflict in the Twentieth Century.* London: Routledge & Kegan Paul, 1960.

———, and Martin Wight, eds. *Diplomatic Investigations.* London: Allen & Unwin, 1966.

Buzan, Barry. *People, States and Fear: The National Security Problem in International Relations.* Chapel Hill: University of North Carolina Press, 1983.

Clark, Ian. *Reform and Resistance in the International Order.* Cambridge: Cambridge University Press, 1980.

Claude, Inis L., Jr. *Power and International Relations.* New York: Random House, 1962.

Cook, Thomas, and Malcolm Moos. "American Foreign Policy: The Realism of Idealism." *American Political Science Review,* XLVI (Spring, 1952), 193–213.

d'Entreves, A. P. *Natural Law.* London: Hutchinson, 1951.

———. *The Notion of the State.* London: Oxford University Press, 1967.

Friedrich, Carl J. *The New Image of the Common Man.* Boston: Beacon Press, 1950.

———. *Constitutional Reason of State: The Survival of the Constitutional Order.* Providence: Brown University Press, 1957.

———. *Man and His Government.* New York: McGraw-Hill, 1963.

Gilpin, Robert. *War and Change in World Politics.* New York: Cambridge University Press, 1981.

———. "The Richness of the Tradition of Political Realism." *International Organization,* XXXVIII (Spring, 1984), 287–304.

Graubard, Stephen R., ed. *The State.* New York: Norton, 1979.

Hare, J. E., and Carey B. Joynt. *Ethics and International Affairs.* New York: St. Martin's Press, 1982.

Herz, John. *Political Realism and Political Idealism.* Chicago: University of Chicago Press, 1951.

Hinsley, F. H. *Power and the Pursuit of Peace.* Cambridge: Cambridge University Press, 1963.

Hobbes, Thomas. *Leviathan.* Edited by C. B. Macpherson. Harmondsworth: Penguin, 1968.

Hoffmann, Stanley. "International Relations: The Long Road to Theory." *World Politics,* XI (April, 1959), 346–78.

———. *The State of War: Essays on the Theory and Practice of International Politics.* New York: Praeger, 1965.

————. "An American Social Science: International Relations," *Daedalus*, CVI (Summer, 1977), 41–60.

————. *Primacy or World Order: American Foreign Policy Since the Cold War.* New York: McGraw-Hill, 1978.

————. *Dead Ends: American Foreign Policy in the New Cold War.* Cambridge, Mass.: Ballinger, 1983.

Kant, Immanuel. *Kant's Political Writings.* Edited by Hans Reiss; translated by H. B. Nisbet. Cambridge: Cambridge University Press, 1970.

Keohane, Robert O. "Theory of World Politics: Structural Realism and Beyond." In *Political Science: The State of the Discipline,* edited by Ada K. Finifter. Washington, D.C.: American Political Science Association, 1984.

————, and Joseph S. Nye. *Power and Interdependence: World Politics in Transition.* Boston: Little, Brown, 1977.

Knorr, Klaus. *The Power of Nations.* New York: Basic Books, 1975.

————, and James Rosenau. *Contending Approaches to International Relations.* Princeton: Princeton University Press, 1969.

————, and Sidney Verba. *The International System.* Princeton: Princeton University Press, 1960.

Lebow, Richard Ned. *Between Peace and War: The Nature of International Crisis.* Baltimore: Johns Hopkins University Press, 1981.

Lefever, Ernest, ed. *Ethics and World Politics.* Baltimore: Johns Hopkins Press, 1972.

Lieber, Robert J. *Theory and World Politics.* Cambridge, Mass.: Winthrop, 1972.

Lippmann, Walter. *U.S. Foreign Policy: Shield of the Republic.* Boston: Atlantic–Little, Brown, 1943.

————. *The Cold War: A Study in United States Foreign Policy.* New York: Harper Torchbooks, 1972. Original ed., 1947.

————. *The Essential Lippmann.* Edited by Clinton Rossiter and James Lane. New York: Vintage, 1960.

Lucas, J. R. *The Principles of Politics.* Oxford: Oxford University Press, 1966.

Machiavelli, Niccolò. *The Prince and the Discourses.* Edited by Max Lerner. New York: Modern Library, 1950.

MacIntyre, Alasdair. *A Short History of Ethics.* London: Routledge & Kegan Paul, 1967.

————. *After Virtue: A Study in Moral Theory.* Notre Dame: University of Notre Dame Press, 1981.

Macquarrie, John. *Twentieth Century Religious Thought.* London: SCM Press, 1971.

Mannheim, Karl. *Ideology and Utopia.* London: Routledge & Kegan Paul, 1936.

Meinecke, Friedrich. *Machiavellism.* Translated by Douglas Scott. New Haven: Yale University Press, 1952. Reprint. Boulder, Colo.: Westview, 1984. Original ed.: *Die Idee der Staatsräson in der Neueren Geschichte.* Munich, 1924.

Midgley, E. B. F. *The Natural Law Tradition and the Theory of International Politics.* London: Paul Elek, 1975.

Mitrany, David. *A Working Peace System*. 4th ed. London: National Peace Council, 1964.

Nardin, Terry. *Law, Morality and the Relations of States*. Princeton: Princeton University Press, 1983.

Nye, Joseph S., and Robert O. Keohane. *Transnational Relations and World Politics*. Cambridge, Mass.: Harvard University Press, 1972.

Osgood, Robert E. *Ideals and Self Interest in America's Foreign Relations*. Chicago: University of Chicago Press, 1953.

————, and Robert W. Tucker. *Force, Order and Justice*. Baltimore: Johns Hopkins Press, 1967.

Porter, Brian, ed. *The Aberystwyth Papers: International Politics, 1919-1969*. London: Oxford University Press, 1972.

Potter, Ralph B. *War and Moral Discourse*. Richmond, Va.: John Knox Press, 1969.

Ramsey, Paul. *War and the Christian Conscience: How Shall Modern War Be Conducted Justly?* Durham, N.C.: Duke University Press, 1961.

————. *The Just War: Force and Political Responsibility*. New York: Scribner's, 1968.

Ruggie, John G. "Continuity and Transformation in the World Polity: Towards a Neo-realist Synthesis." *World Politics*, XXV (January, 1983), 261–85.

Schlesinger, Arthur M., Jr. *The Vital Center: The Politics of Freedom*. Boston: Houghton Mifflin, 1949.

Schuman, Frederick L. *International Politics*. New York: McGraw-Hill, 1933, and six later editions.

Schwarzenberger, Georg. *Power Politics: An Introduction to the Study of International Relations and Post-War Planning*. London: Jonathan Cape, 1941.

Speier, Hans. *Social Order and the Risks of War*. Cambridge, Mass.: Massachusetts Institute of Technology Press, 1969. Original ed., 1952.

Spykman, Nicholas. *America's Strategy in World Politics: The United States and the Balance of Power*. New York: Harcourt Brace, 1942.

————. *The Geography of the Peace*. New York: Harcourt Brace, 1944.

Stevenson, Leslie J. *Seven Theories of Human Nature*. Oxford: Oxford University Press, 1974.

Tannenbaum, Frank. "The American Tradition in Foreign Relations." *Foreign Affairs*, XXX (October, 1951), 31–50.

————. "The Balance of Power vs. the Co-ordinate State." *Political Science Quarterly*, LXVII (June, 1952), 173–97.

Thompson, Kenneth W. "The Study of International Politics: A Survey of Trends and Developments." *Review of Politics*, XIV (October, 1952), 433–43.

————. *Political Realism and the Crisis of World Politics*. Princeton: Princeton University Press, 1960.

————. *American Diplomacy and Emergent Patterns*. New York: New York University Press, 1962.

————. "Idealism and Realism: Beyond the Great Debate." *British Journal of International Studies*, III (1977), 159–80.

————. *Ethics, Functionalism and Power in International Politics.* Baton Rouge: Louisiana State University Press, 1979.

————. "Moral Reasoning in American Thought on War and Peace." *Review of Politics,* XXXIX (July, 1977), 386–99.

————. *Masters of International Thought: Major Twentieth Century Theorists and the World Crisis.* Baton Rouge: Louisiana State University Press, 1980.

————. "Science, Morality and Transnationalism." *Interpretation,* IX (September, 1981), 415–26.

————, ed. *Moral Dimensions of American Foreign Policy.* New Brunswick, N.J.: Transaction, 1984.

Thucydides. *History of the Peloponnesian War.* Edited by M. I. Finley; translated by Rex Warner. Harmondsworth: Penguin, 1972.

Vasquez, John A. *The Power of Power Politics: A Critique.* New Brunswick, N.J.: Rutgers University Press, 1983.

Vincent, R. J. *Nonintervention and International Order.* Princeton: Princeton University Press, 1974.

Waltz, Kenneth N. *Man, the State and War.* New York: Columbia University Press, 1959.

————. *Theory of International Politics.* Reading, Mass.: Addison-Wesley, 1979.

Walzer, Michael. *Just and Unjust Wars: A Moral Argument with Historical Illustrations.* New York: Basic Books, 1977.

Wight, Martin. *Power Politics.* Edited by Hedley Bull and Carsten Holbraad. Harmondsworth: Penguin, 1977.

————. *Systems of States.* Edited by Hedley Bull. Leicester: Leicester University Press, 1977.

Wolfers, Arnold. *Discord and Collaboration.* Baltimore: Johns Hopkins Press, 1962.

IX. Historical Works

Acheson, Dean. *Present at the Creation.* New York: Norton, 1969.

Ambrose, Stephen E. *Rise to Globalism.* Baltimore: Penguin, 1971. Rev. ed., 1984.

Aron, Raymond. *The Imperial Republic: The United States and the World, 1945-1973.* London: Weidenfeld and Nicolson, 1974.

Divine, Robert A. *Second Chance: The Triumph of Internationalism in America During World War II.* New York: Atheneum, 1967.

Feis, Herbert. *From Trust to Terror.* New York: Norton, 1970.

Gaddis, John Lewis. *The United States and the Origins of the Cold War, 1941-1947.* New York: Columbia University Press, 1972.

————. *Strategies of Containment: A Critical Appraisal of Postwar American National Security Policy.* New York: Oxford University Press, 1982.

Halle, Louis J. *The Cold War as History.* New York: Harper & Row, 1967.

Knapp, Wilfrid. *A History of War and Peace, 1939-1965.* London: Oxford University Press, 1967.

LaFeber, Walter. *America, Russia and the Cold War.* New York: John Wiley, 1967. Four later editions.

Maier, Charles S. "Revisionism and the Interpretation of Cold War Origins." *Perspectives in American History,* IV (1970), 313–47.

May, Ernest R. *Lessons of the Past.* New York: Oxford University Press, 1971.

Schlesinger, Arthur, Jr. "Origins of the Cold War." *Foreign Affairs,* XLVI (October, 1967), 23–52.

Steel, Ronald. "Did Anyone Start the Cold War?" *New York Review of Books,* XIX (February 24, 1972), 22–28.

———. "The Power and Old Glory." *New York Review of Books,* XX (May 31, 1973), 33–35.

———. *Walter Lippmann and the American Century.* Boston: Atlantic–Little, Brown, 1980.

Taylor, A. J. P. *English History, 1914–1945.* London: Oxford University Press, 1965.

———. *Origins of the Second World War.* 2d ed. London: Hamish Hamilton, 1966.

Taylor, Telford. *Munich: The Price of Peace.* Garden City, N.Y.: Doubleday, 1979.

Thompson, Kenneth W. *Cold War Theories. Vol. I: World Polarization, 1943–1953.* Baton Rouge: Louisiana State University Press, 1981.

Ulam, Adam B. *Expansion and Coexistence: The History of Soviet Foreign Policy, 1917–1967.* New York: Praeger, 1968. 2d ed., 1973.

———. *The Rivals: America and Russia Since World War II.* New York: Viking, 1971.

Yergin, Daniel. *Shattered Peace: The Origins of the Cold War and the National Security State.* Boston: Houghton Mifflin, 1978.

Index

Abyssinia (Ethiopia), invaded by Italy, 63–66
Acheson, Dean, 91, 149, 154, 165, 175
Adler, Mortimer J., 60
Americans for Democratic Action (ADA), 111, 119
Aron, Raymond, 2, 17, 28, 32, 223, 230
Augustine, Saint, 1, 126–27, 218

Baldwin, Stanley, 64, 93
Barth, Karl, 101, 128
Bebel, August, 36
Becker, Carl, 60
Beetham, David, 31
Bentham, Jeremy, 95
Bethmann-Hollweg, Theobald von, 11, 48
Bismarck, Otto von, 34, 35–37, 52, 166, 210
Bodin, Jean, 70
Briand, Aristide, 57, 61–62, 169
Brinton, Crane, 68
Bull, Hedley, 21, 219
Burke, Edmund, 139, 164, 168
Butler, Nicholas Murray, 55, 57, 61–62

Cambodia, invasion of, 214–15, 216
Carnegie Endowment for International Peace, 57
Carr, E. H.: 68–99; and appeasement, 83–87; compared to Morgenthau, 138; compared to Weber, 17, 70, 76, 93; compares U.S. and U.S.S.R., 90–91; criticized by Morgenthau, 138; criticizes idealists, 69–74; critique of, 92–99; on morality, 77–79; on morality of states, 79–83; defends Munich agreement, 84, 96; follows Niebuhr, 74–75, 80, 95; discusses power, 74–77; and sociology of knowledge, 70–72; predicts fewer sovereign states, 89–90; on U.S.S.R., 88,

90–92; on post-1945 world, 87–92;
Castlereagh, Robert Stewart, Viscount, 201–202
Cavour, Camillo di, Count, 80
Chamberlain, Neville, 17, 81, 84–85
Chiang Kai-shek, 149
China, 149
Churchill, Winston, 96, 155
Clausewitz, Karl von, 232
Cleon, 8
Congress of Vienna, 199–200, 202, 209
Corcyrean Civil War, 9
Czechoslovakia, 83, 85, 87, 91

Davies, David, 56, 59, 60
De Gaulle, Charles, 41
Democracy: 88; Niebuhr on, 111–12, 122–23; Weber on, 39–41
Dickinson, G. Lowes, 55–56, 58
Diodotus, 8
Dulles, John Foster, 124, 180

Ebert, Friedrich, 52
Eisner, Kurt, 42, 50
Engels, Friedrich, 37
Ethiopia. See Abyssinia

Fosdick, Raymond D., 57
Friedrich, Carl J., 10, 12
Fulbright, J. William, Senator, 185

Gavin, James M., General, 185
Geneva Protocol (1924), 57, 61
Germany: 26, 71, 117, 227, 228, 229; Carr on, 83–86; French occupation of Ruhr, 75; and Locarno Treaty, 75; Morgenthau on, 150–51; and Munich Agreements, 83–86; Niebuhr on, 117–120; reoccupies Rhineland, 65; Weber on, 34–39, 42–44, 50–51;